THE
ADVERTISED
mind

GROUND-BREAKING INSIGHTS INTO
HOW OUR BRAINS RESPOND
TO ADVERTISING

ERIK DU PLESSIS

KOGAN
PAGE

London and Sterling, VA

First published in Great Britain and the United States in 2005 by Millward Brown and Kogan Page Limited.

120 Pentonville Road
London N1 9JN
United Kingdom
www.kogan-page.co.uk

22883 Quicksilver Drive
Sterling VA 20166-2012
USA

© Erik du Plessis and Millward Brown, 2005

The right of Erik du Plessis to be identified as the author of this work has been asserted by him in accordance with the Copyright, Designs and Patents Act 1988.

ISBN 0 7494 4366 9

British Library Cataloguing-in-Publication Data

A CIP record for this book is available from the British Library.

Library of Congress Cataloging-in-Publication Data

Du Plessis, Erik.
   The advertised mind : groundbreaking insights into how our brains respond to advertising / Erik du Plessis.
       p. cm.
   Includes bibliographical references and index.
   ISBN 0-7494-4366-9 (alk. paper)
   1. Advertising—Psychological aspects. 2. Advertising—Research. 3. Human information processing—Research. I. Title.
   HF5822.D8 2005
   659.1′01′9—dc22

                                                                              2005001178

Typeset by Saxon Graphics Ltd, Derby
Printed and bound in Great Britain by Scotprint

Contents

Figures

Tables

Foreword

I was aware of the existence of this book (published in Dutch) even before Erik du Plessis' company, Impact, became part of Millward Brown, and have since urged him to update it and get it published in English. The result is essentially a new book that expands on the original to provide new insight.

This book is unlike any other book about advertising previously published. Most previous books have considered advertising as a process, but given little attention to the processor of advertising: the human brain. And yet, over the past two decades, the human brain is arguably the area in which science has made its greatest discoveries. So much has been learnt that it now makes sense to consider the implications of those discoveries in the context of how advertising works.

Concurrently over the past two decades, our understanding of how advertising works has also progressed. New insights into the relationship between advertising spending and sales effects (both short and long term), are beginning to change the way advertisers think about the value of that investment. New insights into the factors that influence the success of advertising have allowed advertisers to place greater confidence in pre-testing (the discipline of judging an ad before it is broadcast, to determine if it is likely to achieve its objectives). For the most part these new insights are entirely compatible with the new learning on how the brain works.

This book seeks to explain the insights in these two fields, and relate the findings on how the brain works to the findings on how advertising works. The aim is to inform readers of the scientific developments, and to encourage them to find their own ways to apply them in the context of advertising. While Millward Brown has sponsored the book, we have not sought to influence the content. We did not need to. While Millward Brown and Impact have used slightly different research methodologies in the past, serving slightly different objectives, our underlying philosophies and resulting insights are very compatible.

Let me give you a preview of the book's contents, and explain how it has led me to some new thoughts about how advertising works and a greater clarity on some of our observations from research, both pre-testing and in-market tracking.

EMOTION IS CRITICAL TO ADVERTISING BECAUSE IT IS CRITICAL TO ALL HUMAN THOUGHT

Emotion plays a critical role in guiding our instinctive reaction to events happening around us.

We monitor our environment constantly and automatically, but with so many things going on around us, we need some means to determine what to pay attention to. This cannot be a conscious process – it would take too long. So the monitoring process constantly references existing memories as those memories are spontaneously triggered by what is happening at the time. Memories can include any feeling, association or idea triggered by what is happening at the time.

It is the emotional properties of those memories that determine whether we pay attention or not, and how much attention we pay. The more intense the emotional charge of the associated memories, the more attention we pay. If the charge is positive, it is likely we will feel attracted to what is happening. If it is negative, we will feel repelled.

So when we watch television or read a magazine, hoping to be entertained or informed, our brain constantly monitors the process in order to decide if what is being shown is likely to result in entertainment or edification. If the indicators suggest that it will, then we will pay more attention. Maybe not much more, but enough to follow along with what is being shown and said. This is one reason why advertising that creates a positive emotional response performs better than that which does not – a fact repeatedly born out by tracking studies the world over.

EMOTION IS CRITICAL TO ADVERTISING BECAUSE IT HELPS DETERMINE THE DEPTH OF PROCESSING THAT TAKES PLACE

Advertising works by establishing feelings, associations and memories in relation to a brand. These associations must come to mind when we think about a brand, ideally when we are considering a purchase, if they are to have any effect on our behavior. Emotion, by helping to stimulate and guide attention, helps to create and reinforce the associations created by advertising. This is a learning process, but not the one that we are used to from school. In the context of most advertising, particularly passively consumed media like television and cinema, learning is incidental, not deliberate. This is why people tell you they are not influenced by advertising. They are not actively trying to take anything away from the experience, and therefore are not influenced at that time, but the effects will show up later, long after a particular viewing experience is forgotten.

DEPTH OF PROCESSING AND REPETITION COMBINE TO ESTABLISH NEW MEMORIES AND FEELINGS ABOUT A BRAND

Most of our learning in relation to brands or ads is incidental. We do not set out to learn; it simply happens as a matter of course. Just as with deliberate learning, however, repetition will help establish the memory more firmly. It will typically take more exposure to establish a new memory than to confirm an old one, particularly if the new memory is in some way incompatible with the associations already established for the brand. Again, this is entirely consistent with what we observe from tracking studies. Awareness of advertising accessed by the brand name tends to increase quickly in relation to exposure, because the brand itself is familiar, and the exposure automatically triggers existing associations (even prompting recall of previous advertising from years ago). Recall of memories specific to an execution tends to increase more slowly as the new ideas become established in relation to the brand.

BRAND EQUITY IS THE SUM OF ALL FEELINGS, ASSOCIATIONS AND MEMORIES RELATED TO A BRAND

Just as with all things we experience, exposure to a brand will trigger all its related feelings, associations and memories to create an initial emotional response that then shapes our more considered reaction. The origin of these associations does not matter – it can be nostalgia created by childhood experiences, antipathy based on who we see using the brand, or simply a positive reaction to the look of the product. All of these things have the potential to shape our more rational consideration of a purchase.

BRAND MEMORIES ARE STORED IN A WAY THAT RESEMBLES AN UNTIDY, OVERSTOCKED CUPBOARD

Too many theories about advertising are based on the belief that brand associations are buried in our subconscious, and assume that complex psychological methods are required to dredge them up. A far better analogy, consistent with real-life observation, is an overstocked cupboard to which the brand is the key. Hearing the brand mentioned, seeing the logo, watching an ad – any of these can turn the key and open the cupboard door. As the door opens, memories and associations will tumble out, and they will continue to do so as long as the door is kept open. Advertising memories are among the items cascading out; there is no separate cupboard specifically for associations created from advertising. In fact, unless advertising memories are kept in the same cupboard as all other brand associations, they will not benefit the brand in any way.

ADVERTISING CONTRIBUTES DIRECTLY TO A BRAND'S EQUITY

Advertising seems such a trivial event in the context of all our potential experience of a brand, but it plays two important roles that make it a powerful marketing tool.

First, it can create new associations for a brand. In this case, a positive emotional response and repetition will increase the likelihood that the new impressions will become established as part of the brand's equity.

Second, advertising can help to keep existing brand associations fresh in peoples' minds, simply by stimulating the automatic referencing process, or, better still, by focusing attention on those associations in a new way. By stimulating positive associations it helps to ensure that the right feelings, associations and memories fall out of the cupboard when people think about the brand. The results are less obvious than when new ideas are established but they are fundamental to ensuring the long-term success of the brand.

ADVERTISING RESPONSE IS THE COMBINED EFFECT OF CREATIVE AND MEDIA PLANNING

The interaction of the creative and the media strategy is critical when trying to establish new impressions for a brand. The two must work together to allow learning to take place. For some people this may be accomplished on their first exposure, for others it may require several exposures, and for some it may never happen. The average rate of learning will be governed by four factors:

▮ *The emotional response created by the ad.* How much people like an ad will determine the degree of attention and shape the response to what is shown and said.
▮ *How well the impression created by the ad is established in relation to the brand.* This is critical if the impression is to have any influence on the response to the brand. Ads vary dramatically in the degree to which what is liked is integrated with the brand, and only if the associations are stored as memories related to the brand will they have an effect.
▮ *The number of and interval between exposures to the ad.* Cheap impressions will have no value if they simply create excessive frequency for an ad that is well branded and is not seeking to change impressions of the brand. On the other hand, frequency may well be what an ad needs in order to firmly link the impression with the right brand or to establish new ideas.
▮ *The degree to which the new impressions must compete with existing memories to become established.* To return to the cupboard analogy, if there is already a lot in the cupboard, the ad may need many more exposures to force its associations to the front than if there is nothing in there.

THERE IS NO 'ONE SIZE FITS ALL' MEDIA STRATEGY THAT CAN MEET DIFFERENT ADVERTISING NEEDS

In the past we have worked with the concept of 'effective frequency' – typically three exposures – and now 'recency' planning. The truth is that the most effective media schedule will vary dramatically depending on the task and creative involved.

As a result, the media strategy and creative should be managed as one entity, and managed over time. All too often, however, media plans are made and executed without reference to the nature of the creative. This is understandable given the development of separate media agencies charged with 'cost-effective' planning, but the potential opportunity cost involved is massive. How many new product launches fail because the advertising did not create enough brand awareness? How many brands lose share because the competition created a far stronger media presence? The answer is far too many. Proper research can significantly reduce the risk involved by informing the teams involved as to the difficulty of the advertising task, the potential of the creative vehicle, and the actual performance in-market.

Lastly, I want to leave you with a couple of thoughts that are relevant to the practice of market research. After all, both Erik and I are researchers at heart.

THE EMOTIONAL RESPONSE TO BRANDS AND ADS CAN BE RESEARCHED

For emotion to fulfil its evolutionary role of ensuring we pay attention to the right things, it must work quickly and simply. Essentially the emotional response to any event makes us feel positive or negative, attracted or repelled. We may use different words to classify the strength and nature of the emotional response once it has happened, but the emotions themselves are easily recognized, if not easily described. This means that simple introspective questions can provide good insight into the emotion created by a brand or ad. In other words, people may have trouble describing what love feels like, but they can easily discriminate between love, fondness and pleasure when they see the words in front of them.

THE FIRST RESPONSE IS THE TRUEST RESPONSE

When people talk about brands or ads they often start off by saying, 'I like it because…'. Based on what we now know of how the brain works we should accept this statement at face value. Further probing may well just lead to a rationalization of this response. The real challenge for research then is to discover the origins of that initial reaction, be they childhood memories, a desire for status, or even the fact that they liked the brand's advertising, without being misled by people's desire to appear rational.

I am proud to have been involved in the development of this book. It is both an entertaining and educational read, and I am sure you will enjoy it.

Nigel Hollis
Millward Brown

Preface

Every quest towards understanding begins at the point at which interest first starts to develop, and with the reason for wanting to learn more about the subject. This is where my quest began, and why it took shape as it did.

MEDIA PLANNING IN 1980

In 1980 I was appointed media director of BBDO, one of South Africa's leading advertising agencies, and found myself responsible for spending hundreds of millions of rands on our clients' behalf. I had previously worked as research manager and then senior product manager for a major wine and spirits company. South Africa at that time did not permit the advertising on television of hard liquor (including the whisky brands in my portfolio), so I found myself in the unique position of being a media director without any experience of the country's major advertising medium.

I began by inviting the major media owners to give me a crash course. This resulted in four invitations to lunch and one sales pitch, none of which left me any the wiser. It was clear I would have to find out for myself what terms such as 'effectiveness' meant in the context of television advertising.

In the meantime this was how I worked. I would painstakingly compile a media schedule, analyse how many people were likely to see the advertisement and how often, prepare the best presentation I could with the technology available in those days, and present it to the client as convincingly as possible. In the debate that followed the presentation, clients would often ask, 'How do I know that this is the best way to invest my money?' I soon learnt that the only 'effective' media schedule was one the client signed up to.

What worked for me at this point was to tell the client, 'In my experience, this works.' Not once did a client challenge me on what my 'experience' entailed. I was the media director; that seemed to satisfy them. I was also only 30 years old, but nobody quibbled about what that implied about my experience.

Of course what I really meant by 'this works' was, 'In my experience, this is the type of media schedule that most advertisers sign.'

I did have one fallback: a book entitled *Effective Frequency* by Mike Naples (1979) which was sponsored by the Association of National Advertisers, to the effect that it is important to optimize the percentage of people who are exposed to an advertisement three or more times. In presenting my media schedule, I could use the audience data to demonstrate the percentage who would be exposed to the commercial three or more times, and if anyone asked me why this mattered, I could answer, 'American research has proved conclusively that this is the optimal level of exposure.'

The clients signed up. This was more than 20 years ago, admittedly, but have things changed? In 1994 Leckenby and Kim published an article in the *Journal of Advertising Research* (Sept/Oct) in which they reported on the results of a study of media directors in the 200 largest advertising agencies in the United States. The directors were asked how they evaluated the effectiveness of a media schedule. As Leckenby and Kim put it:

> *It is worth noting that more respondents rated 'frequency distribution' and 'effective reach' as the most important factors in evaluating media schedules...*
>
> *[For] the respondents who checked they used 'effective reach' for media evaluation the most frequent definition of 'effective reach' was 'levels 3 and above'.*

Another 10 years later, media directors are probably still defining effectiveness the same way – except they might now be quoting Erwin Ephron and recency planning theories.

IMPACT INFORMATION AND ADTRACK

After four years I resigned from BBDO to start my own research company, Impact Information. I reckoned there was a need for a feedback system to tell advertisers and media directors what really was an effective way of scheduling advertisements, and now I had the chance to develop one.

Our methodology, which we called Adtrack, was to record all the new television commercials in the country as they appeared each week, then telephone a weekly sample of 200 people. For each new commercial we asked the respondents whether they had seen a television commercial for brand X, and if so, to describe it.

At BBDO, when we showed prospective clients our agency show reel, they would often say, 'I always liked that ad.' They appointed us to handle their business because they liked our advertising. Then when we proposed new commercials for them, which we said would be liked by consumers, they became super-critical. 'It is not advertising's job to entertain, advertising must sell!' This intrigued me: liking the advertisements on our show reel had sold us to them, after all. So because the Adtrack questionnaire had the space, we asked respondents who had recalled and correctly described a commercial to rate it on points out of 10 for likeability.

DISCOVERING AD-LIKING

By 1986 we had a database of over 1,000 commercials. Two academic studies were done using our data. They both showed that the best predictor of the rate at which a commercial converted 'exposed audience' to 'people remembering the advertisement' was whether the audience *liked* the commercial or not. In other words: people watch advertisements they like. This may appear to be trivial and obvious, but at that stage to the best of my knowledge there was no evidence in the world that it was true, and no advertising copy-testing methodology worked from this premise.

We thought this conclusion would popularize our advertising tracking system amongst the advertising agencies, and we spread the news extensively. As we went from agency to agency, something interesting happened. Again and again we had to listen to agency people telling us which advertisements they thought would be liked and which not. Usually they gave us reasons. Now we knew the answers from the consumers, and the agency people were just as often wrong as right in their predictions. One reason was that no agency person could conceive of consumers not liking one of the agency's own advertisements, or liking an advertisement created by a rival. But besides this professional jealousy, they also drew a line between what they defined as 'liked' advertising and 'effective' advertising, and this was a very shaky line indeed. We quickly realized that the definition of 'ad-likeability' would be a very arbitrary one if one had to rely on the advertising agency people's judgement!

CLUTTER REELS LET US DOWN

At this time we were asked to test a commercial that a major multi-national client had developed in South America for a product it was planning to launch in South Africa. Part of this test involved a clutter-reel recall measure. The commercial (in its final South American form) was embedded in a reel with a number of other commercials, to simulate a television commercial break. Respondents were approached in shopping centres, taken to a room, asked to view the reel, then afterwards asked to name the commercials they had seen. To counter the effects of recency and primacy, the position of the test commercial was rotated in the reel.

The simplistic logic is that the post-exposure recall is a measure of the penetrative ability (or mcmorability) of the commercial. This commercial did exceptionally well in the test. It was flighted, and we tracked its awareness on Adtrack. After the first week no one remembered seeing it.

We recommended that the intensity of flighting the commercial be increased. It was, and still no one remembered it. We then recommended that the branding in the commercial be increased, and the intensity of the flighting be increased, and still no one remembered having seen it.

At this stage we seriously had to question whether the results of the clutter reel were as predictive as we (and plenty of others) had assumed they were. Fortunately we had plenty of data on recall of ads, and a database of copy tests using clutter reels. We analysed the data – and found that the clutter-reel recall measures are not predictive of real-life advertisement recall.

This meant we could not reliably predict the ability of a commercial to 'penetrate' via the simple method of clutter reels. It left us in a difficult position. We could either be a pre-testing company or a post-tracking company, but if we could not predict the penetrative ability of a commercial from a pre-test, we could not realistically be both.

One alternative was to leave other research companies to do pre-tests using clutter reels, and when Adtrack measures showed that they were wrong in their prediction of the advertisement's memorability, leave them to explain why to the client. A better alternative was to find ways to increase the predictive ability of pre-tests.

The logical answer to why people give attention to commercials in a natural viewing environment was already in our hands: based on more than 1,000 advertisements we knew that people look at (and remember) what they like. Unfortunately we also knew that we were as wrong as the advertising agencies when we tried to predict subjectively what people would or would not like.

COMMAP – UNDERSTANDING AD-LIKING

We then set out to develop a system of copy-testing that was based on a better understanding of what comprises likeability. From this experiment we developed COMMAP, which I shall come back to later in the book.

A few years later Millward Brown also announced that it had found clutter reels not to be predictive of the in-market ability of a commercial to be memorable. It developed the Link pre-testing methodology based on its experience with tracking advertising. Link is remarkably similar to COMMAP, understandably so because both are based on experience with tracking the in-market performance of advertising.

LEFT- AND RIGHT-BRAIN ARGUMENTS RELATED TO RECOGNITION AND RECALL

Towards the end of the 1980s we tracked the awareness of another multi-national client's commercial. When we asked people, 'Can you remember seeing a commercial for [the brand]?' virtually no one said yes. This was not a popular result with the agency or the brand group. They quoted substantial sales increases for the brand. The advertisement was again tracked over subsequent bursts – and the results still showed very few people remembering it.

The client's research department then did a recognition test as part of an omnibus study managed by another research company, and this came back with significantly higher scores. The research company was asked to explain the difference, and it cited a paper by Herb Krugman (1977). This argued that recall is a left-brain measure and recognition a right-brain measure, and therefore recall is appropriate for 'logical' advertisements and recognition is appropriate for 'emotive' advertisements. Krugman argued that print is logical and television is emotive, therefore recognition should be used to measure television advertisements and recall should be used for print. (Quite a convoluted argument.)

We showed the client that what it had done was to repackage the product, reduce the price, and put it on promotion during the launch of the commercial; and that the 'massive increase in sales' was really only a market share increase from 3 to 4 per cent on A C Nielsen measures. However, the damage was done: our competitor did a talk at the South African national research conference saying that recall is only an appropriate measure for right-brain advertising.

We knew from our database (now of approximately 30,000 commercials) that the most memorable advertising over the years is based on emotion (as measured by advertising likeability). But this empirical evidence was obviously not going to stand up against convincing arguments based on quotes from Krugman, Zielske (1982) and especially Larry Gibson's 'Not recall' (1983). It seemed to me we needed to learn as much as possible about left-brain/right-brain theories (also called brain hemispheric theories) so that we could understand how this influenced advertising measures.

THE AMERICAN ADVERTISING RESEARCH FOUNDATION 'DISCOVERS' AD-LIKING

At this stage a remarkable exercise, the Copy Research Validation Project (CRVP), was completed by the US Advertising Research Foundation (ARF). The objective of this major study, managed by Russ Haley and undertaken by a body that had no axe to grind, was to find out which copy-testing research question was the most predictive of a commercial's actual selling ability. It measured advertisements on all the commonly used copy-testing measures, and found that the simple question 'How much do you like the advertisement?' was the best predictor.

This was a total shock to the whole industry. According to Haley, this question had not even been included in the original design of the questionnaire; it was an afterthought. Obviously it led to a lot of interest. During the early 1990s a paper by Alexander Biel, 'Love the ad. Buy the product?' (1990) was one of those most quoted by advertising agencies.

This was good news for us, since it vindicated the use of the ad-liking measure in Adtrack. It was less good news for the big copy-testing companies in the United States, where there were three schools: persuasion versus recall versus recognition. These companies' extensive databases of commercials generally did not include 'likeability' as a measure, and obviously it was not in their interests to change their assumptions of how advertising works and should be measured, even if it would have led to further insights into how advertising works, and more effective use of advertising money.

As a result of these experiences, it was perhaps inevitable that I would become even more interested in the workings of the brain, and in whether what was now known about it validated our results. The research I went on to do led to this book taking its first shape.

THE ITINERARY

My journey to the writing of this book has taken more than two decades, and during the second of them I have read many books, journals and papers about the mind and the brain, and many more about advertising. At the same time my company has continued to build and update the now-massive Adtrack database.

The book begins with a brief look at the problems confronting us, then continues with a review of some of what has been learned about the workings of the brain. The final section attempts to put this research to the service of advertising, and in the process ties it in with research from the advertising sector.

Most of this book does not comprise my wisdom. It draws on the insights others have achieved, and in some cases received Nobel prizes for. I am merely trying to show readers interested in advertising how the 'newer' insights into the brain relate to their area of endeavour. I hope they will find it useful.

Introduction

Many advertising books avoid asking a very basic question: 'Does advertising work?' Obviously nobody is going to write a book about advertising if they believe it does *not* work, but to avoid answering this simple question can create misunderstanding, because the implication is that *all* advertising works. In my experience this is not so. Some advertising works much better than other advertising, some advertising really does not work at all (in the sense of prompting consumers to buy goods, or at least be predisposed towards them), and some advertising works negatively. I am in a position to know, because much of my career has been spent in advertising research, trying to measure the effect of advertising, and to figure out how to predict what advertising will work.

The advertising industry is a major one in all developed countries. It involving megabucks of spending on the part of companies whose goods and services are being advertised. It creates a great deal of employment: in client companies, in research organizations, in advertising agencies, and in the media. And much of the money and the effort is wasted in creating and scheduling advertisements that seem to have no particular effect.

Perhaps this is no wonder when you think of the sheer amount of advertising that each of us encounters every day, to say nothing of other promotional efforts, and of all the kinds of information that assault us. Nobody could pay attention to it all; there is simply too much of it. So the first task for the producer of any brand (a product or service) is to ensure that its advertisements are noticed.

The second task is to ensure that the advertisements go on to do the job they are intended to do – which is, in crude terms, to prompt purchase of the brand. And the third task is to ensure that the purchases continue, that the brand image remains positive, that word spreads – in a phrase, that the whole enterprise is a success.

It would be too simplistic to say the industry is not good at this. The thought, the ingenuity, the creative and technical skill that goes into producing advertisements is enormous, and from many perspectives the quality of the output is remarkably high. Anyway, as I said, there is no way that every advertisement can be a winner. We all only have so much ability to pay attention; not every ad can 'grab' us. Similarly, if one brand is the category leader, then other brands by definition end up as the category also-rans. But that is not to say we cannot get better, and one of the spurs to make us better as an industry is feedback from advertising research.

In research, I think few would disagree that there is plenty of room for improvement. The industry has not proved tremendously good as yet in measurement and prediction. Our measures have been crude, our predictions as often wrong as right. My starting point in writing this book is advertising research, since that is my field, but I go on to look at how changes in the paradigms to which researchers operate will feed back into wider changes in advertisers' understanding of *how to produce advertisements that work.*

Let me first explain how the book is structured. I look first at the scale of the problem: the difference between advertising that works and advertising that does not work. I also look at some of the ways in which attempts have been made to predict before the event how advertising will work, and to measure after the event how it did work. Much of this will be familiar to those involved in advertising research, but I hope it will provide an useful scene-setting refresher to them, and it may well be new to others among my intended audience.

Who am I writing for? Anyone and everyone who wants to understand advertising. This includes those in the advertising industry (those who make and place or schedule advertisements, and those who research the results of advertising), those who need to advertise to sell their goods or services, students and anyone else who takes an interest. After all, we all see advertisements, and whether we like it or not, we are all influenced to some extent by them. This is not a textbook, it is a book of insight.

After the initial scene-setting, I go on to look at some of the fields I have trawled in search of insight. Advertising works on our minds: it prompts us (if it works) to make purchases. So to find out how to make it work better, and what measures we might use to find out how well it works, I have researched the fields that deal with the workings of the brain, both from the black-box perspective (psychology and its offshoots) and from the inside-out perspective (neurology and artificial intelligence). Exciting new developments have taken place, and are continuing to take place, in these fields, and the shifts in the paradigms to which they work can point the way to shifts in the paradigms that shape advertising research, and a new level of accuracy and insight in its output.

I look at how we come to pay attention to part of the huge volume of sensory stimuli that we receive every day, with the aim of helping advertisers create ads that will attract attention. I also look at how we learn and remember, with the aim of helping advertisers create ads that will be remembered. (The purchase act usually comes some time after the advertisement is seen: if it is not remembered, how can it affect that act?)

An advertisement is one thing and a brand is another, though the two are clearly linked, or perhaps more accurately the advertisement is part of the totality that is the 'brand value'. (At least, if they are not linked, the advertisement must be a total failure.) With a view to helping discover how best to ensure that seeing (and/or hearing) the advertisement feeds into purchasing the brand, I look at how concepts take shape in the brain. How can we strengthen the linkage between the concepts, so we can ensure that consumers do not just like the advertisements, they also like (and buy) the brand?

And here I come to the core of the book. The heart of what I have to outline is this. Advertisements that work are advertisements that are liked.

THE NEW PARADIGM FOR ADVERTISING

A *paradigm* is 'the way that we view things'. Once in a while a 'paradigm shift' occurs. Basically this means that the world does not change, but the perspective from which we view the world changes. Major paradigm shifts in history include the discoveries that the earth is not flat, but round, and that the earth is not the centre of the universe: it is only one of many planets, orbiting around one of many suns.

Historians have studied paradigm shifts, and identified some features that are common to all of them:

1. The world does not change, but the way the world is understood changes.
2. The paradigmatic shift derives from a discovery in one field, but a major shift affects many other fields as well.
3. By the time the paradigm shifts, there is already a lot of evidence supporting the new paradigm, but it has not previously been interpreted in the context of that new paradigm.
4. Many people cling to the old paradigm even after it is clear that the new one is a better fit with experience, because of their heavy vested interest in it.

5. When there is a shift to a new paradigm, a lot of previous knowledge makes more sense – because it is seen from the perspective of the new paradigm.

I make no claims to be Galileo, and although I can point to some small innovations made by my company, the research I outline is in large part not my own. Nor is it, on the whole, research specifically about advertising. But the paradigm shifts that have occurred in neurology, psychology and artificial intelligence – some of them small, at least by Galilean standards; some of them, it seems to me, pretty major – have very clear applications in our field of advertising, and it is these that are my subject here.

I explore them all in more depth in the chapters to follow, but let me set out at this point the bones of my argument.

▮ There has been a major shift in neurologists' understanding of how we pay attention; which is, if you like, a facet of the wider question of how we come to be conscious beings. The old paradigm, which can be dated back to Descartes, is that there is some higher entity in us, a 'homunculus', as he called it, which directs the activities of our brains, and through our brains, of our bodies. (Another way of suggesting the same thing is that there are two different entities: the brain, which is physical, and the mind, which is non-material, and directs the workings of the brain.) The new paradigm, which draws both on neurological research and on experiments in creating 'artificial intelligence', shelves the idea of a 'higher' intelligence, and turns instead in the opposite direction: to our most primitive and instinctive reactions.

▮ At the centre of this new paradigm is the thesis that it is *emotion* that governs all our behaviour: driving our unconscious reactions, but also *determining what becomes conscious*. Emotion feeds into, shapes and controls our conscious thought.

▮ What we pay attention to, we remember; that is, it has a permanent impact on the contents of our brain. And what we have paid attention to and remembered in the past, we are more likely to pay attention to in the future, so attention and memory create a feedback system. But the first task of the advertisement is to be attended to, in order that it can be remembered.

▮ Since emotion plays a key role in the directing of our attention, the task of the advertisement is to evoke emotion in us.

▮ 'Emotion' is a difficult concept. (We look later at some definitions of it.) At their simplest level, according to this thesis, all 'emotions' can be analysed down into one of two basic emotions, which might be described as positive (pleasure, or an inclination in favour of something) and negative (fear, or an inclination against something).

▌ We are all programmed to seek out the positive, and shun the negative. So it goes without saying that the emotions that the advertisement generates in us need to be positive ones. In simple terms, we need to 'like the advertisement'.

There are other things to be looked at too: how repetition plays a role in memory, how concept formation feeds into brand value, and much more, but that is the core of it. I go on now to take a first look at the state of knowledge about advertising and its effects.

1

How advertisements work

The fact is that until recently, most advertisers did not have much, if any, evidence that their advertising worked for them. They also did not have systems that really held their advertising agencies accountable for producing advertising that worked.

Just as other sectors have focused increasingly in recent years on measurement and assessment, so there has been a trend in advertising towards trying to measure the effect of advertising, and to prove whether it works. As a spur to this, a number of countries have introduced award schemes which encourage marketers to submit case studies containing indisputable evidence that their advertising works. Even so, much advertising is not rigorously tested (indeed, much advertising is not tested at all) to see if it has the intended effect. We might still be left wondering why there are so few case studies, if there are so many advertisers.

I look in this chapter at some ideas about what advertising is intended to achieve, then I look at some of the research which gives a pointer to whether or not it has succeeded.

HOW ADVERTISING WORKS

Gordon Brown is one of the founders of Millward Brown, now one of the 10 largest market research companies in the world, and a company that specializes in measuring advertising. The view of how consumers use advertising – in other words, how advertising works – that I put forward here derives in large part from him.

A simple mechanistic model of how advertising works might postulate that consumers see a commercial, this changes their perceptions of the brand (or creates a perception, if it is a new brand), and as a result they purchase the brand. (I talk here mostly of television advertising, but unless I indicate otherwise, my argument applies equally to print, radio and other forms.)

This might seem to imply that most of the effect of the advertisement occurs at the time of exposure to it. However, it should be borne in mind that most advertising breaks on television contain between three and eight commercials. It is highly unlikely that a consumer will concentrate on all the commercials during a break, and 'update' his or her perceptions of each of these brands. Most people simply do not behave like this, and they often do not pay much attention to advertisements in magazines, on billboards or on the radio either.

The more likely situation, surely, is that consumers absorb something from the advertisement, perhaps without consciously thinking much, if at all, about it at the time. Then at the time they are making purchase decisions they 'use' that impression to influence their choice. We could say that the consumer 'remembers' the commercial, but this does not mean that the consumer memorizes the commercial, and could describe even directly afterwards all the scenes and words that made it up. (We look later in more depth at exactly what *is* remembered from it.)

To understand how the commercial then has an effect on purchasing behaviour, we next need to consider the buying process. A good starting point is Gordon Brown's description of the purchase of a fast-moving consumer good (FMCG).

The consumer goes to a shop because he (or she, but let us take this sample consumer to be a man) needs something. He takes a trolley and starts to wander up and down the aisles, being shunted by other shoppers' trolleys, and trying to get past slower customers. While he is doing this, the thought that is going through his head is unlikely to be, 'I saw an advertisement for Colgate toothpaste last night and must go to the toothpaste section to buy some!' Rather, most shoppers let themselves be prompted by the display on the shelves. You most likely know this from your own experience, as do I. Thus as we make our way past the dog food display we remember that we have run out of dog food; as we pass the toothpaste stand we remember that we need some toothpaste; and as we walk past the snacks we remember that we intend to entertain some people in the next few days and it would be useful to stock up on crisps and nibbles.

Retailers know this, and arrange brands in product categories in a way that is intended to reflect customers' decision-making processes and prompt them to buy as much as possible. Of course stores could arrange the brands in terms of their advertising shares, so that when shoppers enter the store the first brand they see is the one that was advertised the most in the past week, the second brand is in a different product category, but was advertised the second most in the past week, and so on. Logic suggests that this would work well if shoppers actually made their purchases based on how much advertising they had seen in the past week; but retailers do not generally do it, because they and you and I all know that this is not how you, or anyone, shops.

Let us go back to the shopper in the supermarket, reaching the tooth-paste display as he remembers there's hardly any toothpaste left in the tube in the bathroom. It is at this point that he considers the brands on display, and picks out a tube to put in the trolley.

How much thought goes into this process? The sight of the different brand packages is likely to stir some memories, but probably nothing as clear-cut and thorough as a second-by-second recall of the last television commercial. Often it is enough for the consumer to think, 'This is the brand we used last time, and it was OK.' Sometimes a little more thought is involved: perhaps 'We were disappointed with this', or 'The children hated the taste', or 'Mary next door said her children like this brand.' Sometimes what comes to mind will include the advertisement: perhaps a key image or fact from it, perhaps little more than the memory that the brand *did* advertise.

In short, what determines whether a shopper will buy a brand is largely memory, and memories derived from advertising are among the memories that are liable to come to mind.

ADVERTISING AND NON-FMCG PURCHASES

Of course, this description assumes that the product is sold in a supermarket and displayed alongside competing products. That is not so for all products, but we might think of there being a 'virtual supermarket' for services (banks, insurance, hairdressers or whatever) and also for durable goods (stoves, tyres and the like), in which consumers identify in some way (walking through a mall, combing the *Yellow Pages*, checking out prices on the Internet) what is available, then come to a buying decision based on just the same types of memory.

THE ROLE OF ADVERTISING

In short, as I have tried to show, the job of advertising is to make itself remembered so that it can in some way influence the purchase decision. And the job of those planning advertising campaigns is to plan them in such a way that they will be remembered. Let us now go on to look at how campaigns actually are planned.

PLANNING AN ADVERTISING CAMPAIGN THAT WILL WORK

An advertising budget contains two components, the money for making the advertisement, and the money invested in the media to expose the advertisement to consumers. Most of the time around 80 per cent of the budget will be used on media placement, and only 20 per cent on production. It seems intuitively obvious that the impact an advertisement has will depend on both its content and its scheduling.

As well as how often an advertisement is scheduled, its size (for a print advertisement) or length (for a radio or television advertisement) is clearly a significant factor.

A beautiful quote I read in *Admap* goes:

> *Bad advertising is as good as no advertising. It just costs more!*

An ineffective media schedule can make an effective advertisement totally ineffective. However, the media scheduling cannot make an ineffective advertisement effective. So first of all an advertiser needs to be sure that the advertisement that is being made will be effective, and then it needs to be sure that the media schedule is appropriate for it.

Many advertisers appear to forget that the effectiveness of a campaign depends on both these components. I have come across research (by other companies than my own) which condemns an advertisement for its content, when the problem was not the advertisement but the media schedule.

MEDIA PLANNING

Media planning is simply a process of determining where and when the advertisement will appear. The where and when determine:

▍ how many people might be available to see (and/or hear) the advertisement;
▍ whether or not these are the types of people the advertisement is directed at;

■ how many times the audience will have seen the advertisement before;
■ the cost of the slot: as a broad simplification, the larger the audience, the higher it will be;
■ whether the medium itself is able to attract audience attention.

Media research has progressed over the past three decades to the extent that in most countries media professionals know how many people are in the room with a particular channel on the television screen at any time, and how many people are likely to look at a specific magazine or newspaper. They also know quite a bit about the demographics of the audience for a television or radio programme, or the readers of a newspaper or magazine, and about their product usage. This means that media planners can easily work out how many people will be exposed to an advertisement if it is placed in a particular medium at a particular time and/or in a particular position. They can also work out how best to reach target customers (in demographic terms) for the product being advertised.

The size of a campaign can be described in terms of gross rating points, or GRPs. Mathematically, the GRP of a campaign is its reach (that is, the estimated audience that would have an opportunity to see the advertisement one or more times) multiplied by its average frequency (how many times on average these people see the advertisement). Thus a campaign with 100 GRPs could reach 50 per cent of the audience on average twice, or 25 per cent of the audience on average four times.

In simple terms, the job of the media planner is to accumulate as many GRPs as possible (in other words, to provide as large a potential audience as possible) as cheaply as possible, focusing on the type of people that the advertiser is interested in. As media shops have become more popular, the importance of the GRP/money equation has grown: this is a prime area of competition, and advertisers increasingly evaluate the media planning/buying function in terms of how many GRPs they get for their money.

FREQUENCY

This leaves what is arguably the bigger question: how many GRPs do advertisers actually need to accumulate to make their campaign effective, and over what time period?

To take two extremes, it is intuitively clear that advertising is not so efficient that there is no need ever to repeat it. It does not work for an advertiser to only show an advertisement once, then sit back and wait for people to rush off to buy the product. First, the one showing will not have caught all the potential audience; and second, most people need a few exposures to an advertisement before they establish a firm impression from it and it impacts on their buying behaviour. (These are issues we shall be exploring in depth.) Similarly, it is clear that it is not true that more and more advertising will produce more and more return: there is likely to be a saturation point. In between these two extremes there will be a level at which the return on the advertising spend is at its greatest.

The return from advertising is known as its 'response curve', and there is a point at which the payback from the advertising spend is at its greatest. What makes finding this point more difficult is that the optimum has to be balanced along two axes: as many people as possible need to register the advertisement, and those who do register it need to register it a sufficient number of times to establish a strong memory of it and a good link with their concept of the brand.

There are of course various theories about where the optimum frequency level lies. Surprisingly, most of the answers in current theories are very close to being very wrong. It might be thought that advertisers who invest billions of pounds, dollars or rands would have figured out the right answer by now. They have not. To make this clearer, let us review the history of the frequency debate, and the state of the art today.

Run-up to the frequency debate

The 1950s, 1960s and 1970s were remarkable for the strides forward that were made in audience measurement. Media owners and even industry bodies in some countries invested big money in research systems that measured what people viewed, read and listened to. Before this research became available, media planners largely had to recommend media placements based on what publishers said they had sold (that is, on audited circulation figures), but subsequently they had reliable independent data to work with.

As audience and readership information became available, companies like Telmar and IMS developed computer systems which gave media planners the ability to analyse the audiences in different ways. As the analysis capabilities became more extensive, media planners and advertisers started to ask more complex questions of the data. Thus there was an evolving process of information becoming available, leading to new questions, leading to new information.

Throughout this process advertisers were asking the obvious question, 'How many times do I need to show my ad to people in a given period?' They never got a clear and authoritative answer.

Dr Simon Broadbent won the Thomson Silver Medal in 1967 for a paper discussing the shape of the response curve for advertising. The papers he refers to in his award-winning paper refer back to papers published in the 1940s which were trying to answer the same question, so it is one that has been asked (and not adequately answered) for a very long time.

An answer of sorts came from Herbert Krugman (who was then head of advertising research at General Electric) in a paper entitled 'Why three exposures may be enough' (1972). Most advertisers and agencies reacted violently against his paper, although in many cases this was probably because they had only read the heading and had not digested Krugman's argument in detail. The popular interpretation was that a major organization was saying that all that was necessary to sell anything was to make an advertisement, then show it to people three times, and never again. Understandably advertising agencies (who make the bulk of their income from the 16.5 per cent commission they earn on media placements) thought this would lead to a lower overall level of advertising, and they did not like that.

Krugman subsequently concentrated on trying to put across the message that what he meant was that there were three stages of 'psychological exposure' in people's reaction to advertisements:

- At exposure 1, people say 'What is this?'
- At exposure 2, they say 'What does it say?'
- At exposure 3, they say 'I've already seen it', and a process of disengagement begins.

The psychological exposures do not correlate one-to-one with actual physical exposures; they are stages in reaction which might each contain a number of physical exposures. So people might, for example, reach the 'exposure 2' phase after having been exposed to the advertisement half a dozen times; and the third 'psychological' exposure, in Krugman's words, might be the third actual exposure or might equally be the twenty-second actual exposure. At the time, however, his explanation of what he meant had much less impact than the title of his paper.

Mike Naples and 'effective frequency'

One effect of Krugman's paper was to bring the whole issue of frequency of exposure to the fore in the 1970s. As one result of this, Mike Naples was commissioned to review the available research, and he produced a book entitled *Effective Frequency* in 1979. He concluded that there is little response to an advertisement the first or second time people see it. Only after the third time is there any response, and thereafter there is a diminishing response for each subsequent exposure. So the response to exposure to advertising takes the form of an s-shaped curve, as in Figure 1.1.

A careful reading of Naples' book shows that it is based on only four studies, and that the only empirical study that really led to these conclusions was one carried out by Colin McDonald in the early 1960s. Naples' book first appeared in 1978, and from then on the rule of thumb for media planners became, expose people to the advertisement more than three times, because exposures to people who only see it once or twice are effectively wasted.

Naples did not give any recommendation about the period over which these three exposures should be made. The planning industry mostly assumed it should be over a purchase cycle, although this made no sense for items that are bought daily, or for items like motor cars that are only bought once every few years. Nor was there any consideration of what would happen between bursts of advertising: if a person was exposed twice in the first burst, would his or her first exposure in burst two count as the first or third exposure? Clever media directors chose the answer depending on the size of the client's budget; less clever ones probably did not even think about it. Finally, there was no recommendation that the rule of 'three plus' be adapted to take account of the creativity of the advertisement, or its length, or any other factor.

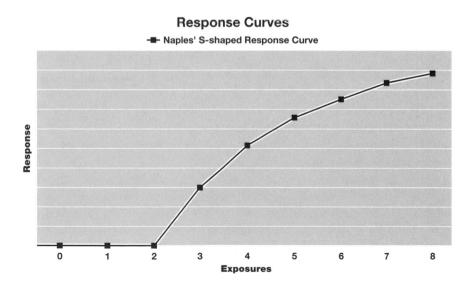

Figure 1.1 *The response curve to advertising*

In 1994 Leckenby and Kim carried out a piece of research in which they asked the top 200 US advertising agencies how they judged the efficacy of a media schedule. The usual answer was, 'How many people had an opportunity to see the advertisement three times or more', so this thinly based rule was still accepted as gospel 16 years on.

In short, in the 1960s and 1970s media researchers developed techniques that perfected audience measures, software suppliers supplied new ways to analyse the data, and 'effective frequency' provided a rule of thumb that media planners could using in running optimization programmes. Everybody was happy, and no one really seems to have questioned the paradigm.

AND THEN CAME JONES

All of this was working reasonably well until in 1995 Professor John Philip Jones published the results of his ground-breaking research in a book entitled *When Ads Work: New proof that advertising triggers sales*. His breakthrough was in the use (in conjunction with the US-based A C Nielsen Company) of 'single-source' data. This provided a way to measure for the first time whether a consumer had had an opportunity to see a brand's television commercial, and then whether the same respondent had bought the brand within the next seven days. Of course, for decades before this advertisers had been working on comparing sales before and after advertising campaigns as a crude attempt to find out whether the advertising was actually influencing sales, but this was the first time that a direct link between the individual's seeing the advertisement and the individual's purchases could be explored.

It is pretty self-evident that there could still be many factors that affect purchase decisions apart from the opportunity to see an advertisement for a brand, but at least with the link made between possible sight of advertisement and purchase of brand, the influence of these other factors on the data is minimized.

The analysis used data from 2,000 US households in which meters were attached to home television sets, providing information on the times the set was in use, and the channel to which it was switched. In each of these households there was also a hand-held scanner that could record the bar codes of products purchased. The experiment was done over a two-year period, and the data was analysed for 78 advertised brands.

From this data Professor Jones calculated a measure of short-term advertising strength (STAS). This was based on the differential between 'stimulated' purchases (the brand's share of purchases among households that had received at least one television advertisement for it in the seven days prior to the purchase) and the baseline (the brand's share among households in which it had not received any television exposure in that period). This is an elegantly simple measure: it purported to show exactly how much impact the advertisements had on people's propensity to choose the brand.

The major finding by Professor Jones was that the average STAS index for advertised brands was 124. In other words, during the seven days after exposure to an advertisement, the brand's share of spend was 24 per cent higher among those who had been exposed than among those who had not. Not only was there a short-term (seven-day) effect, there was also a long-term effect for all advertised brands: their market share increased by 6 per cent over the year following an advertising campaign.

However, this is an average statistic, so the 24 per cent increase is not necessarily the outcome for all brands. It does not mean that any marketer choosing to advertise on television can expect a 24 per cent increase in sales as a result. The variations in response were quite dramatic.

To demonstrate the variation, Professor Jones divided the brands into quintiles, so the 20 per cent with the highest STAS effect were placed in Quintile 5, and the 20 per cent with the lowest STAS effect in Quintile 1. Table 1.1 shows how great the variation was between quintiles.

Table 1.1 *The STAS effect: increase in share of spend for different advertised brands*

	Average STAS index
All brands	124
1st quintile	82
2nd quintile	100
3rd quintile	112
4th quintile	130
5th quintile	198

As you can see from the table, the findings were that for 20 per cent of advertised brands, advertising works phenomenally well. Advertising leads to a doubling in share of spend among those who saw the commercial! Even more importantly, for 60 per cent of advertised brands there was evidence of more than a 12 per cent increase in share of spend in the seven days after the advertisement was seen. Professor Jones also concluded that this sales effect occurred even when there had only been a single exposure to the commercial in the previous seven days. (This was to lead to Erwin Ephron's concept of 'continuity planning': see page 18.)

It would be difficult to exaggerate the shock this caused to the advertising system. Suddenly media directors who had been confidently telling clients they needed a schedule based around at least three exposures had to start telling them something completely different – and something that would, in many cases, mean less advertising in total! They had every motive to find fault with Jones's database or his research findings, but the database was too big and the research too well constructed, and no one managed to invalidate the findings.

The subtitle of Professor Jones's book makes it clear what contribution he felt this mammoth experiment made to advertising theory. He expected to trigger a backlash against the drift away from advertising and towards other forms of promotion that were believed to be more effective, with his 'new proof that advertising triggers sales'. You might expect advertising agencies to have created a lot of noise about these results, in an attempt to restore the confidence of advertisers in their product. You might also think advertising professions would have invested heavily in finding ways to make *their* advertising appear in the top quintile. After all, the flip side of the good news of Professor Jones's work for the industry was that 40 per cent of advertisements do *not* seem to have a significant impact on sales. Unfortunately these two aspects of Professor Jones's work were largely glossed over, and it was the media recommendations that were developed out of the research that received a lot more attention and debate. (We come back to these in Chapter 18.)

The implications of Professor Jones's work for the response curve are shown in Figure 1.2.

SPOT'S RESEARCH

SPOT is the acronym for the Dutch Foundation for Promotion and Optimization of Television advertising. In 1997 it conducted a tracking experiment to determine the effectiveness of television advertising. It tracked 67 brands among 50 respondents, each week for a 20-week period. The experiment measured quite a large number of issues, including 'ad memory' and purchase intent, for all the brands in the category.

The Jones experiment specifically looked at individuals' exposure to advertisements and their resultant behaviour. In contrast, the SPOT research did not try to ascertain whether the individual respondents had

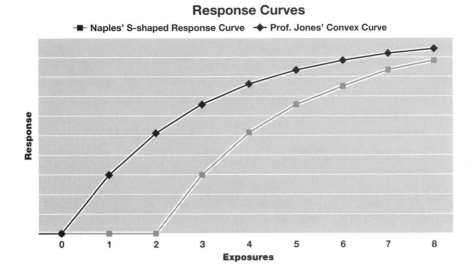

Figure 1.2 *The impact of Jones's research on the advertising response curve*

actually had an opportunity to see the advertisements. It worked on the general assumption that a predictable proportion of the respondents would have seen the advertisements, based on the GRPs in the media schedule. The focus of the research was on what happened in the minds of the respondents: did they remember the advertisement, and did it affect their intention to purchase the brand?

The main conclusions of this research were:

▌ Television advertising is effective.
▌ However there is a big variation in effectiveness between advertisements.
▌ The impact on ad memory varies between 1 per cent and 17 per cent per 100 GRPs.
▌ The impact on purchase intent varies between 0.5 per cent and 24 per cent per 100 GRPs.
▌ The extent to which people 'liked' an advertisement explained 40 per cent of the variation in effectiveness.
▌ Advertisements that were not well liked had an average of 3 per cent impact on ad-awareness per 100 GRPs.
▌ Advertisements that were moderately well liked had 10 per cent impact per 100 GRPs.
▌ Well-liked advertisements had an average impact of 33 per cent per 100 GRPs.
▌ In short: ad-liking influences the purchase intention.

These two pieces of research used quite different methodologies, but one thing should be glaringly obvious about their conclusions: they both agree that not all advertising works equally well.

SPOT also has something to say about why some advertising works and some does not: and the factor that comes out most strongly is that 'ad-liking' is a major determinant.

COLIN McDONALD

Further damage was done to the validity of Mike Naples' 1978 recommendations when in 1996 Colin McDonald (on whose research Naples' findings were largely based) rejoined the debate and claimed that Naples had misinterpreted and misrepresented his findings. He reanalysed his original data and found that it actually supported what Jones was saying. In fact, at an ARF Conference McDonald spoke in a session chaired by Mike Naples, and said he had always been surprised by the conclusions Naples had reached. (I was in the audience at the time.) This pretty much signalled the end of the 'three strikes' era.

ERWIN EPHRON AND 'CONTINUITY PLANNING'

The story does not stop here, however. Erwin Ephron, a respected independent media consultant in New York, looked at the Jones data with a view to making practical recommendations for media planners. He proposed a very simple approach, based on the assumption that the central objective of a media schedule should be to minimize wastage. If the main effect of an advertisement results from just one exposure, and subsequent exposures deliver a lesser return, then to provide any consumer with more than one exposure could be defined as wastage. So Ephron's recommendation was to aim to schedule the advertisement so that as many people as possible receive only one exposure to it.

Ephron's name for this approach to media scheduling was continuity planning, and the methodology he proposed was to take the available budget, divide it by the number of weeks the campaign was intended to last, then try to optimize the reach of the schedule and minimize its frequency distribution. Given the simple and unarguable nature of Jones's results, this rather simplistic application of them makes a fair amount of sense.

WHY IS THERE ANY DEBATE?

It would be too neat, however, if that were the end of the debate, and it certainly has not been. However, it does make some sense to ask, why? If advertisers have been asking questions about frequency of exposure for more than 50 years; if audience measures have been available since the 1960s; if the answers affect the real impact of advertising budget expenditure, why is there still serious and wide-ranging argument about how best to plan a campaign? How come the broad outlines at least of campaign planning have not been firmly agreed, and the debate has not narrowed down to argument about the details?

The answer is probably very simple. Advertising theory is a complex beast, calling for input (as this book will show) from many different fields. For all the effort that has been put in, for all the work of the research industry in measuring the effects of advertising, there seem to be some big questions that have not yet been answered.

Maybe, too, there is a real resistance in parts of the advertising industry against boiling down their 'creative' endeavour into something that is capable of definitive measurement. And clearly there are vested interests that work against conclusions that might lead to a reduction in advertising budgets.

Still, we must be fair: the fact that these studies were carried out at all is indicative of a changed attitude, and an increased willingness to take accountability seriously, among advertisers and agencies over the past three decades.

A degree of cynicism is permissible too, though, not least among clients. When the media planning community tell them for years that it is absolutely proven that the 'Naples effective frequency rule of thumb' is the firm basis for effective scheduling, then they turn around and tell them that actually, no, this research never quite stacked up, and it looks like 'Ephron's continuity planning rule of thumb' is much nearer the mark, they might be forgiven for thinking maybe there is something to be said for going with their own gut instincts instead.

In addition, one thing that all the research has agreed on is that different advertisements have different degrees of effectiveness. This makes instinctive sense to most people, anyway. If both intuition and all the empirical evidence show that advertisements have different rates of efficacy, logic would say that probably they will need different exposure schedules if the best is to be gotten out of them. Ephron's rule might be on the right lines, but it is clearly a very broad brush for dealing with a very complex problem.

Perhaps one problem is that advertisers expect their agencies to give them all the answers, and at the same time, the agencies do not have the resources to research in detail what would be best for each individual campaign. The only realistic option for the agencies is to rely on rules of thumb, even if it is clear that they provide no more than a very loose fit. Arguably what is needed is for advertisers to invest in determining the right media strategy for each of their products.

2

Approaches to the human mind

Now that I have outlined the questions to be answered, it is time to look at some of the insights that I believe can provide some answers to them. The next few chapters of the book concentrate on research in fields other than advertising, and on what they have taught us about the workings of the brain.

For any tour to be successful one should have an overview of the area to be toured. I have drawn heavily on Professor Stan Franklin's book *Artificial Minds* (1997) to provide the structure for my overview, in the form of a schematic of how the sciences involved in the new understanding of the mind relate to each other. (His book is highly recommended for its wider content too.) Professor Franklin is Professor of Mathematical Sciences and Co-Director of the Institute for Intelligent Systems at the University of Memphis. The schematic he outlines is shown in Figure 2.1. As you can see, it places the sciences along two axes, one indicating whether they tend to take a top-down or bottom-up approach, and the other indicating whether they take an analytical or a synthetic approach.

NEUROLOGY

Professor Franklin places the neurologists in the bottom-left quadrant of his schematic. The neurologist's starting point is the physiological. Neurologists cut open brains, remove tumours, look at the inside of the brain, and do pathological tests to see which areas of the brain are damaged.

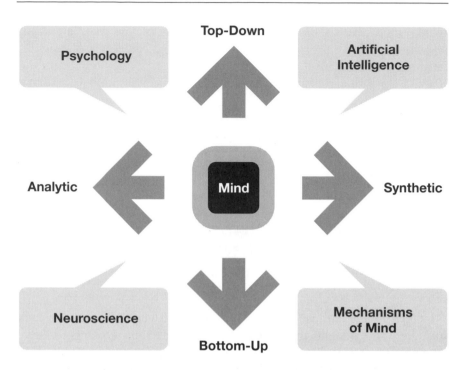

Figure 2.1 *Sciences involved in the new understanding of the mind*

Perhaps surprisingly these people seldom show any interest in finding out how this organ they dissect actually works; that is, how the brain thinks. They have, in the main, been more interested in discovering details of the 'building blocks' of the organ. However, some have become more involved in how these building blocks might work, and have started to publish in this area. Professors Damasio and LeDoux are among these, and I later refer to their work specifically in this regard.

The basic physical building blocks of the brain are neurons, so the core interest of neurologists who investigate brain function is in what the neurons do. They work from the details, and the structures, up towards the output of the organ. (In Franklin's terminology, they research from the bottom up.)

PSYCHOLOGY

In the top-left quadrant Professor Franklin places the psychologists. They really work from the top down. They look at the output from the human mind, especially as it is demonstrated by behaviour, and speculate about the underlying functioning. Some psychological studies are aimed at defining what a normal mind is like, and also what deviates from the normal. Psychologists also spend a lot of time trying to identify how the mind learns to behave the way it does.

This top-down method is much like looking at a television set and drawing conclusions about what its components must be: there must be a picture-making unit, there must be a reception unit, there must be a sound-receiving and sound-making unit, there must be a colour-changing unit, and so on. It does not tell us what these components look like or consist of, it simply hypothesizes that they must exist.

Because they specifically look at the output of the mechanism, psychologists' contribution to the new science of the mind is invaluable, because their insights set up the validation framework for the new insights that are being gained from the bottom up. If bottom-up models of the brain do not produce output that squares with the 'real' output psychologists have measured, then something has to be wrong.

ARTIFICIAL INTELLIGENCE SCIENTISTS

On the right-hand side of Professor Franklin's schematic is a different breed. Generally these are the people who are classified as computer scientists, and who are trying to emulate human intelligence on a computer. Professor Franklin divides them into two categories, artificial intelligence scientists and 'mechanism of mind' scientists, though most authors view them as two variants of the same species.

Many universities offer courses on artificial intelligence, and there are a lot of books on the subject. In the serious literature, the starting point is usually an attempt to define what intelligence is. This can become a very laborious exercise. Obviously a chair has no intelligence, but does an amoeba? Does a snake? Does your dog? Does a dolphin?

I asked my wife, a psychology major, these questions, and she said the difference was emotion. (Humans have emotions but computers do not.) Some scientists and thinkers feel that the difference between human intelligence and animal or other intelligence lies in the use of language, or in the use of mathematics or logic, or in something that could be described as 'consciousness'.

One old and established test for artificial 'intelligence' in a computer is to put a human being behind one curtain and a computer behind another curtain, and start asking them questions. The computer could be argued to be as 'intelligent' as the person if another person cannot tell the computer and the person apart.

Certainly a computer can now be as knowledgeable as a human being, and can carry out many mental tasks as well as – sometimes better than – human beings. A computer can beat even Grand Masters at chess; it can do any sum faster than a human being, it can correct grammar and spelling. Maybe this is why my wife selected 'emotion' as her differentiator, since we do not think of emotion as a property of computers.

The problem with computers is that they are limited by their programs. Computers cannot do what they have not been programmed to do – and they have to be programmed by a human programmer. Computers are good at definable and predictable tasks such as playing chess, but they tend to be stumped much more easily when it comes to naturalistic conversation.

Professor Franklin sees the work of these artificial intelligence scientists as top-down. It starts with the output of the human brain – intelligence – and then tries to emulate this, mostly by writing heuristics which make the computer appear intelligent.

'MECHANISMS OF MIND' SCIENTISTS

The 'mechanisms of mind' scientists in the fourth quadrant of Professor Franklin's schematic are in a sense what this book is all about. They start their thinking from the 'bottom up', by designing and programming devices in ways that replicate our knowledge about the structure and function of the brain, and seeing what this produces. We shall learn later in the book what kind of results they are achieving.

The true depth of knowledge, however, comes from the interaction of all the many sciences that are interested in the human mind. This interaction is leading to a much greater understanding of the mind.

In the chapters that follow, I try to pull together some of the divergent strands of knowledge from each of these different sciences, and reach some conclusions about how the brain works – and in particular, how it processes advertising. But in essence this book is largely about the approaches of mechanisms of mind scientists, and what they can teach us about the human mind.

3

Psychologists' models of learning and memory

INTRODUCTION

Let us look first at the area in the top-left quadrant of Professor Franklin's schematic, the field of psychology.

Psychology is a very large field, and all I can do here is draw on some theories and insights which are directly relevant to my argument. For more information, readers are referred especially to Professor Alan Baddeley, who has written some of the most user-friendly books on the topic, especially *Your Memory: A user's guide* (1996). However, most standard books on cognitive science (or learning) cover the basic material I introduce here and expand upon it.

You will recall that Professor Franklin viewed psychologists as approaching the mind from the top down, rather than being driven from the perspective of the components of the brain. They largely restrict their studies to the output of the mechanism (that is, human behaviour), and derive models that fit it. The behaviour that is of most interest to us at this point is the behaviour of our memory. How do we learn things, how do we remember them, and how do we forget them? Answers to all these questions have an obvious relevance to advertising, since one of the key questions we need to answer is how advertisements come to be remembered so that they can subsequently impact on the buying process.

EBBINGHAUS (1896)

One of the first cognitive psychologists (although the term did not exist in his day) was Hermann Ebbinghaus. He studied the process of learning by giving himself the task of memorizing nonsense syllables. He compiled a list of them, then repeated them until he could do so perfectly from memory, recording the number of rehearsals that were required. The next day he would repeat the exercise again (with the same nonsense syllables), recording the number of rehearsals required, and the same again the next day. Not surprisingly, he found that each day he required fewer rehearsals, as shown in Figure 3.1.

This experiment, done in 1896, has been repeated in a variety of ways by cognitive scientists to determine the rate at which people learn different things, and also the rate at which they forget them. Advertising and media specialists are familiar with it because it has found its way into advertising literature. It was quoted – virtually the only evidence from cognitive scientists – by Mike Naples in his book *Effective Frequency* (see page 12), and was still the main reference in Colin McDonald's update of Mike Naples' book in 1995.

Ebbinghaus's work has been taken further in similar studies in which people are asked to repeat the contents of a list immediately after exposure to it. In all this work a U-shaped response has been found to exist: the items early in the list and the items last in the list are remembered better than those in mid-list positions. An example of such an experiment by my own team can be found in the *Journal of Advertising Research* (du Plessis

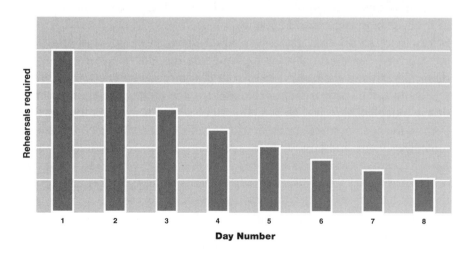

Figure 3.1 *Ebbinghaus's memory experiment*

1994a). We asked respondents to view 12 advertisements and tell us which they remembered.

The better memory of the first words (or advertisements) in the list is called the *primacy effect*, and the better memory of the last words (or advertisements) is termed the *recency effect*.

SHORT- AND LONG-TERM MEMORIES

Working from the 'outside in' – that is, taking the evidence and looking for a theory to fit it – psychologists put forward the theory of short-term memory. They hypothesized that there is a place in the brain in which immediate sensory experiences are received and analysed. They postulated that the recency effect is the result of the most recent words on the list 'replacing' the previous contents of the short-term memory.

Everybody knows that people can remember things for a very long time. All of us can remember things that occurred when we were very young, or people from our youth. If it this is true, and it is also true that we remember recent experiences, and forget recent experiences, then there should logically be two types of memory: short-term memory, which holds information for a few seconds (although psychologists are typically vague in defining how short short-term is), and long-term memory. The information in our short-term memory is immediately available to us, but the information in our long-term memory is not: we have to retrieve it in some way in order to be able to use it.

Other mechanisms are needed to complete this model. Obviously if information is moved from short-term memory to long-term memory, and then retrieved when it is required, there has to be some kind of filing and retrieval device. Since it is unlikely that a system such as this will work of its own accord, there also needs to be an element that tells the filing and retrieval device what to do. This can be called the central executive, and in the model it acts rather like a computer's operating system.

Even with the central executive in place, the system will not be able to 'switch attention'. It runs the danger of simply doing whatever it starts to do for the rest of its natural life. Therefore, like a computer, it needs an interrupt or escape button to stop it doing what it is doing. This is called the *supervisory attentioning system*.

Figure 3.2 shows how these elements logically fit together. The arrows in the schematic show the 'connections' that must exist between the

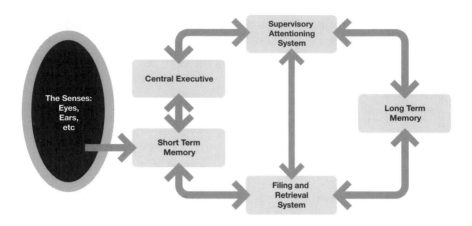

Figure 3.2 *A psychologists' model of the brain*

various functions. The double-pointed arrows denote flows of information that have to go in both directions.

This whole system makes intuitive sense. It also looks very similar to the way that a computer is organized, and therefore we might be forgiven for thinking that this model of the human memory has been strongly influenced by computer development.

A lot of research has been done by cognitive psychologists using this model. Their research is especially marked by attempts to record the input and output of this system under different circumstances: or in less computer-oriented language, how it learns and forgets.

It should be borne in mind at this point that this model is not based on any knowledge about the areas that have been found in the human brain. It is an abstract model of what kinds of elements there *might* be in a brain, or logically *should* be in a brain if the model is correct. Of itself the model makes no attempt to map the 'central executive' or the 'supervisory attentioning system' onto the upper brain or the lower brain, or any more specialized part of the brain for that matter, although this is an exercise that might be done to see if the model is validated by knowledge from the bottom up.

THE SUPERVISORY ATTENTIONING SYSTEM

I shall not say much about short-term or long-term memory, since these are familiar concepts to almost everyone, but I shall discuss the supervisory attentioning system here, because relatively few people have been exposed to the concept, and it is a vital concept for advertisers. It is central to much of the content of this book.

Imagine yourself at a cocktail party. Everybody is talking. Your ears are being assaulted by noise, from a lot of people all speaking at about the same volume. All the same you are pursuing a conversation, and you can mostly follow what your companion is saying, despite the fact that she is not talking any louder than everyone else. This is because you are concentrating on your companion. Then someone in a nearby conversation mentions your name. You involuntarily switch your attention to the person who mentioned your name, and listen to a few words of that conversation. You realize the participants are not talking about you, but about someone else with the same first name, and switch your attention back to your companion.

The question is, how come, if you were concentrating on what your companion was saying, and actively ignoring the background noise, you were able to identify your name in another conversation?

Let us take another example. Imagine you are driving a car – a complex learnt behaviour – on a narrow road, and at the same time having a conversation with your passenger. You come up behind a slow-moving tractor and need to pass it. So you stop talking and concentrate on driving; then when you have overtaken successfully you pick up the conversation at the point you left off. Again the question is, what made you switch your attention from talking to driving if you were doing both so comfortably before?

Let us consider an even more amazing (when you think about it) piece of human behaviour. You are the passenger in the car, and you are saying something when the driver (non-verbally) signals his intention to pass the tractor. You stop talking until the driver has overtaken and is back in lane, then continue the conversation. In other words, you intuitively recognize from experience that the driver will switch from listening to you to concentrating on the manoeuvre, then switch back to the conversation. Again the question is, how did you know you should be switching from talking to not talking, and back to talking again?

Now let us close in on our main focus. You are reading a newspaper in front of a television set. The television is on, but you would not describe yourself as watching it; you are concentrating on an article in the paper. But occasionally an advertisement, news item or announcement on the television catches the edge of your attention. If a researcher asked you afterwards what you had been doing, you would probably say, entirely honestly, 'I wasn't watching the television, I was reading the paper. Advertisements? I always ignore them.' If they then asked, 'Did you notice the Audi ad?', you might equally honestly say, 'Yes.'

In all these instances, your supervisory attentioning system is at work. And if it is to work, it needs to get input from your senses, or at least from your short-term memory's information derived from your senses, about things happening in the environment that are not your main focus of attention.

INTERPRETATION

The most important thing your brain has to do is to interpret the incoming data that you receive via your senses: sight, hearing, smell and touch, plus your broader sense of your body and its position. Without interpretation your brain would simply be a recorder of experiences. However, the simplified psychologists' model of the brain in Figure 3.2 does not tell us a lot about how this interpretation is done.

Think of an elephant.

Most people have a pretty clear sense of what an elephant is: a large grey animal with a trunk and big ears, native to parts of Africa and Asia. Most people have seen an elephant, if only in a zoo or on the television. The more often you read this paragraph and the more you think about an elephant, the more clearly you are likely to visualize an elephant.

Now think of an ndlovu.

Unless you're Zulu-speaking, that is likely to be trickier. You can probably figure out roughly how the word is pronounced, but it will not conjure up a picture in your brain. Of course, if you do speak Zulu you will be at an advantage; you will have a picture of a large grey animal with a trunk.

The concept of an elephant is, when you think about it, a pretty complex one. It contains quite a few elements – the ones we mentioned above, the size, the trunk, the flappy ears, for instance – that will be common to everyone who in any sense 'possesses' or 'knows' that concept. But at the same time it is *your individual* concept of an elephant. It will take its shape from the things that you know about elephants, either from seeing them, or from reading about them, or watching television programmes about them, or hearing other people's stories about them – and because your experiences are unique, that concept is likely to be subtly but meaningfully different from anyone else's concept of an elephant.

My concept of an elephant differed from yours up to now, most likely, because it included the word 'ndlovu' and yours did not. In future yours will contain it too.

A year ago I drank a pint of Guinness, and there was still some caustic soda in the tap when it was poured, so it tasted of caustic soda. Ever since, when I taste Guinness, I get the taste of caustic soda. (This would be your experience if you had my memories.) So somewhere in my brain the taste of Guinness continues to be linked to the memory of the taste of caustic soda. If you have never drunk Guinness that has been poured through contaminated pipes, your concept of Guinness will have that difference from mine.

One kind of question that market researchers often ask is along the lines of, 'When I say Coca-Cola, what comes to mind?' When you are asked that question, a whole host of associations are likely to come to mind. Some of them will be the 'brand signature' of Coke, the kinds of things that marketers want you to think of when you think of Coke: brown liquid, thirst quenching, squiggly logo, red can and so on. Among these brand associations there will almost certainly be some memories of advertisements for Coca-Cola, since you are (I assume) a consumer in a market in which Coca-Cola advertises heavily.

What comes to mind will also include some of your own more specific associations (that time you drank two cans of Coke when you were six and were sick at the seaside, maybe).

We can describe a word such as 'Coke' or 'elephant' as a *trigger* for the concept of Coke, or of an elephant. That is, when you are given the word 'elephant' your brain automatically gets to work and what you know about elephants (or at least, a fair bit of all that you know – there might be things you were told about elephants that you have 'forgotten', or at least cannot 'bring to mind' right then) comes to awareness. This business of using language as a trigger for concepts is not a trivial one: to make it work you need the conceptual framework that language provides. You need to know how individual letters work, how words work, and you need to know the specific word 'elephant' (or 'ndlovu') and link that with the animal it signifies. Unless all these components are in place, the black squiggles on the page will conjure up nothing for you.

Similarly, the squiggly logo of Coca-Cola can act as a *trigger* for the whole Coca-Cola concept, and so can the taste of the brown fizzy liquid itself.

So in some way, the supervisory attentioning system takes the trigger and uses it as a kind of 'index card' to haul out of long-term memory all that you know about Coca-Cola, or an elephant, or your grandmother, or anything else of which you have a memory.

All this background knowledge lives in our long-term memory, and as a result our interpretation of incoming observations is *dependent on* our long-term memory. The incoming stimulus can only be interpreted by recall of the information required for interpretation from long-term memory.

This process of interpretation needs to be very fast: there is no discernible gap between seeing the word on the page and visualizing an elephant. Obviously the speed with which you interpreted the word 'elephant' was not crucial to your existence, but in other circumstances our speed of interpretation and reaction is vital. When you see a road sign that says 'Stop!' you need to react and stop promptly if you are to avoid an accident.

But how does the supervisory attentioning system identify the trigger? How does it decide what should be the trigger, what your attention should focus on, out of all the inputs you receive through your senses?

When you think about it, that is not an easy question to answer.

Let us return to the example of a cocktail party. You are talking with your companion. To understand what she says, you need to interpret the words you hear. To do this you are continuously using your long-term memory to identify words, identify sentences, and interpret their meaning.

At the same time your supervisory attentioning system is monitoring the environment for cues to make you change your focus of attention, such as someone nearby mentioning your name, or your spotting a familiar face somewhere else in the room. It needs to be able to identify these cues out of the infinite number of stimuli that you are receiving. And to do this, it too needs to draw on your long-term memory. However, how does it know where in your long-term memory to look? *How does it know what is important enough to make you change your focus?*

That is one of the core questions I hope to come close to answering in this book.

4

The structure of the brain

As Professor Franklin's schematic (page 22) showed us, the psychologists whose insights we looked into in Chapter 3 take a 'black box' view of the brain, and do not attempt to find out what it is actually made of. But most of the researchers whose work we shall be looking at take a less opaque view, and in order to put their insights into perspective, it will be useful to explain at this point how exactly a brain is put together.

The brain is a hugely complex organism, and there is barely any limit to the detail with which it can be described. My aim here is not to be exhaustive, but simply to introduce the terms that will appear later in the book.

You may find it useful to refer to Figure 4.1, which is a schematic of the main areas of the brain.

THE CENTRAL NERVOUS SYSTEM

The brain is a core part of a larger system in the human body (and of course, an analogous system in the body of other animals, although they are not our subject here). This is the central nervous system, and it also includes both the spinal cord and the 'peripheral' nervous system, which includes all the elements that convey sensory information to the brain. In very simple terms, the brain receives sensory input from the rest of the body via the nervous system: on what is seen, what is heard, what is smelled, the position of the body in relation to its environment, what it touches, and so on. The cells that obtain this sensory input connect to the cells in the central nervous system, and ultimately in the brain. The brain then processes that information – in ways we shall begin to consider in Chapter 5 – and sends output signals via the central nervous system. In short, we react. The brain is also in some way

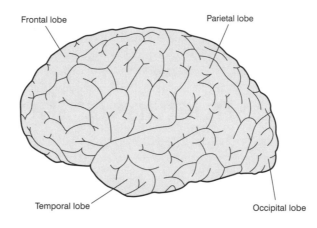

Frontal lobe

Parietal lobe

Temporal lobe

Occipital lobe

a) The lobes of the cerebral cortex

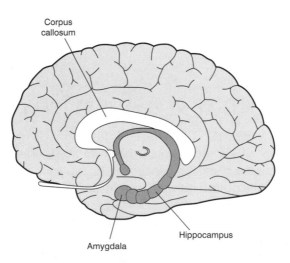

Corpus
callosum

Amygdala

Hippocampus

b) Cross-section showing the corpus callosum, the hippocampus
and the amygdala

Figure 4.1 *The main areas of the brain*

lastingly affected by the input and its processing, and it is this that we describe as 'memory' or 'knowledge'.

The 'lower brain' (that is, the part that sits lowest in the skull, at the head of the spinal cord) is mostly concerned with vital functions like breathing, and we do not need to consider it much in our context. Our main concern will be with the upper brain, or the cerebral hemisphere, and to some extent with the 'midbrain', the strange and complex set of structures that links the cerebral hemisphere to the rest of the central nervous system.

The cerebral hemisphere (so called because it is a roughly hemispherical structure, like an upturned bowl inside our heads) has a heavily wrinkled outer layer, the *cerebral cortex*, which is divided into four *lobes*. As we shall see, there are many pitfalls in suggesting that any area of the brain 'deals with' any specific function, because almost any function seems to involve activity across many sections of the brain. Even so, it is clear that the different lobes are primarily involved in different types of activity. The *frontal lobe* has a specific role in planning future action and controlling our movements. The *parietal lobe* is concerned with 'somatic sensation': that is, forming our body image and relating it to the space we occupy and our surroundings. The *temporal lobe* has a specific role to do with our ability to hear, and the *occipital lobe* is concerned with our sight.

Two other areas of the cerebral cortex that have been identified will also play a role in our story. The *posterior association area*, which is found at the margin of the parietal, temporal and occipital lobes, appears to deal with the use of information derived from the sensory system for perception and language. And the *limbic association area*, at the medial edge of the cerebral hemisphere, is concerned with emotion and memory storage.

The hemisphere is also bisected from the front to back, across the middle of our skull, into what are often known as the 'left brain' and 'right brain' (or 'left hemisphere' and 'right hemisphere'). These are not entirely separate, because they are linked in a normal brain by a large bundle of nerve fibres known as the *corpus callosum*.

An important area of the inner cortex is the *hippocampus*, which broadly speaking seems to be involved with aspects of memory storage.

Several deep-lying structures beneath the cerebral cortex, in the area of the midbrain, will also be of interest to us. The *basal ganglia* seem to help regulate motor performance, but of more concern than that (to us as advertisers) is the *limbic system*, located in the lower midbrain, which appears to be the area of our brain that controls our feelings of pleasure on the one hand, and of fear and pain on the other. It is sometimes referred to as the 'reward centre', and sometimes called the 'lizard' brain, because the limbic system is a very primitive part of the brain which is found in all animals, even reptiles. One part of the limbic system, the *amygdala*, has a particular role in handling our fear responses.

THE CREATURE THAT EATS ITS BRAIN

Only a creature that moves from place to place requires a brain! The sea squirt ascidian has a brain and a nerve chord to control its movements. As it reaches its sedentary mature form, these structures are gradually absorbed and digested, leaving only those needed for filter feeding. This little example in nature really explains the importance of brains in evolution.

Now let's go on to look in more detail at how our brains actually operate.

5

Neurons: the building blocks of the brain

Now we have some overview of the general structure of the brain, we can home in on a lower level, and look at its basic building blocks. In effect we are now moving to the bottom left of Professor Franklin's model (page 21–22), and considering the contribution of neuroscience. My overall aim here is to build up a picture of how the brain actually handles the processes of paying attention and remembering, so we can consider later in the book what relevance these insights have to those involved in advertising.

NEURONS

Neurologists know that the basic building block of the brain is a particular type of cell that is known as a *neuron*. Like all cells, neurons have a cell body containing a nucleus, and they also have two other core components: one or more *dendrites*, and an *axon*. (See Figure 5.1.)

Dendrites are thin fibres that project from the body of the neuron. They receive signals from other neurons: so to use a term also applicable to computers, they perform an *input* function. A single neuron can have any number from one to several thousand dendrites.

The axon is usually the longest of the fibres projecting from the cell body. It directs electrical information away from the neuron, so (again in computer terminology) it provides an *output* function. Although the neuron generally has only one axon, its axon generally has a lot of branches, and it is able to pass on information through these branches to as many as a thousand other neurons.

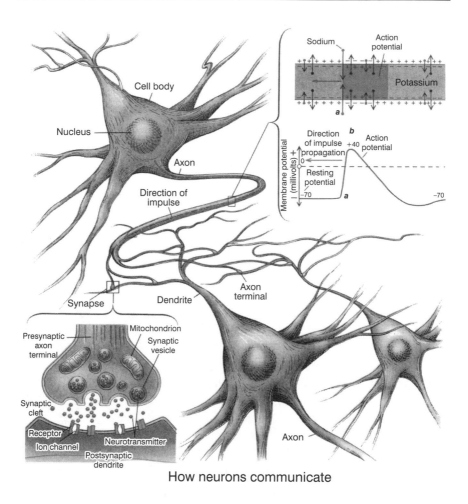

How neurons communicate

Figure 5.1 *The structure of neurons*

The human brain is made up of around 10 to the power of 10, or 10,000,000,000, neurons. In fact, there are more neurons in your brain than there are stars in the Milky Way. And the interactions of the dendrites and axons of these neurons make up the incredibly dense network of cell activity that takes place in your brain.

Although the dendrites of some neurons receive information from the axons of other neurons, they are not physically in contact with each other. There is a very small gap between the two, which is known as a *synapse*. Neurons are able to communicate by sending chemicals called *neuro-transmitters* across the synapse. These neurotransmitters either excite the receiving neuron to send out (or continue sending out) a signal, or they inhibit it from sending out a signal.

Put simply, the main function of a neuron is to carry 'messages' from one part of the body to another, and to do this the nervous system uses two basic processes – an electrical process and a chemical process. The electrical process is an impulse that travels through the neuron, but does not itself travel between two neurons. The actual transmission between two neurons takes place chemically.

The electrical charge within a neuron (as with the electrical charge in, say, a battery) is the result of the unequal distribution of ions between a negative pole and a positive pole. When a neuron is 'resting', or in other words it is not transmitting information in the form of impulses, the inside of the cell is negatively charged and the positive pole is outside the cell. The resting potential of a neuron is a minuscule minus 70 millivolts. (Compare this with a torch battery, which has a potential of 1.5 volts.) When the neuron is stimulated it generates an impulse of 40 millivolts. This impulse travels down its axon towards the neurons it is in contact with (which might include itself), and depending on the state of the chemicals at the synapse, the next neurons may or may not be stimulated.

This electrical impulse travels at a speed of between 1 and 100 meters per second, which might sound very fast considering how small the neuron is, and in fact the brain itself is, but it is very slow compared with a computer. If telephones carried signals at this speed we would have great difficulty having transatlantic conversations. A neuron can fire up to 1,000 times per second. Again this might seem a very impressive statistic, but it is slower than the cycles of even the first generation of computers.

Once a neuron has 'fired' it returns to its resting state of minus 70 millivolts. There is no change to the electronic state of the neuron after it has fired. In other words, there exists no 'memory' in the electronic state of the neuron.

SYNAPSES

As was mentioned above, the electrical impulse flowing down an axon is not in itself passed on to the next neuron. It activates a chemical process in the synapse, and it is this that is transmitted to the second neuron. Whether the second neuron fires in response to being stimulated by the first (or in reality, in response to being stimulated by the many neurons that send signals simultaneously to it) depends on whether the (composite) signal exceeds a certain threshold, which is called the *limen* of the synapse. (This term has the same derivation as the word 'subliminal'.)

However, each time the neuron does fire, the chemical state of the relevant synapse is altered. It becomes more sensitive: in other words, the limen is lowered. This means that each time two neurons fire in sequence they will be more likely to fire next time there is stimulation of the synapse. This increased sensitivity between the neurons is the only trace of there having been some experience. So our memory is not stored as electrical settings of the neurons; it is embodied chemically in the greater likelihood of a particular set of neurons reacting to a new sensory input.

NEURONS IN ACTION

Let us go on now to see what neurologists have discovered about the ways in which neurons combine to build up the functioning of our brains. Then we will consider how their models of how the brain works compare with the psychologists' model of the way the human brain appears to work, judging from human behaviour.

This explanation is centred on the approach used by Rummelhart and Hinton, which is explained in more detail in Gillian Cohen, George Kiss and Martin LeVoi's book *Memory: Current issues* (1993).

HINTON DIAGRAMS OF NEURONS

The basic way in which neurons function can be represented very simply in diagrams based on squares and arrows. These are called Hinton diagrams, and the representations of neurons in them are known as *nodes*.

Figure 5.2 represents four neurons (or nodes) as simple squares. (Of course, this is a representation of four neurons, not the billions that make up our nervous system, but in reducing down to this tiny number we can still get a sense of the how the neurons interact.)

The next step is to show the dendrites and axons that connect the neurons as arrows. Each of these arrows connects with another neuron (node) at a synapse. The synapses are shown as little squares inside the nodes in Figure 5.3, and the small letters indicate the originating node (for

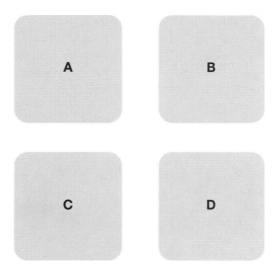

Figure 5.2 *Four neurons as simple squares*

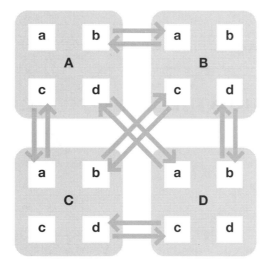

Figure 5.3 *Dendrites and synapses*

example, synapse b in node D indicates that the axon from node (neuron) B impacts on node (neuron) D). Each neuron/node can also feed its own signals back into itself, so these synapses are also shown.

As I explained, synapses vary in sensitivity to the incoming signal. In Figure 5.4 some of the small synapse squares have been shaded to show that they are 'sensitive' to electrical impulses from the relevant neuron. When the incoming signal stimulates a sensitive (or shaded) synapse, it will cause the neuron to fire. What we have here is a simple *neuronal network*.

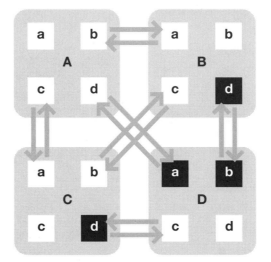

Figure 5.4 *A simplified neuronal network*

MAKING THE NEURONAL SYSTEM DO THINGS

Let us know look at what happens if (say) node A fires. (See Figure 5.5.)

Cycle 1

Node A sends an electric impulse to its synapses with other neurons with which it is connected – including itself. We show this by shading node A to indicate its firing, and also shading the arrows leading outwards from it, to indicate that they are transmitting a signal.

Cycle 2

All of the neurons that have sensitized synapses will now fire. In this example synapse a in node D is sensitized, so only node D fires and sends

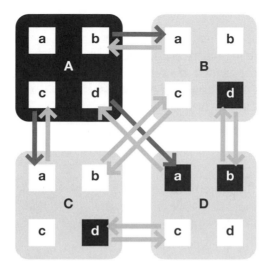

Figure 5.5 *What happens when node A fires*

the signal onwards. (The synapses in nodes B and C are not sensitized, so these nodes do not fire.) Again this is indicated by shading node D and the arrows leading from it. (See Figure 5.6.)

In the terminology used by brain scientists, node A has *recruited* node D. At the same time node A has finished firing, and reverts to its resting state.

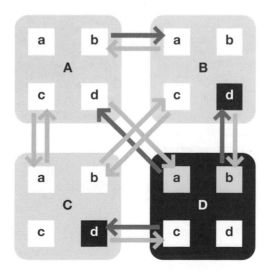

Figure 5.6 *Cycle 2 of the sample system*

Cycle 3

Figure 5.7 shows the result of node D's firing. These electrical impulses from node D cause nodes B and C to fire, because their synapses for signals from node D are sensitive. So node D has now recruited nodes B and C, and returns to its resting state.

Cycle 4

In cycle 4 (not illustrated), the impulse sent from node B again causes node D to fire. (Note that node D is not sensitive to node C, so it does not fire as a result of node C's firing.)

Cycle 5

This will in turn cause nodes B and C to fire, as they did in cycle 3, so the system settles into a repeating cycle where first nodes B and C, then node D, fire repeatedly. This is called a state of 'reverberation'.

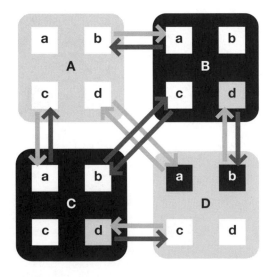

Figure 5.7 *Cycle 3 of the sample system*

EXAMPLE OF A SYSTEM WITH DIFFERENT SYNAPTIC SENSITIVITIES

Simple neuronal systems like this eventually settle into a reverberative pattern, but if a different set of synapses were sensitized, the system would settle in a different state of reverberation. Figure 5.8 shows a similar basic neuronal network but with different synapses sensitized. In this example, when node A fires it recruits node D, which recruits node B, which recruits node C, which recruits node B; and the system settles in a state of reverberation between nodes B and C. You may find it useful to work through this example.

The neurons that fire repeatedly in a reverberative state are described as a *neuronal cloud.*

It is also worth noting that in the second example, although nodes A and D were involved in starting the process, they were not part of the final cloud of reverberating neurons. This is a good representation of what happens in the brain. Typically, say, the optic nerves start the process of recruitment, but they do not become part of the resulting cloud of reverberating neurons.

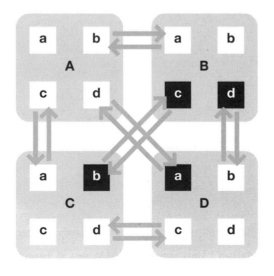

Figure 5.8 *A neuronal network with different sensitivities*

RUMMELHART AND BIGGER NEURONAL SYSTEMS

This is a very simplistic example, so now let us move on to a slightly more complex example: an experiment by David Rummelhart, a Nobel Prize winner. He identified 64 adjectives and nouns related to items commonly found in a house. His students had to identify how often they found these descriptors occurring at the same time when walking through a house – for example, how often the word 'large' would be associated with 'sink' and how often it would be associated with 'wall'. From this information Rummelhart programmed a neural network, which is shown in Figure 5.9. The sensitivities of the synapses are simulated by the frequency with which pairs of words appeared in the students' reports. This is a Hinton diagram using the same conventions as those used in the examples above, only this one has 64 nodes. The arrows are not shown for clarity, but the black squares indicate sensitized synapses.

The rest of the experiment consisted of 'firing' two of the neurons/nodes and then seeing what happened to the whole system. (This is not literally brain surgery: recall that we are talking about simulations here, so the experiment is a logical process of working out 'if this…, then that'.) Figure 5.10 shows what happened when the nodes 'oven' and

Figure 5.9 *Hinton diagram of Rummelhart's experiment*

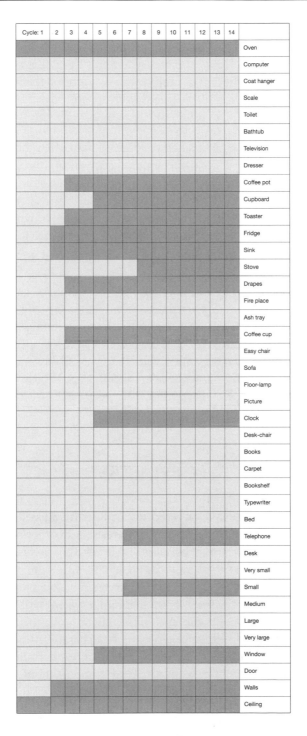

Figure 5.10 *Firing patterns for Rummelhart's experiment*

'ceiling' were fired. The grey cells indicate the nodes that are activated in each of the cycles, so it is easy to see the process of recruitment. The original two nodes recruited the nodes 'walls', 'refrigerator' and 'sink', which then fired in cycle 2. This activity then recruited the nodes 'coffee-pot', 'toaster', 'drapes' and 'coffee-cup' in cycle 3, and by cycle 8 the system had settled into reverberating mostly around the types of things found in a kitchen.

Rummelhart's team then repeated this phase of the experiment, activating the nodes 'desk' and 'ceiling'. The outcome is shown in Figure 5.11: the initial two nodes recruited other nodes until by cycle 6 the system was reverberating around words descriptive of a study.

The significance of Rummelhart's experiment is that it seems to provide a good analogy for how our brains work in real life. We walk around in different houses and we observe things. When we go into a kitchen we see a stove, clock, refrigerator, walls and so on. The neuronal systems that enable us to identify these items fire at the same time, and this means that their synapses increase in sensitivity. The same thing happens in a living room, for example: our simultaneous response to a couch, cupboards, pictures and the like increases the synaptic sensitivities between the neuronal systems involved when we see these items. In short, we make an increasingly close association between these items: so our brain links the concepts 'stove' and 'refrigerator' more readily than it links the concepts 'stove' and 'easy-chair'.

GESTALTS

To summarize what we have covered so far: in artificial systems designed to be analogous with neurons, the firing nodes recruit other nodes until the system settles into a 'neuronal cloud' of reverberating nodes (or neurons). This happens in similar ways in systems with only four nodes, and in slightly bigger systems with around 40 nodes; and we can hypothesize that it happens not too dissimilarly in the brain's system with its billions of neurons. It is typical of these systems that the nodes that started the process are not part of the final cloud of reverberating nodes. It is also typical for the resultant cloud of reverberating nodes/neurons to contain a lot more nodes/neurons than were involved in the firing at the beginning of the process.

Professor Susan Greenfield calls these 'Gestalts', a term derived from psychology, referring to the concept that the sum of the parts is more than the individual parts.

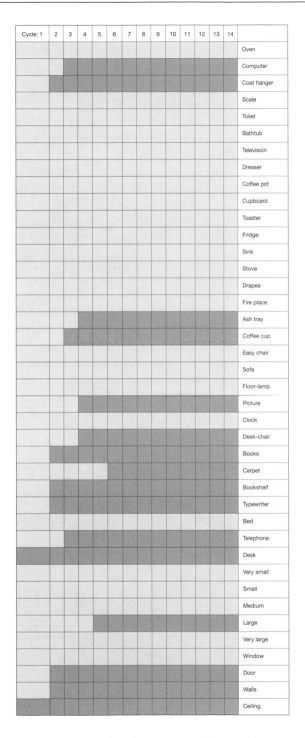

Figure 5.11 *Firing patterns for the re-run of Rummelhart's experiment*

Take a look at Figure 5.12. It is a simple line sketch made up of three ovals, a vertical line and a bent line. This is what our optical system experiences: but we interpret it as a smiling face. So somehow the activity in our brain starts with the optic neurons that register the lines, then recruits other neurons and knits them into a neuronal cloud that represents the idea 'smiling face'. The neurons that make up this pattern are recruited because their synapses make them sensitive to signals from the neurons at the start of the process. In other words, we have seen faces before; we have seen simple diagrams before and learnt to interpret them as faces; and our brain draws on this previous experience. So the neuronal activity that looking at this figure prompts settles down (so quickly that we do not even register the process) into the thought, 'Ah – it's a smiley.'

The mnemonics (that is, little pictures that denote concepts) in Figure 5.13 do the same thing. We see a few lines, and our brain effortlessly does the rest of the work to tell us what they are supposed to signify.

If you think back to Chapter 3, when we looked at the way in which the brain interprets information from a psychologist's viewpoint, you might feel that these ideas can be phrased in a different way. A Gestalt is in a way a concept, except that in some way it is a stripped-down concept. It is more like a complex *trigger* for a concept.

I recently received the e-mail in Figure 5.14 from my daughter (which means that everyone in the world has probably seen it). Can you make sense of it? I thought so.

Figure 5.12 *Gestalt: a few lines become a smiling face*

Which city?

Which country?

Figure 5.13 *The Gestalt effect*

Subject: this is bizarre

Aoccdrnig to rsceearch at an Elingsh uinervtisy, it deosn't mttaer in waht oredr the ltteers in a wrod are, the olny iprmoetnt tihng is taht the frist and lsat ltteers are in the rghit pclae. The rset can be a toatl mses and you can sitll raed it wouthit a porbelm. Tihs is bcuseae we do not raed ervey lteter by itslef but the wrod as a wlohe.

Figure 5.14 *The Gestalt effect and words*

At first sight this looks as if a real oddity of the brain has been discovered, but when you understand the Gestalt concept and how the brain works, it is not so odd after all:

- When we are learning to read as children, first we learn letters and their sound, largely through repetition.
- Next we learn combinations of letters – that is, words and their meaning. We learn to identify words as a whole – as Gestalts – rather than puzzling them out letter by letter.
- Then we learn to read on a sentence by sentence basis, so we interpret each word in the context of the sentence.

Soon we get so good at making out the message from a glance that there is actually plenty of redundancy in it: we do not really need all the letters to be present in the right order in order to make out the meaning. (And the 'meaning' of course, is a complex beast: it is not just a question of being able to speak the words out loud, it is a question of drawing on all the concepts that they signify.)

You might think this is not so different from being shown the squiggly logo of Coca-Cola, or hearing the word 'ndlovu': they are all we need in order to retrieve an extraordinary amount from our brains.

SUMMARY: IMPORTANT FEATURES OF NEURONAL SYSTEMS

The important features of neuronal systems that we have demonstrated here are:

▌ Our knowledge and memories are not stored as 'on' or 'off' states of the neurons themselves, but in the sensitivities between the neurons – that is, the state of the synapses.

▌ The state of the synapse is set by experience: that is, it is sensitized in relation to the number of times the two neurons have fired in conjunction in the past.

▌ The system comes back with more than it started with. For example, if you stimulate it with 'bath' and 'wall' it is likely to come back with all the items in a bathroom. This leads to the Gestalt effect: the whole is more than the sum of the initial components.

▌ Within two or three firing cycles the system has already stimulated most of the nodes that will be present in the final Gestalt (or the final state of reverberation).

▌ The brain does not use a separate set of neurons to store each individual concept (like a bathroom, or a kitchen). It is the pattern of neuronal activity that embodies the concept.

▌ The process of observation leading to interpretation is itself the process of laying down memory traces.

DISTRIBUTED MEMORY

The question you might reasonably ask at this point is, what does 'the neuronal system that is used to identify "Coca-Cola"' look like, and where is it found in your brain? That is a good question, but researchers have not yet reached the point where they can give a full answer to it.

As I explained in Chapter 4, neurologists have been able to identify the specific functions of some areas of the brain. There is no specific area, though, that can really be identified as our 'memory'. You might think that because we all hold so much information in our brains, it would have become apparent pretty early on where exactly it is stored; but it turns out not to be as easy as that.

This does not mean that neurologists know nothing about how memory works. As well as investigating patients with brain damage, they conduct open brain surgery with patients who are fully conscious. (The patients are not anaesthetized, first because there is no sensation in the brain, so they feel no pain during the surgery, and second because remaining conscious enables them to give feedback to the surgeon during the operation.) During these operations neurologists have found that when they probe certain parts of the brain, patients have very specific 'experiences of memories'. For instance a patient might say that she has suddenly has a strong recollection of standing in the kitchen as a child at Christmas, watching her mother cooking a meal, and can smell the food.

What appears to happen in these cases is that the stimulation of the neuronal cells by the surgeon leads to a recollection, or recall of memory, of events. Most importantly, this recall includes everything about the event: memories of words, faces, smells, emotions and so on. It is rather like when we hear a few notes of a song we know: it acts as a prompt and we sometimes recall the whole song, the words and the tune (or at least an overall sense of them), and often our experiences and feelings at the time we first heard it.

Scientists have agreed for a long time now that memories are not stored in a specific location in the brain, but are stored *throughout* the brain. This is understood best against the background of the neuronal system outlined earlier in this chapter. The power of the system lies in its high degree of interrelation, with many neurons able to transmit messages to many other neurons. So most likely there are no *specific neurons* that are associated with 'Coca-Cola' (rather like the individual letters c, o, l and a are not specific to the name: they also appear in many other words), but there is a *specific pattern of neuronal activity*, which might spread widely across the brain, that is associated with 'Coca-Cola', and which in turn triggers other associations: the red can, the squiggly logo and so on.

It does appear that there is a limited amount of organization in the way the brain stores information. As an example, when PET scans (see Chapter 6) are being done and patients are exposed to the word 'spoon', particularly intense neuronal activity can be seen in an area close to the area that is known to control the movement of the hands. This seems to suggest that the core neuronal activity related to concepts is located close to areas where there is related neuronal activity when those concepts are needed.

The Hinton diagrams we have used in this chapter are obviously simplifications. The initial set of diagrams shows only four nodes, each with four synapses, compared with the billions of neurons, each with thousands of dendrites, that exist in the human brain. But the pattern of transmitted activity that Hinton diagrams show (and that is extended in Rummelhart's experiment) seems to reflect (in its very simplified way) the pattern of activity in the brain itself.

If each 'node' in the Hinton diagram was taken to represent not one neuron but several thousand neurons, the analogy would still hold. The neuronal system the 'node' represented would still be connected to other neuronal systems, would still transmit signals to them, and would still be recruiting other neuronal systems in exactly the way the Hinton diagram proposes.

Rummelhart's experiment goes a step further in showing how our complex system of overlapping and interlocking concepts – our way of making sense of sensory input and of thinking, one might say – might work. It suggests, for instance, that there is a sense in which our brain identifies 'window' as a general concept, and uses this concept in a potentially infinite range of different contexts: kitchen window, bedroom window, window of the mind or window of opportunity, for instance. The pattern of neuronal activity that is 'window' relates to other patterns of neuronal activity, to narrow down to the specific (my kitchen window) and to expand outwards to the analogous (window of opportunity), just as it meshes in some way with related and overlapping concepts like 'large' and 'small', 'ceiling' and 'walls'.

NEURAL NETWORKS

A statistical technique called *neural networks* is based on programming a computer in exactly this kind of way, then feeding it data which it analyses. It is especially good in providing predictions (of stock exchange prices and the like) and also in grouping objects (what is known as *cluster analysis*). (A good book which outlines some of this is *Neural Network Solutions for Trading in Financial Markets* by Dirk Baestaens, Douglas Wood and Willem Van den Bergh (1994).) The important point is that neural network programs will always provide an answer – even if the answer is wrong. In other words: if there is an input, there will be an output.

This is important, again, because of the analogy with our brains. The neural systems in our brains will always provide an output for any input stimulus. We all know this is true: when we see something it is interpreted, even if the interpretation is wrong. Thus every advertisement I see is interpreted against my own experiences (memories), and my interpretation might be very different from yours, but I will still have interpreted the advertisement. This is often quite fun when traveling in a foreign country where you do not know the brands or the culture.

The fact that neural networks are very powerful clustering tools (indeed, they are generally agreed to be better at clustering than at predicting) is also very important to understanding the brain. LeVoi uses a very nice example of this (and in this book we use many examples to keep people thinking about the brain):

> *Question: Describe the difference between a dog and a cat without reference to the sound they make.*
>
> *Or: Write a heuristic for a computer to deduce from pictures of dogs and cats which are which.*

This is virtually impossible for a computer to do. Size does not help, because there are very small dogs and much bigger dogs, a range that spans that of cats. The number of legs and ears, or their shape, does not help because again, how do you distinguish dogs from other animals on these criteria? The dietary needs of dogs and cats are not that different. The length of their hair is not unique. Yet every toddler can walk into a strange house where there is an animal he or she has never seen before, and say 'Nice doggy' or 'Nice kitty', and be right 95 per cent of the time!

How can a toddler be so accurate when no one has sat down and explained the difference? The answer is neural networks. Almost every time the toddler has seen a cat or a dog, someone will have said, 'Nice doggy' or 'Nice kitty', effectively providing information on which is which. The child learns the differences, not by being told point by point how dogs and cats differ (as we have seen, neither a child nor most adults can do that), but simply by taking in a mass of gestalt information.

This is what neural networks do very well. They are programmed by being shown pictures, or told about characteristics, and given a classification. Soon the neural network will do its own classification and with a massive degree of accuracy. It will do this to every example it is introduced to, never saying 'I don't know', although like the toddler, it will occasionally get the answer wrong.

Our brains are brilliant classifiers. They need to be, because we have to classify the things that surround us quickly so that we can generalize from previous experiences with similar things or situations, and react appropriately!

Obviously this has a lot to do with how we interpret advertising. It also has a lot to do with how we invoke a memory of an emotion when we are exposed to something, as we shall go on to find out.

6

Learning and emotion

Now let us go on to look at how our brains operate on a rather more complex level, by considering the processes of learning and emotion.

If individuals, and the species as a whole, are to develop and adjust to their environment, they must not only acquire, but also retain (and in a general sense, 'learn from') information. We have seen this process taking place at an elementary level in simple neural models; the same process takes place, at several levels and to an infinitely higher degree of complexity, in the human brain.

We all start off with an initial endowment of information, in the form of our genetic code. The genes encapsulate (or encode, in the form of strings of DNA – deoxyribonucleic acid) the information necessary for the organism to grow to maturity from a single cell. Geneticists now understand to some degree how our genes 'program' us, so as our body grows, and the number of cells in it multiplies (from the single cell of a newly fertilized human embryo to the billions that make up the adult human body), different cells automatically take on different forms and functions. Just as we all (unless our genetic code is damaged in some serious way) grow two legs, two arms, one head and so on, so we all acquire a brain with a number of specific areas (on a macro level), which seem to perform broadly the same functions in all of us.

As individuals, we all have a fixed genetic code. However, the genetic code we pass on to our children will be different, both because it selects elements from both parents' genetic codes, and because random mutations occasionally take place. Sometimes these mutations cause defects in the offspring, but on other occasions they are beneficial, leading to the process of Darwinian evolution.

We have touched too on concept development, the Gestalt effect, and the question of how we learn to pay attention. You might reasonably argue that the very simple artificial neuronal systems we have looked at have not yet told us a great deal about any of these complex activities. One question that is worth asking is can bigger systems on these lines 'learn' complex behaviour, or does it take a degree of 'hard-wiring'? By analogy, how much of the activity in a human brain is inbuilt (that is, arises as a result of our genetic code), and how much is learnt activity?

Professionals in different areas do not agree on the answer to this question, and perhaps they never will. There is still much debate, for example, on how far the ability to use a language is 'hard-wired' into our brains, and to what extent it is 'soft-wired': that is, learnt as the result of our early exposure to language. To some degree both processes must be involved, but nobody is entirely clear where the dividing line comes.

Although the genetic code lays down to some degree the shape of the human brain, from birth onwards (or arguably even before birth, to some extent) we receive sensory input. Our response to this sensory input is in the form of patterns of neural activity, which become stored in the form of synaptic sensitivity, and thus help to shape the patterns of future responses.

It is generally agreed that our genetic inheritance also predisposes us to some extent to classify and conceptualize our sensory input. So although all of us are different in our individual thought patterns, pretty much all of us come to differentiate other individuals, and to acquire a sense of pleasure and pain, or liking and dislike. Language gives human beings a much enhanced way of conceptualizing and thinking about their experience, and those of us who share a language learn to categorize things in, if not the same way, at least broadly similar ways. Language also leads us towards another ability: the ability to learn at second-hand, not just from our own sensory experiences, but from the communicated experiences of others.

As we have seen, all the information that we acquire (as opposed to that which is encoded in our genes) is acquired through our sensory systems, and it is stored (again, 'encoded', if you like) in the developing pattern of neuronal sensitivity in the brain. And as I have also explained, each piece of sensory input impacts on the neuronal pattern in our brains to a greater or lesser extent, not only triggering an immediate pattern of neuronal firing, but also predisposing our brains to respond in certain ways to future input. So we can think of our 'knowledge' or our 'memories' as being stored in this pattern.

Much of this information acquisition is not intentional. We have sensory experiences all the time, whether we choose to or not. For example, close your eyes and try to 'see' everything on the road from your home to your office. If you are anything like me, you will be able to visualize every turn, all the road signs, the traffic lights, the significant buildings you pass, and so on. I certainly never wanted to learn the road in such detail. In fact, if I were a computer I would consider this a great waste of memory. But because I have travelled along the same route so many times, it has in a very real sense 'burnt' itself into my memory, and become a part of my knowledge base.

However, we also have in some way the ability to 'pay attention', or what I have described as a 'supervisory attentioning system'. We have the ability to *choose* to pay attention, to choose to learn (not just from our own experience, but from books, television programmes and other ways in which the knowledge of others is encapsulated and communicated), as well an innate tendency to pay attention to (which means, or at least leads to, learning from) some things without conscious choice.

Advertisements, of course, are a specialized form of communication, and we can think of them too as a resource from which individuals 'learn'.

It has been estimated that more than 80 per cent of what we as individuals 'know' has been learnt incidentally, rather than through a formal and conscious learning process. As a result, this form of learning is very important, not least to those who are concerned with influencing what others learn (as advertisers are).

'MAKING' A BRAIN

We have moved quite rapidly from considering the wetware of the brain (neurons and synapses) to how memories are laid down, then to how Gestalts are formed (memory retrieval) and even to how we interpret mnemonics (little pictures) and words. One obvious question is, if neurologists have reached this point in their understanding of the brain, is it possible to make an artificial brain 'learn' something? The answer is yes: it has been done (at least up to a point), and we now look at one example.

This relatively simple 'brain' uses an analogy of the human optical system, and first we need to look very briefly at how the optical system works.

As we all know, visual signals are registered by our eyes. The cells in the retina can detect light (and even colour), and they fire when they are struck by these light rays. In themselves these cells do not interpret anything. The retinal cells connect to the optic nerve, which is really two nerve bundles (that is, neuronal systems with dendrites and axons) that connect the retina to the area at the back of the brain known as the occipital region. As a result, the disordered visual information that hits our eyes begins a system of processing which might end with our thinking, for instance, 'I am looking at a television advertisement for Persil.'

DARWIN III

An experiment to see if a neural network could be made to 'learn' like a human being was carried out by Professor Gerald Edelman (who won a Nobel prize for his work). Essentially what Edelman did was to set up a neural network system on a computer that had no pre-programmed knowledge. He was looking to generate a form of 'intelligence' that lies in versatility and initiative: the ability to learn different things without being programmed to learn anything specific.

When a baby is born it has a full set of neurons. The number of neurons does not increase with age. However, the weight of the brain increases up to age 20 mainly due to the growth of dendrites. Thus, a newborn baby has all the tools with which to learn and only needs to be *able* to learn. Think of this as being similar to when you buy a new computer before you load software and operating systems. The computer has the tools with which to play chess or edit your documents, but it cannot yet do so. Only when the software is installed can it carry out any of these tasks. Every application, however, needs its own software. A newborn baby does not have 'software' loaded but it eventually learns how to 'carry out tasks'. The child psychologist Piaget states that a newborn baby does not at first even recognize its hands as belonging to him, or even that they can be used. They are just objects floating around in his field of vision. A newborn baby also has only two outputs: Displeasure (crying) and Pleasure (not crying).

Edelman's model simply consisted of a lot of nodes (again, analogous to neurons) connected broadly as they were in the Hinton diagrams I used in the previous chapter. Some of the nodes were connected to a 'field of sight'. They were intended to represent the human optical system, so when there was something in the field of sight, these nodes received it as input. Some of the nodes were sensitized so they fired when a colour appeared in the field of sight: red-sensitive nodes fired when something red entered the field and blue-sensitive nodes fired when something blue entered it.

Another set of nodes controlled an 'arm'. When these nodes were activated they caused a movement in the arm. In Edelman's program this arm also moved across the lines of sight, so that as it moved it activated the sight nodes, which sent signals to the core of the 'brain'.

However, the sight nodes and the movement nodes were not pre-programmed to work in harmony. All that the system could 'see' was what happened in its line of sight. All that happened was that when a node that moved the arm fired, the arm moved and triggered some 'sight nodes'.

The system itself was 'activated' by sending minor random impulses to the nodes activating the 'arm' so that it made random movements. Obviously these were recorded by the optical system. The program that was simulating this neuronal network also sent little 'missiles' towards the entity. These were little blue blocks (which the researchers called bottles) and little red blocks (called bees) which stimulated the nodes sensitive to red and blue.

Think of Darwin III as a newborn baby. Darwin III was given a 'mood measure': each time a bottle reached him he felt better, each time a bee stung him he felt worse. The only 'programming' that was done to Darwin III was that it wanted to optimize its mood, ie to feel good.

The system was set to run with bottles and bees randomly approaching Darwin III, arms flailing randomly in the air, the eyes recording the visual activity by sensitizing nodes, and the mood meter recording each time Darwin III is hit by a bottle or a bee.

Quite soon, due to the synapses strengthening (associations being formed), Darwin III learnt that when a bottle comes his ways he will soon feel good, and when a bee comes his way he will soon feel bad. He also formed the associations that each time an arm hit a bee he did not feel bad, and when an arm directed a bottle to his mouth he felt good sooner.

Let's reword this: when the synapses indicating a bee fires at the same time as the synapses that moves the arm he did not feel bad. When the synapses indicating a bottle fires at the same time as the synapses that moves the arm he felt good.

Obviously it would have been a trivial task to write a program instructing Darwin III what to do with his arms, but then Darwin III would only have been able to swat bees and not been able to learn anything else without a program. The triumph of Edelman's experiment is that he created a machine that could learn anything which has to do with making it feel better, or avoiding what would make it feel bad.

PLEASURE AND PAIN

We are still looking, you will recall, for something that explains just how the supervisory attentioning system knows what to focus attention on. Darwin III managed to develop a quite complex pattern of behaviour on the basis of a very simple rule of what to focus on: blue good, red bad. We might go a step further and anthropomorphize the little robot by saying that it experienced 'pleasure' at encountering blue objects (or perhaps that it saw them as 'good'), and that it felt 'pain' in encountering red objects, or saw them as 'bad'.

Human beings feel pleasure and pain as well. Could these be the trigger for our brain's focused activity?

Professor Joseph LeDoux, of the Centre for Neural Science at New York University (and author of *The Emotional Brain: The mysterious underpinnings of emotional life* (1996)) has done research into what happens to our brains to make us feel love, hate, anger and joy. Do we control our emotions, or do they control us? Needless to say, he does not have the final answers (yet), but he certainly has a better idea than most.

Despite the alluring title of his book, LeDoux tends to focus on just one emotion: fear. Understanding why we feel fear, and how it affects what we do, gives us many clues to how other basic emotions might work.

Fear – that is, a reaction to danger, or something that warns of potential danger – is a primitive emotion that has an obvious relationship to our ability to survive. It is important that we react with fear when we are in a dangerous situation: and this means that we need to recognize that a situation *is* dangerous.

One example Professor LeDoux uses is going on a hike in the country (in an area in which snakes are sometimes found) and noticing a twig shaped like a snake. Immediately, involuntarily, you are afraid. This produces a physical reaction: you will freeze, and your heart rate will increase. Then, with luck, you will realize that the twig really is only a twig. Slowly your body will return to its normal state, and you go happily on with your hike.

It often takes only a split second before you realize that the fear is unfounded. But even if you quickly conclude that it is only a twig, you will still have reacted with fear before that awareness kicks in. The reason is simple: 'The cost to your survival is much more if you think it is a twig, when it is a snake, than what the cost would be if you thought it was a snake but it turned out to be a twig.' So there is a strong evolutionary advantage in our identifying all conceivably dangerous situations as dangerous, and having our attention strongly drawn (by the feeling of fear) to the source of the potential danger.

Managers are advised to first think, and then react. In nature the rule is, react first, then think.

THE AMYGDALA IS THE KEY TO THE FEAR RESPONSE

LeDoux has done a lot of experiments, and quotes many other experiments, which have traced this emotional reaction back to the amygdala, a part of the limbic system of the midbrain. When the amygdala is damaged, the 'fear' response is absent. The amygdala is directly connected to the mechanisms that cause the body to release adrenaline, the heart rate and rate of breathing to increase, and bodily movements to 'freeze', which is why these are such prompt and strong reactions to anything that stimulates the amygdala.

Some of LeDoux's experiments involved teaching rats what to be afraid of by giving them electric shocks after they heard a bell or saw flashing lights, and finding out (by staining their neurons) how the anticipation of pain (when they next hear the bell, say) affects their neural activity. Based on his experiments LeDoux concluded that any stimulus takes two paths through the brain. It goes into the amygdala, which produces a response on an emotional (that is, fear or not fear) level, and it goes into the hippocampus where the content (including the emotional content) is evaluated. (The hippocampus is the part of the brain where thinking and interpretation appear to take place, a process we consider more shortly.) The amygdala is a very 'insensitive' interpreter: it is not able to differentiate between the nuances of an input stimulus. The hippocampus provides a much more subtle response that does interpret the nuances, but it takes longer to do so, which is why the amygdalal reaction kicks in first.

In neurological terms, then, this is broadly the process when we see something that might be a twig or might be a snake. (Of course, anything else we see will spark at least the start of a similar process.)

1. The image is registered on the retina.
2. This stimulates the optic nerve.
3. The optic nerve stimulates the neurons in the occipital region of the brain (at the back of the head).
4. The neurons in the occipital region start to recruit other neurons, starting the process of interpretation.
5. The process of recruitment moves from the rear of the brain towards the front (there is nowhere else for it to go).
6. When the neuronal activity reaches the amygdala in the midbrain, the image itself is only half interpreted, but that 'broad' interpretation (could be a twig/could be a snake) is enough for the amygdala to work on and react if it matches one of its (probably also broad) patterns that prompt the 'fear' reaction.
7. The amygdala sends two signals. One goes from the limbic system to the muscles, prompting the bodily reactions that we mentioned earlier, and the other goes back to the occipital region, prompting it to pay more attention to this potentially dangerous stimulus.
8. Recruitment of neurons continues towards the frontal lobes (the area of the brain where rational thought takes place). The signals direct from the optic nerve and those triggered by the amygdala combine,

and the frontal lobes complete the process of identification (conceptualization and categorization) and interpretation.

9. The frontal lobe sends signals back to the amygdala which prompt it either to signal the body's alarm systems to relax, or to continue the fear response until the danger is past.

We can call this last step 'post-rationalization' in its truest sense: we rationalize our emotional reaction, and this in turn modifies the emotional reaction.

WHEN MEMORIES ARE LAID DOWN THEY ARE EMOTIONALLY 'TAGGED'

One very big danger in offering this kind of tidy step-by-step analysis is that you, the reader, might assume that as a result there are really two separate memories that operate within the brain: one memory that operates on the amygdala and another that operates on the hippocampus. This does not seem to be the case. The emotional reaction and the rational interpretation, the 'contextual memory', are not only formed at the same time, they are inextricably part of the same system. And the hippocampus does not only draw on the rational information the neuronal Gestalt provides, it also draws on the emotional information that is a part of the Gestalt.

THIS IS NOT JUST TRUE FOR BIG EMOTIONS

A second possible misconception is that this emotional reaction is something that only operates in extreme, potentially life-threatening situations. After all, we do not have the same kind of intense bodily reaction when we see a pack of breakfast cereal as we do when we are shot at or see a venomous snake. However, this does not mean that there is no input from the amygdala in other circumstances.

Of course, the snake example is a relatively extreme one, and fear of our life is an extreme emotion; but we have a whole range of emotions, from mild liking and disliking upwards. All of them appear to derive in some way from the limbic system, of which the amygdala is a part, and for all of them the limbic system sends output to the hippocampus (as well as producing physical reactions).

FROM FEAR TO PLEASURE

If humans fear things, they also enjoy them, and to concentrate on fear alone is to tell only half the story. So at this point I need to introduce the idea of a 'pleasure centre' in the brain. I use as the focus of this explanation a book by Ronald Kotulak entitled *Inside the Brain* (1996). A very large part of the research about the 'pleasure centre' in the brain comes from research that has been done around alcoholism and drug abuse, trying to identify why people continue to seek out things that rationally they know are bad for them.

Although the amygdala seems to deal mostly with fear and pain, the limbic area as a whole seems to handle feelings of pleasure as well. Dr George Koob, a neuropharmacologist at the Scripps Research Institute in La Jolla, California, puts it this way:

The reward system brings limbic information – emotional information – into the area of the brain that makes you do things.

Performing like an emotional thermostat, the limbic system helps the brain sort through the zillions of sensory inputs and thoughts we experience each day by tagging them as emotionally hot or cold, or something in between.

Hot things are to be remembered and they are spritzed with pleasurable sensations ranging from the thrill of sex to the glow of a good deed. Cold sensory inputs and thoughts receive no emotional tag and they drift away to be forgotten.

The reward system affects behaviour. It says 'that was good, let's do it again and let's remember exactly how we did it'. In this way you learn important new things that are good for you.

LEARNING AND FEELING

The physical reactions that the amygdala prompts in us, and those of pleasure that the limbic system mediates, seem to be inbuilt, or 'hard wired' as I put it earlier: we do not need consciously to *learn* how to react physically when we feel afraid, or what it feels like to enjoy something.

However, do we need to learn through experience what to be afraid of? This is not that straightforward an issue.

In South Africa we often have visitors from the UK and the United States, and they are afraid of things like mamba snakes, lions and baboon spiders, but they are not afraid of zebras or giraffes. This fear cannot come from first-hand experience: we don't have to have been bitten by a snake ourselves in order to fear snakes. Is it entirely because they have read books and seen films, and generally been briefed that zebras and giraffes are not dangerous, but baboon spiders are? (In fact, generally speaking baboon spiders are *not* dangerous to human beings, although of course there are some species of dangerous spiders.) It seems like a thin explanation.

When James Bond wakes up in bed and finds a tarantula on the pillow, the whole cinema audience feels his fear, not just because we empathize with him, but because in some way we 'know' that snakes and tarantulas are dangerous. But again, how do we know it? Is it that we are in some way 'hard-wired' to fear things that look like snakes or spiders?

If this is so, perhaps it explains why the limbic system, through which our sensations seem to pass *before* they are fully 'interpreted' or 'thought about' by our higher brain, somehow 'recognizes' things that are pleasurable or scary, and is able to 'tag' them.

ALCOHOL AND THE PLEASURE CENTRES

Using PET (positron emission tomography) scanners that show us what parts of the brain are most active during different activities, University of Chicago scientists have made the first images to show alcohol affecting the reward centre in humans, and watched as alcohol went on to affect other areas of the brain. Dr Malcolm Cooper says: 'We're at the interface between molecular biology and behaviour. It's all rushing down on us in a superb way. We can now begin to relate behaviour to genes and metabolism.'

Alcohol seems to reduce the level of neuronal activity, and at least when only a little has been drunk, to induce a sense of calm. It works in the same way that barbiturates sedate people, and anaesthetics make them unconscious. As more alcohol is consumed, larger sections of the brain are turned off, until the person ultimately does lose consciousness.

Alcohol also prevents new memories from being laid down, which is why it is often difficult to remember the names of people you met at a cocktail party, or to remember at all what you did when you were very drunk.

The mechanism by which alcohol works is tied to the reward system. As a result, associations with drinking tend to become tinged with pleasurable, emotional memories. (The unpleasant part of the drinking experience is not remembered as well due to the interference of too much alcohol with the memory system.) That's why an urge to drink can well up in abstinent alcoholics when they pass the bar where they used to drink or see an advertisement for their favourite beverage. So in some way, the process from enjoying alcohol to suffering from alcoholism is driven by the 'reward' system of the brain. We might say that it is an emotion that drives this, and the emotion itself is formed by the memories of how the body felt before. We discuss this somatic reaction extensively in the next chapter.

DARWIN III IS DRIVEN BY EXPECTED EMOTIONS

This gets us back to the 'machine' that was built by Edelman, which could sort red blocks from blue blocks. The thing that really drove this machine was the unit inside it that said that blue blocks lead to pleasure and red blocks lead to discomfort.

All that Darwin III wanted to do was to increase its pleasure (be happy) – or reduce its level of discomfort. Without this mechanism, Darwin III would have done nothing – just waved its arms randomly, sometimes knocking away bees, sometimes knocking away bottles.

Not only is it necessary to have a 'centre for pleasure' in the brain, this centre also needs to be anticipative. Darwin III needed to 'know' that when it saw a bee approaching it would soon experience pain, and when it saw a bottle approaching it would soon experience pleasure.

What we have learnt of the limbic system and its role in brain activity suggests how human beings come to have this knowledge too.

SEEING ACTIVITY IN THE BRAIN

Until fairly recently it was barely possible to look at a living brain doing the things that a living brain actually does: or at least, doctors could look at it, but all they saw was a lump of inert grey matter. True, brain surgery is generally done with the patient conscious, but the brain itself does not move or visibly change its shape when it works, so doctors do not learn from the sight of it, they only learn from what patients can tell them about the thoughts and memories they stimulate. (Although these are often fascinating, this makes for a rather imprecise kind of knowledge.)

Technology to measure electronic activity in the brain (in the form of EEG scans, in which electrodes are placed on the patient's head and electronic activity is measured) has existed for many years, but the outputs are so gross (that is, they measure such a large section of the brain at once), that they only provide very imprecise information. One advantage of EEG scans, however, is that they can record a sequence of events over time.

Another technology that has been developed enables us to see something of the electrical and chemical activity that goes on inside a working brain, at a degree of resolution that enables plenty of interesting things to be learnt. This technique, positron emission tomography (PET), measures areas as small a cubic millimetre. (Even this is still considered a gross measure, since a cubic millimetre contains billions of cells, but it is a major improvement on what could be done before.) The PET technology works by injecting sugar water that has been made radioactive into individuals. When activity takes place in a specific section of the brain, this section burns energy, which means that it attracts the sugar (and the radioactive isotopes). It is not easy to see the sugar, but the isotopes attached to it can be shown on scanners. As a result, neurologists can see which areas of the brain show the most activity when patients are doing (or thinking) different things.

First, I should like to introduce you to a pattern of EEG activity: the pattern that is generated when a light is flashed into an individual's eyes, or he or she is briefly exposed to a picture. Figure 6.1 shows the typical electronic pattern measured in the rear portion of the brain. There are two lines, one showing activity in the left brain's occipital region, and the other, activity in the right brain's occipital region. The zero point on the horizontal axis indicates when the picture was shown, so the activity to the left of this is the kind of activity we see when the individual is not looking at anything in particular, and the activity to the right is the activity in the brain when the individual is focusing on a picture.

Researchers have shown that the cycle of activity of the visual cortex lasts around 0.3 milliseconds. That is, when a signal from the eye reaches the occipital region the neurons fire, recruiting other neurons (as described in Chapter 5) and setting in train a pattern of neural activity. Once they have fired, the neurons in the occipital region return to their resting state, but 0.3 milliseconds later they receive the next signal from the visual system, and this sets them firing again. This 0.3 millisecond cycle is not specific to the simple task of being shown a picture, it is a very standard feature for the occipital region.

However, the occipital region is not the only region of the brain where activity takes places during this kind of exercise. We know that the pattern of neuronal firing that goes on in the occipital region leads to further patterns of activity, for example in the frontal lobes (where we believe the

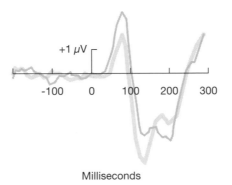

+1 µV

-100   0   100   200   300

Milliseconds

Figure 6.1 *Pattern of EEG activity in the occipital region*

activities of conscious thought and interpretation are focused), and in the limbic system, which, as we have seen, seems to be associated with emotion and the focusing of attention.

FUNCTIONAL AREAS IN THE BRAIN

The fact that there are areas in the brain with specific functions was known long before PET came along, although the sub-units into which neurologists were able to break down the brain were much larger than a cubic millimetre. The functions of these areas were discovered mainly by examining people who suffered physical damage to different areas of the brain. It became clear that damage to different areas correlated with the loss or impairment of specific brain functions. For example, damage to the back of the brain tends to cause blindness or sight impairments, so it is a reasonable deduction that this area of the brain deals in some way with input from the eyes. Back in the 19th century a Dr Broca noticed that many patients who incurred damage to a specific area at the side of the brain tended to suffer speech impairments. This area became known as the Area of Broca.

As I mentioned earlier, it is generally accepted that memories are in some way distributed throughout the brain, and there is no particular section of the brain that can be labelled 'memory', but there does seem to be a degree of organization in areas where often-used memories are stored.

A PICTURE OF SIGHT

Among the information we have learnt with PET is a considerable amount about how the human visual system works.

Students were asked to look at a computer screen with just a small cross-hair on the screen, while PET pictures were taken. Then words were flashed on the screen at the rate of 40 per second. They were just required to keep on looking at the cross-hair, while further PET pictures were taken.

Some similar areas of the brain showed activity during both these tasks, and it seems reasonable to postulate that these are the areas that were processing the same part of the task – that is, looking at the cross-hair. If the similar activity is deleted from both pictures, what is left is (arguably) the activity that resulted from seeing the words as well as the cross-hair. The area that was activated in this experiment is in the back of the brain, and is known as the occipital region. (See Figure 6.2.)

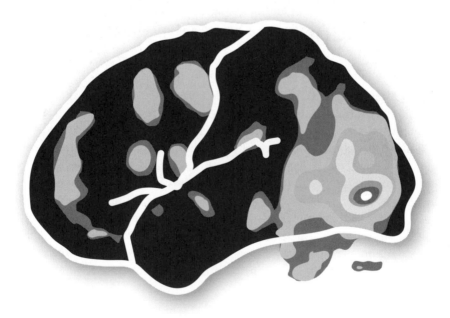

Figure 6.2 *Stimulation of the occipital region when the subject is passively viewing words*

It has long been known that when people suffer damage to the rear of the brain, their sight is affected, and this PET information confirms the previous hypothesis that the occipital region processes visual information.

A PICTURE OF LISTENING

In the next experiment the students watched the cross-hair while the words were spoken to them over earphones. Again the difference between the two pictures (of watching the cross-hair alone, and of watching the cross-hair while listening to the words) suggests which parts of the brain are involved in the verbal processing task (see Figure 6.3).

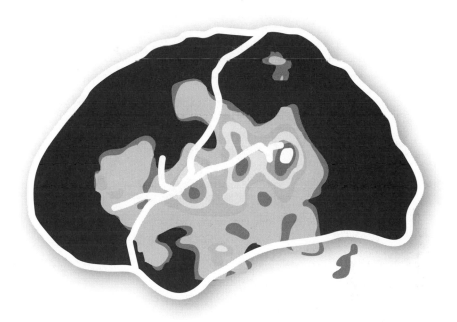

Figure 6.3 *Pattern of brain activity shown by PET when the subject is listening to words*

A PICTURE OF A NAÏVE ACTIVITY

Next the students were presented with the nouns, as before, but this time they were asked to think of and say out loud a verb related to the noun. Thus, if they were given 'nail' they had to say something like 'hit'. This task was termed 'naïve' because the list of nouns was new to the students, so they were required to *think* in order to come up with a suitable verb. The main area that showed PET activity was in the frontal lobes, where it is generally accepted that conscious thinking occurs (see Figure 6.4).

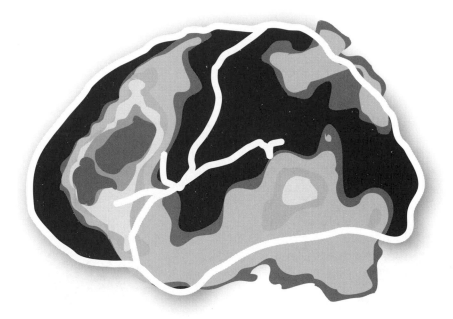

Figure 6.4 *Pattern of brain activity shown by PET when the subject is generating a verb to go with a noun*

A PICTURE OF A PRACTISED TASK

Next the students were given 15 minutes of intense practice in generating verbs to go with the list of nouns, and only then was the PET picture taken. This picture (Figure 6.5) shows very little activity anywhere in the brain that can be directly related to the task. We could perhaps be forgiven

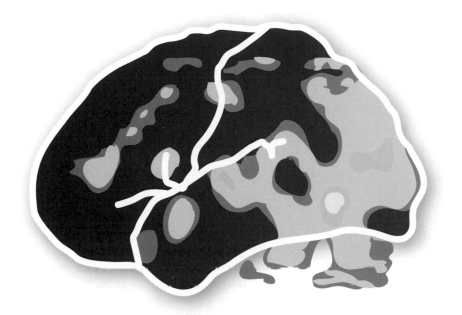

Figure 6.5 *PET scan of brain activity after practice on the word list*

for wondering if this is not what brain activity looks like when worn-out advertisements are being aired.

CONCLUSION

There's still quite a gap between this evidence of how real brains work, and the mechanical models we looked at earlier in the chapter, but at least we are beginning to fill it. In the next chapter we go on to consider another aspect of higher brain functioning, the question of what it means to be conscious, in order to paint a little more of this picture.

7

Arousal and consciousness

We've looked at some of the elementary building blocks of brain function, and briefly at the ideas of learning and emotion. Now it is time to consider in more detail how our brains enable us to focus on, learn about and memorize – everything around us, advertisements included – by looking at some aspects of the tricky subject of consciousness.

For this I turn to Professor Susan A Greenfield's book *Journey to the Centres of the Mind* (1995). Professor Greenfield lectures in neurochemistry at the Department of Pharmacology at Oxford University, and is a leading researcher on Parkinson's disease and mechanisms of neural degeneration. I mentioned earlier her definition of the 'Gestalt', the word she uses for the neuronal clouds that might be thought of as representing concepts in the brain. The work I want to discuss here involves chemical activity in the brain.

Our brain can be likened to the sky on Guy Fawkes Night, with lots of fireworks going off at the same time, as different kinds of sensory input reach it. In order to function at all, we need to filter this input in some way, and subsequently to make sense of it; to conceptualize on the basis of it, in other words. Of all the input you receive, you are only likely to be *conscious* of one or two things at a time.

The study of consciousness is intrinsically related to the study of the state of arousal of the brain. Arousal can be described as a general state of alertness: it is low when we are relaxed, and high when we are frightened.

Arousal can be measured. One way of measuring it is by using an electroencephalograph (EEG), in which a pattern of electrodes is placed on the scalp and used to record the electronic activity in the brain. Another (in some ways more accurate) way is by electrodes attached to the skin in places where the sweat glands are most sensitive to emotional stimuli: the palms, feet, armpits and forehead.

Arousal is a powerful factor in consciousness, although it is not the same as consciousness. When you are asleep your arousal level is very low, and you do not form any consciousness of your environment.

When you are at a high level of arousal – say, very angry – you might find that your consciousness is so overloaded that you are not able to give attention to any single input. It is easier for a person to become conscious of a single sensory experience when at the middle ranges of arousal than when at too low or too high a level. At too low a level of arousal, we do not really have enough neural activity to conceptualize fully; and at too high a level, we suffer from 'information overload'.

DETERMINANTS OF A CONSCIOUSNESS: THE POWER OF AN EPICENTRE

What is consciousness? Different researchers and thinkers have tried to give many answers to this question, but the one I would like to suggest to you is this: consciousness is what you are paying attention to; it is what you are thinking about. It is the epicentre of the neural activity that is going on in your brain, the peak that is the focus of attention.

The bigger, louder or more dominant an input is, the more likely it is to trigger neural activity and in turn to become the centre of your consciousness. Professor Greenfield gives a marketing example: if you walk into a shopping centre and see a mountain of oranges on display, you are more likely to give oranges attention than you would if there was only one orange among a lot of other fruit on display.

A nearby gunshot is much more likely to enter your consciousness than a car backfiring in the distance. However, when you are waiting in a doctor's reception room a lone print on the wall might capture your attention – quite simply because there is usually not much stimulus in this environment, so this low-key object might form the epicentre of your neural activity.

ANOTHER DETERMINANT OF CONSCIOUSNESS: THE AVAILABLE NEURAL NETWORK

The biggest and brashest thing in your field of vision is not always the one that draws your attention, however. Perhaps you are in the supermarket deliberately (consciously) looking for a kiwi fruit for a recipe you are preparing. The kiwi fruit display might not compete with the orange display for size or luridness of colour, but it is still likely to be the one that your attention homes in on. Or perhaps you are at a party full of people when your attention is drawn by someone at the far side of the room. Other people are more immediately 'in your face', but it is the old friend you really want to see again who becomes the focus of your attention.

Why does this happen? Professor Greenfield argues that it is because of the size of the neural cloud that forms in your mind as a result of the sensory stimulus (the sight of the individual, the sight and smell of the fruit). The size of the neural cloud will be determined partly by the strength of the sensory input, but partly too by the size and synaptic sensitivity of the available neuronal network. If there are many neurons available for recruitment, the neuronal cloud has the potential to become bigger, to generate more activity, than when there are fewer neurons to recruit. (It can be argued that the neuronal network that is the most developed for most people is the neuronal network concerned with themselves, which is why you react to your name being mentioned in nearby conversations.)

WHY THE BRAIN NEEDS TO CONTROL ITS LEVELS OF AROUSAL

Let me quote Professor Greenfield (1995) on the importance of the level of arousal to the process of becoming conscious of something:

> *Strength (recruiting power) of the epicentre (of neuronal clouds) might interact with arousal to generate three different situations. For gestalt formation and for consciousness, it is very important if arousal is low, medium or high. When arousal is high and the epicentre strong then only small gestalts are formed because of the rapid imposition of new epicentres bombarding our senses due to high arousal and the constant exposure to new aspects of the external world, themselves due to the attendant high degrees of restlessness and movement. Now imagine a situation where the converse applies. We are readily distracted, less aroused, but the focus of our consciousness is still strong. In such cases, when arousal levels are more moderate, gestalt formation is larger because the epicentre acts as a raindrop in a puddle where the ripples are unopposed. We are paying attention, deeply conscious of a specific object. In the third situation arousal is low. Because we are asleep and the epicentres are completely internal driven, and thus weak, gestalts are again small. Consciousness is composed of mere fragments, we are dreaming.*

It should be fairly easy for you to appreciate why it is important for a being to control its state of arousal if it is to survive. If the level is too low, it will not give attention to environmental threats. If it stays too highly aroused for too long, it will not be able to focus its attention or learn about its environment either. To optimize its chances of survival it is necessary for the organism to be able to be highly aroused in threatening situations, to also be able to reduce this to a state of low arousal to allow the body to rest, and to be able to regulate the level of arousal between these two extremes. This control is achieved chemically in the brain.

CHEMICALS THAT CONTROL AROUSAL

I have shown how the neurons react to being stimulated, and how this stimulation itself creates long-term changes in the chemicals in the synapses that determine future reactions by the neuron when it is stimulated (that is, it creates one of the building blocks of a long-term memory). Besides this long-term reaction in neurons there is also a shorter-term reaction called neuronal modulation, a phenomenon that has been studied only during the past 15 years.

Neuronal modulation is a process that causes the response of a neuron to become biased for relatively short periods of time, ranging from seconds to hours, without changing the response of that neuron permanently. If it was not for neuronal modulation, the response from all neurons would be invariant: that is, a neuron would fire or not fire depending only on its synaptic sensitivity as determined by how often it had fired before. Instead, our response to a stimulus depends on the circumstances in which we encounter it.

Neuronal modulation is caused by the action in the brain of chemicals called amines. There are five identified amines:

- serotonin;
- acetylcholine;
- dopamine;
- norepinephrine;
- histamine.

These chemicals do not work on individual synapses: the level of them affects the sensitivity of neuronal responses throughout specific broad areas of the brain at any given moment. They are disseminated in the most basic part of our brain, the part that is also found in the brain of reptiles. This is not really surprising: even snakes and crocodiles sleep, and become angry or aroused.

AROUSAL AND CONSCIOUSNESS AND ATTENTION

Why is this important in understanding the brain? Professor Greenfield puts it this way:

> *A stimulus, in the simplest case an object in the outside world such as an orange, triggers a series of diverse, idiosyncratic connections in the cortex – for example, eat, seeds, diarrhoea, first peel. The strength and extent of these connections depend on experience. Such connections are long-lasting and not very flexible. Thus there would be reasonable infrastructure for learning certain associations, the basis for enduring significance of objects around us – for example, the intrinsic properties relating to the taste or the methods and consequences of eating oranges. In addition, whatever degree of arousal happens to be prevalent at the time will ensure that a certain amount of particular amines are released within the cortex and that the amines modulate very large groups of neurons to be potentially more excitable. ... Wherever neurons are modulated for a temporary period, to respond easily and sensitively to the corralling signals from the group of associated neurons, a gestalt forms and a unique consciousness is formed for that moment. ...*

> *The orange will be an effective epicentre only if it happens to have temporary significance, perhaps caused by hormones signalling that I am thirsty, in conjunction with no competition plus time to recruit an increasing number of associations which would become stronger, like a flame burning out along a network of fuses. These types of associations could include a trip to Morocco, my mother's tales of the lack of oranges during World War II, and so on. They would deepen my consciousness of the orange as I stare at it in the window. Anyone seeing me would conclude I was concentrating on the orange.*

Especially if you are involved in advertising (and even more so if your role is primarily a creative one), you will recognize this pattern of association forming – and how it ties in, in a broad sense, with the kinds of association that advertisers try to introduce to strengthen consumers' responses.

One other important thing to bear in mind here is that the level of arousal has a real impact on the level of response we get from research done at a time other than the moment of purchase. How individuals react to the name of a brand in one situation need not be similar to how they react to it in a different situation, when the chemically regulated susceptibility of their brain is at a quite different level.

In the next chapter we go on to look at emotion, and its role in this complex system.

8

Emotion and reason

I told you at the start of the book that the main predictor of the success of advertising was 'ad-liking'. We have now reached a point at which emotion enters the story, so you may feel that we are heading towards an explanation of this phenomenon. But we need to look carefully at what emotion is, before we can bridge the gap between the instinctual fear response that we make when we encounter a snake, and our mild fondness for one brand of shampoo over another.

First, I want to tell you a marketing research story that is true, and which demonstrates a very important point.

In the late 1970s I was asked by South African Breweries to propose a research methodology to prove that South African black people see fewer colours than white people do. My contacts at SAB explained that the firm had just used a well-known Dutch psychologist/qualitative researcher to conduct focus groups for its intended new packaging. In his conclusions he expressed the opinion that South African black people see fewer colours than whites. My brief was to find a way to verify this, because of my interest in neurology.

It was only when my wife was discussing our new living room decorations, in Afrikaans, explaining where the beige and the maroon curtains would go, that I realized although she was speaking Afrikaans she was using the English words 'beige' and 'maroon'. I also realized that each time I had to 'think about' what colour she meant. Afrikaans does not have words that specifically mean the same as 'beige' and 'maroon': instead we would be more likely to use a descriptive phrase, such as 'a yellowish, brownish colour' or 'a sort of dark purple and red'.

Even people who are virtually bilingual tend to think in one primary language and translate the words that come to mind into the other, and those less fluent in a second (or subsequent) language do this even more. They tend not to use words for which there is no close equivalent in their first language, because these do not fit their conceptual structure. Thus many Afrikaans-speaking people would not use the word 'beige' (although my wife was clearly an exception), but would use the word 'yellow', which maps neatly onto an Afrikaans word, and qualify it as necessary. Similarly they would use 'purple' (which has an Afrikaans equivalent) rather than 'maroon' (which does not).

The average black South African speaks at least four languages. One of these is generally English, but it is likely to be his or her third or fourth language. (Very few 'developed' countries can say this about their average citizens.) The first language will generally be something like Zulu.

In Zulu there is just one word denoting both 'blue' and 'green'. This does not mean that Zulus do not see different shades and hues of blue and green, it simply means that the Zulu conceptual system uses different ways of differentiating shades and hues than English does. Zulu also lacks different words for different degrees of comparison: just one word is used to represent the English terms 'far', 'farther' and 'farthest', for example. However, Zulus can indicate the degree of distance through voice intonation, so they actually say the equivalent of 'far', 'faar', 'faaar' or 'faaaaar': a continuous system rather than a discrete one, so one that is rather better at indicating the exact grades of farness.

I did not need to do detailed physiological research to make the point: South African black people are not genetically unable to see as many colours as Caucasians, but they have fewer words in their lexicon with which to describe them.

The same is true of emotions: different languages have different sets of words to describe emotions, and some of the sets contain more words than others. The English language has a large dictionary, and lots of different words to describe emotions, Afrikaans has a smaller dictionary, and Zulu has a smaller one still. However, this does not mean that Zulus experience fewer emotions than Afrikaners, who experience fewer emotions than English people at Oxford University reading for a degree in the English language; it just means that these different people have different ways of thinking about and verbalizing their emotions.

By the same argument: a baby has no vocabulary, but certainly has a range of emotions. We know this because we see it crying or gurgling contently or laughing or banging the cot bars to express frustration. These are all fairly broad-brush ways of indicating what the baby is feeling, but the baby probably feels a range of different degrees of a wide range of identifiable emotions: discomfort, pain, joy, fun, playfulness, irritation and so on.

DEFINING 'EMOTIONS'

At this point it is perhaps worth looking at what emotions actually *are*. How can we define them? Can we measure them, and if so, how? To answer these questions I shall use as a guide *Understanding Emotions* (1995) by Keith Oatley and Jennifer M Jenkins.

Fehr and Russell (1984) stated that: 'Everybody knows what an emotion is, until asked to give a definition'. Chapter 4 of *Understanding Emotions* is devoted to defining 'What is an emotion?', and reading it rapidly makes it clear how difficult it is to define an emotion. Obviously if we cannot define an emotion, we cannot measure an emotion either.

If you are an advertising practitioner, you have most likely discussed emotive advertising, emotive appeals of advertising, and the effectiveness of emotive advertising. You probably thought you knew what you meant, but this probably does not mean that you could offer a good definition of the word 'emotion'.

However, people can easily give examples of emotions. To demonstrate that point, Fehr and Russell (1984) asked a class of 200 undergraduates to write down, in one minute, all the terms they could think of in the category 'emotions'. The researchers merged syntactic variants (sad, sadness, sadly) in adding up the total, but still found that the students gave 383 different examples of emotions. The most common examples, all mentioned by more than half the students, were happiness, anger, sadness and love.

We would probably all agree that emotions are feelings, but are all feelings emotions? Before we look at psychologists' definitions of emotions, let us do a simple self-inspection. Table 8.1 contains a list of affective words: that is, words describing a feeling. They should all be familiar to you, and most or all will be words you have no difficulty in using to describe yourself or other people. Try to classify them into one or more of the following categories:

1.   A facial expression.
2.   An emotion.
3.   A mood.
4.   An emotional disorder.
5.   A personality trait.

Table 8.1 *Categorizing feelings*

The feeling of:	1. Facial expression	2. Emotion	3. Mood	4. Emotional disorder	5. Personality trait
Being in love					
Hate					
Fear					
Being interested					
Being startled					
Being distrustful					
Depression					
Sadness					
Deceitful					
Deceived					
Happy					
Warm-hearted					
Contented					
Pleased					

You probably found that when you placed a word in two categories, or had to think about which of two categories it should be classified in, you were choosing between:

▌ a facial expression and/or an emotion;
▌ an emotion and/or a mood;
▌ a mood and/or an emotional disorder;
▌ an emotional disorder and/or a personality trait.

Since these form a neat sequence, it looks like there is a scale of some kind in the classification system I suggested. Oatley and Jenkins (1995: 124) suggest that a general consensus is emerging among psychologists that this scale can be used to classify feelings, and that it is concerned with the duration of the feeling. So an emotion is more short-lived than a mood, an emotional disorder or a personality trait, but longer-lived than a facial expression. (See Figure 8.1.)

Besides the duration of the feeling, it might also useful to consider the cause of the feeling. Moods and emotional disorders are primarily caused by the chemical state of the brain at a point in time. This chemical state might occur naturally, but people also use mood-changing drugs (recreational drugs like tobacco and alcohol, prescription drugs like Valium and Prozac, and illegal stimulants like Ecstasy and

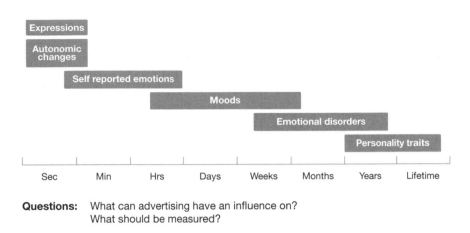

Questions: What can advertising have an influence on?
What should be measured?

Figure 8.1 *A spectrum of affective phenomena in terms of the time course of each*

cocaine) to change their brain's chemical state. Exercise and eating tend to affect it too, and some people consciously use these activities for that purpose.

Mood-changing drugs give us a sense of how chemical changes work to affect our moods. Their effects on our state of mind last for a while, but not indefinitely (from a few minutes to a few hours at most). The drugs generally take a while to have an effect, and it is difficult to identify exactly when a certain mood starts or stops.

DEFINITION

Oatley and Jenkins (1995) settled on the following definition of emotions:

It has been difficult to define emotions, and this difficulty continues. We will be rash and start this chapter with a working definition of a kind that has been gaining acceptance. It goes something like this.

1. An emotion is usually caused by a person consciously or unconsciously evaluating an event as relevant to a concern (a goal) that is important; the emotion is felt as positive when a concern is advanced and negative when a concern is impeded.

2. The core of an emotion is readiness to act and the prompting of plans; an emotion gives priority for one or a few kinds of action to which it gives a sense of urgency – so it can interrupt, or compete with, alternative mental

> *processes or actions. Different types of readiness create different outline relationships with others.*
>
> 3. *An emotion is usually experienced as a distinctive type of mental state, sometimes accompanied or followed by bodily changes, expressions, actions.*
>
> *The major step forward for science, is that a necessary condition for an emotion is the change in readiness for action.*

Oatley and Jenkins also state that 'Attention, for instance, is a result of the emotion, not its cause' (1995: 100). For advertising practitioners this is a profound thought:

> *Advertising does not first get attention, and then create an emotion.*
>
> *Advertising creates an emotion, which results in attention.*

The philosopher Gilbert Ryle gave a description (rather than a definition) of emotion: 'Emotions are described as turbulences in the stream of consciousness, the owner of which cannot help registering them.' This description stresses the fact that emotions are involuntary – also an important issue to advertisers.

How many emotions?

I mentioned that Fehr and Russell managed to generate a list of 383 words denoting 'emotions' from 200 students in one minute. Presumably if they had had more time, and the use of a thesaurus, they would have generated many more. Does the fact that there are so many emotions one can name mean that the brain generates so many different emotions?

The answer to this has to be, why would it? What would be the benefit of having a multitude of emotions?

It is highly unlikely that animals (or people) need to have a multitude of emotions. It is also highly unlikely that new emotions have appeared in the past few millennia. (I cannot think of any.) There is a very active debate among psychologists about whether there exists only one emotion, or several base emotions, or a multitude of emotions that are combinations of the base emotions.

A long tradition of work on emotions postulates that an emotion is a feeling that cannot be reduced further. Wundt (1897) supposed that there were just two such feelings, pleasure and pain. Descartes believed that there were a small number of basic emotions, which were not reducible. The definition by Oatley and Jenkins describes an emotion as resulting in a 'positive' or a 'negative'. Some analysts use the words 'pull towards' and 'push from'. This is very similar to Wundt's pleasure and pain.

Nobody seems to doubt that the area of the brain involved with emotions is the limbic system. Arguably we could reduce the definition of an emotion to stating that an emotion is the output of the limbic system, and does not arise in any other way. What the limbic system does is to send out a warning signal to the body – preparing it for action, and focusing attention – and then add some kind of 'tag' to the developing interpretation of what is perceived. To do this the limbic system has to make a simple decision regarding every piece of sensory input. It can either:

1. Ignore it.
2. Classify it as worthy of an emotional reaction, and give it a positive emotion.
3. Classify it as worthy of an emotional reaction, and give it a negative emotion.

There is no need for the limbic system to consider the *type* of emotion, and there seems to be no benefit to be derived by the limbic system encoding the perception with something called love, jealousy, hatred, fear, or anything similarly specific. All that is required is a positive or negative encoding (or a pain/pleasure, or a pull towards/push from, or other binary way of differentiating). However, when the signal passes on through to the upper brain, more complex thought processes go on, and on this level we certainly can distinguish love, jealousy and all the rest of the emotions we conceptualize.

Multiple emotions are a negative to the organism

Recall LeDoux's model of the role of the limbic system, and his example of a snake (page 62). It should be clear that if the limbic system even tried to differentiate between emotions in any way more complex than positive and negative, it would be detrimental to the organism. The point of the amygdala and the limbic system generally is to react quickly (if sometimes wrongly, as in the twig/snake example), and simplicity is an essential element of this. The same is true for the emotion that is generated. First, the limbic system is reacting to a half-developed inter-pretation, so it would be difficult for the emotion to be fully formed at this stage; and second, it would waste valuable time.

If there is only one 'emotion', however, why can we name so many? Obviously once an emotion has been generated – whether positive or negative – it becomes the subject of processing by the upper brain. This is where the labelling occurs, in the higher thought processes that focus on the emotion and interpret it. So the limbic system makes a sufficient iden- tification of 'something that might be a snake' (or might be a twig, or something else broadly similar in appearance) to be able to tag it as 'nega- tive' and generate the 'fear' response, but it is for the upper brain to analyse the sensory input more carefully, and come to the definitive version: 'Yup, definitely a black mamba.'

As I explained earlier, research shows that television commercials that are liked get more attention than those that are less liked. Logic says that if this model is true, the limbic system must register something about the commercial, sufficient to tag it positively, and pass the message on to the upper brain. In a strange way, people must know *whether they are going to like the commercial* before they pay attention to it. Then their predisposi- tion to like it somehow makes them pay attention.

I wrote in the Introduction to this book about a paradigm shift, and here we are coming to the core of it. Something strange and non-intuitive (to those of us used to an older paradigm) is going on here.

Before we look in more depth at the new paradigm, perhaps it is worth looking a little at the paradigm that preceded it.

RENÉ DESCARTES (1596–1650)

Descartes was the founding father of a lot of today's philosophical think- ing. He was a physician, like many philosophers concerned with the func- tioning of the brain, and he philosophized about how we think, live and make decisions – the issues of brain, mind, matter and soul. (In fact he did not write that much about the soul because the Church was very powerful in those days, and sane men and women avoided anything that could be interpreted as heresy. It is still speculated today how much he toned down his views to accommodate the Church.)

Back in the 17th century, Descartes got an amazing number of things right. Unfortunately he also got some things wrong, and this influenced a lot of philosophies afterwards. The main issue he got wrong is that the 'rational' and 'emotional' are not just different but in a real sense opposed, so that emotional reactions should not be confused with rational thought.

Descartes also speculated on what it means to be conscious, and his proposal was that we each have what might be thought of as a little man, or a homunculus (the Latin for 'small man') residing in our brain. The homunculus effectively represents our consciousness, and decides what we do. For example, it manoeuvres our body by using some kind of levers which pump vitae (the juices of life) through the nerves to the muscles. That part of Descartes' model might sound humorous today, but it made a fair amount of sense in light of the anatomical knowledge of his day, and the fact that at that stage electricity had not been discovered, so there was no way to measure what nerves do. (And he did get it right that the nervous system communicates movement to muscles.) Even though the homunculus-and-levers aspect of Descartes' model was discredited long ago, however, the idea of a higher awareness that controls our actions has continued into modern times. This hypothesis is often referred to as the Cartesian Theatre.

You can see an echo of the Cartesian Theatre in the view I outlined earlier in the book of a supervisory attentioning system. It is easy to imagine that there is some 'higher level' or controller in the brain that is aware of, and controls, what is going on at lower levels. But as you can perhaps sense by now, the model of the brain that is emerging is one that seems to put the 'attentioning system' not on some higher, supervisory level, but on a lower (at least in physiological terms) level of the brain, the limbic level at which emotion is processed. This is the core of a sizeable paradigm shift in our ideas about how emotion and thought are related to each other.

BRAIN HEMISPHERIC THEORIES

Epileptic fits are basically electronic storms in the brain, which happen when neurons start to fire out of control. The difference between a minor attack and a major attack is in the number of neurons that become involved in this activity. During the 1960s a treatment for extreme cases of epilepsy was developed. It consisted of severing the corpus collosum, a powerful cable comprising a few billion neurons, which connects the left and right hemispheres of the brain. Doctors noticed that as well as in some cases finding relief from their epilepsy, those who had this operation performed differently from normal people. Their behaviour changes were analysed, and this led to the hypothesis that the two hemispheres have broadly different functions. The right hemisphere was concerned primarily with the rational and logical, while the left dealt with the more emotional and creative side of human thought.

The operations stopped after the 1960s (because it was clear by then that, on balance, they had a negative effect), and as a result scientists have not been able to access a continuing pool of people with severed corpus collosum on whom they can conduct experiments. Other methods of trying to identify the roles of the two hemispheres generally give pretty shaky results, which is not surprising given the massive interconnectivity between the hemispheres in a normal brain. By the 1970s most neurologists had discarded the hypothesis that there is much specialization between the hemispheres. A typical comment is this one from Steklis and Harnad (1976), 'The simplistic dichotomies of the function of the brain discussed here bear about as much relation to the known facts about hemisphere functioning as astrology does to astronomy.'

However, one obvious question is why did brain hemispheric theories become so popular, and why have they remained as a popular paradigm long after scientists have discounted them?

Descartes has to take a lot of the blame, because the left brain/right brain thesis seemed to encapsulate the well-worn differentiation between the emotional and the rational that, as we have seen, dates right back to Descartes.

DAMASIO – THE EMOTIONAL IS RATIONAL

It is a truism (that is, a part of our paradigm so fundamental that we rarely think to question it) that some people seem to react more emotionally than others, and some more rationally. (This does, as I just explained, significantly predate the 'left-brain'/'right-brain' model and dates right back to Descartes.) However, in 1994 a new viewpoint saw the light of day. According to this paradigm, emotions cause decision making and also determine the outcome of the rational decision making process. This was not propounded by a creative director in an advertising agency, or an emotionally gifted psychologist; it came from a member of the hardest of logical and unemotional schools, a professor of neurology. Professor Antonio Damasio put it forward in a book entitled *Descartes' Error*.

In simple terms, Damasio's suggestion is that human beings, when faced with a decision, use at heart only one criterion: 'How will I feel if I do that?' Of course, no one really knows the answer to how they will feel in the future, since it depends on something that has not yet happened (and might never happen), so we rely on similar past experience to give us a guesstimate of what our feelings will be.

In fact, when someone says to you, 'You are allowing your emotions to cloud your rational decisions', they are exactly right.

Maybe the choice is something like (this is Damasio's example) either buying a Porsche or using the money to send a child to university. It might seem at first as if one of these is an emotional choice (nobody really needs a car as expensive as a Porsche, it's a feel-good choice) and one of them purely practical (it benefits someone else, not you), but in fact either choice (for one and against the other) will generate emotion. The sensory gratification of driving a fast and luxurious car, guilt at letting the child down, pleasure at his or her gratitude: how do you balance those against each other? Consciously it is next to impossible, but even if there is a conscious element to the decision, there are unconscious forces at play too, and your limbic system does its own sums (and sends out its own signals), though your conscious mind may not fully appreciate that this is happening.

As I have already suggested, the fact that this is in some sense quantifiable (in terms of the limbic reaction) means that at heart, the emotions the limbic system deals with are very primitive ones. Guilt and the thrill of speeding in a fast car might not be measurable along the same axis to your conscious mind, but your limbic system reacts to the memory of how you felt in crudely similar situations, and sends the message out as a basic plus or minus: no good choosing the car, you will feel rotten if you do; much better to pay the university fees, you will feel pleasure as a result. (Or, if your past experiences and mental set-up are different, no good giving up the car for the child, your resentment at him or her will make you feel bad; much better to buy it, and your pleasure at having this status symbol will outweigh the little guilt you feel.)

Rather like the fear response, this could be argued to have its roots in a survival instinct, a simple predilection for pleasure (which is associated with surviving and thriving) and against bad feelings (associated with danger and pain), even if sensory pleasure and pain are not obviously involved.

'HOW DO I KNOW WHAT I THINK BEFORE I KNOW WHAT I FEEL?'

This is a line from a French play, and it summarizes to a large extent the scientific argument that we have been building towards.

There are more dendrites leading from the limbic area in the brain towards the frontal lobes than there are dendrites leading the other way.

In other words: there is more information flowing from the area of emotion towards the area of rationality than there is dendrites feeding back into the system that generates our emotions.

When researchers interview respondents, either individually or in groups, briefly or in depth, and we ask them 'What do you think of...', their answer will invariably be: 'I like it, because...', or 'I don't like it, because...'. The answer they give us reflects the processes in their brain: what comes to mind first is the emotional reaction, then the rationalization of it. As researchers we call this 'post-rationalization'. However objective we think we are being, the emotional context set by our limbic reaction colours (according to Damasio, determines) the decision we make, and our rational thought processes arguably do no more than rationalize and justify that emotional choice.

We all know from experience that when we feel emotionally in favour of or against something or someone, it is virtually (perhaps completely) impossible for us to rationalize our way out of that emotion. You must like Jim, a friend says. But maybe you don't, and all your friend's arguments about how kind, thoughtful, lively and interesting Jim is are unlikely to change that fact.

DAMASIO'S SOMATIC MARKER HYPOTHESIS

Damasio called his theory the somatic marker hypothesis, and he calls the somatic marker (that is, the emotion) that is attached to the interpretation the 'soma'.

Later in the book I shall provide a lot of empirical data from advertising research that supports this hypothesis, and discuss its implications. First let me quote Damasio's description of the somatic marker hypothesis:

> *Consider again the scenarios I outlined. The key components unfold in our minds instantly, sketchily, and virtually simultaneously, too fast for the details to be clearly defined. But now, imagine that before you apply any kind of cost/benefit analysis to the premises, and before you reason toward the solution of the problem, something quite important happens: When the bad outcome connected with a given response option comes into mind, however fleetingly, you experience an unpleasant gut feeling. Because the feeling is about the body, I gave the phenomenon the technical term* somatic state *('soma' is Greek for body); and because it 'marks' an image, I called it a* marker. *Note again that I use* somatic *in the most general sense (that which pertains to the body) and I include both visceral and nonvisceral sensation when I refer to somatic markers.*
>
> *What does the* somatic marker *achieve? It forces attention on the negative outcome to which a given action may lead, and functions as an automated*

alarm signal which says: Beware of danger ahead if you choose the option which leads to this outcome. The signal may lead you to reject, immediately, *the negative course of action and thus make you choose among other alternatives. The automated signal protects you against future losses, without further ado, and then allows you to* choose from among fewer alternatives. *There is still room for using a cost/benefit analysis and proper deductive competence, but only* after *the automated step drastically reduces the number of options. Somatic markers may not be sufficient for normal human decision-making since a subsequent process of reasoning and final selection will still take place in many though not all instances. Somatic markers probably increase the accuracy and efficiency of the decision process. Their absence reduces them. This distinction is important and can easily be missed. The hypothesis does not concern the reasoning steps which follow the action of the somatic marker. In short,* somatic markers are a special instance of feelings generated from secondary emotions. *Those emotions and feelings* have been connected, by learning, to predicted future outcomes of certain scenarios. *When a negative somatic marker is juxtaposed to a particular future outcome the combination functions as an alarm bell. When a positive somatic marker is juxtaposed instead, it becomes a beacon of incentive.*

Descartes' error

Damasio's first book is entitled *Descartes' Error*, but obviously by modern standards Descartes made plenty of errors, largely because of his lack of knowledge of how the brain actually functions. However, the 'error' that Damasio refers to is the separation of the 'emotional' from the 'rational'. This is one of Descartes' errors that has persisted right up to today. It is easy to trace its influence, for example, in advertising and advertising research!

The effect of Descartes on all our thinking since early 1600s

As you read the following section think about what the situation might have been if people had never adopted Descartes' distinction between the emotional and the rational:

▌ Imagine we had known all along that our instinctive emotional responses shape our rational behaviour.
▌ Imagine we had known all along that the rational cannot occur without the emotional response that directs our attention.
▌ Imagine we had known all along that emotion is the most important part of human behaviour.

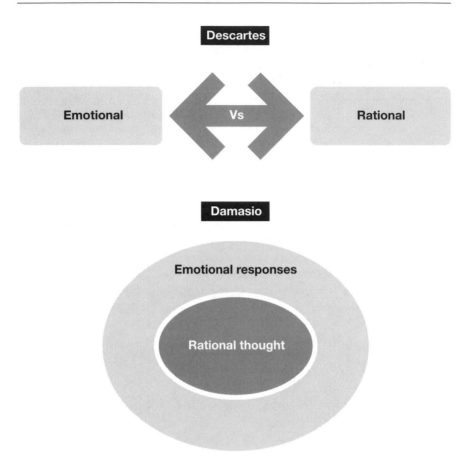

Figure 8.2 *How the emotional and the rational relate to each other: Descartes' and Damasio's views*

Figure 8.2 offers a visual interpretation of the difference between Descartes' view and Damasio's.

SIGMUND FREUD (1859–1939)

While Descartes' views had a profound effect on psychology, it was only 200 years later that Wilhelm Wundt established a laboratory for psychology in Germany in 1879. This date is usually considered to mark the formal beginning of psychology as an autonomous science.

There is no space in this book for a review of the entire history of psychology, but I do want to consider Sigmund Freud in the perspective of the paradigm that Damasio has put forward. His model of the subconscious and its effect on our conscious behaviour had a profound impact, and many advertisers and researchers still draw on it to some extent. So it is part of the paradigm that we work to today, the one that Damasio and fellow brain scientists are in the process of overturning.

Freud too started his career as a physician – more specifically as a neurologist – and he stated in his writings that his theories of the human mind were only mere stop-gaps, paradigms that could prove useful until we understood more about the structure of the brain. His books still make interesting (and far from difficult) reading today, and offer far more than the trite paraphrases that are sometimes put forward.

An example of Freud's that is often used to show how the subconscious works is a story about a man with a phobia about horses. Phobia means 'unreasonable fear': someone with a phobia does not have a normal slight reaction to something that could conceivably be dangerous, but an absolute and paralysing terror of it, disproportional to any threat it poses. Freud's concern was to find out why the man was so afraid of horses, and through hypnosis he discovered that as a small child the man had been bitten by a horse. The man was not 'consciously' aware of the experience – in other words, he had no readily accessible memory of it – but it seemed clear to Freud that it was affecting his subsequent behaviour. Freud's paradigm identified the *subconscious* as the area in our brain which holds memories that affect our behaviour, but are not normally accessible to our conscious mind.

It is interesting to consider how Damasio's somatic marker hypothesis would explain the events:

1. At some stage a horse bit the man.
2. The man associates fear (pain) with a horse.
3. When the man sees a horse an emotional memory ('soma') is raised, and this travels to the hippocampus together with the visual and other sensory information about the horse.
4. While the memory of the actual event might not be readily retrievable, the emotional reaction will remain, and possibly get strengthened each time the man encounters a horse.

The differences are subtle, but no less important for that. Freud pinpointed an interesting phenomenon that needed explanation; however, it is Damasio and LeDoux who have begun to explain (in physiological terms) what is actually happening in the brain. It is clear too that Freud's thought was shaped by the Cartesian model which saw the emotional and the rational as opposed tendencies, and this encouraged him to see the subconscious and conscious minds as also separate and opposed. As we are beginning to see, they are in fact nothing of the kind. This is a crucial insight which, as I am trying to argue, advertising researchers need to keep very firmly in mind.

9

Incidental learning – and forgetting

Now we need to go on to look at how the things that are tagged by emotion (by Damasio's somatic markers) as worthy of our attention go on to become our memories. In other words, we are returning (but at a different level) to the question of how we learn. In particular we need to look at 'incidental learning', the kind of learning that involves our just happening to acquire a memory, or knowledge, rather than the deliberate learning that is involved in formal education, not least because it is this kind of incidental learning that applies most obviously to the advertising context.

Unfortunately it is easier to study the learning process by asking someone to learn something, then studying what happens, than it is to study incidental learning. As a result most of what is known about learning appears to have little application to incidental learning, and by extension to advertising.

However, the good news is that there is no evidence of two separate mechanisms in the human mind, one for conscious learning and another for incidental learning. The mechanism with which the learning is done remains the same, and the only difference is in the way that the mechanism is used: for conscious learning we 'force' our attention towards something, and in incidental learning our attention is directed involuntarily – or at least less consciously.

Learning can be seen as a process of internalizing knowledge. To phrase it differently, it is the process of forming memories. As we sometimes put it, 'I have learnt, therefore I know that…'. Knowledge is in a sense nothing more than memory: memories that are used to interpret new input.

You might argue that learning and knowledge are both broader concepts than the mere formation of memories, because they include the process of understanding. But that is exactly the point. Understanding is the process of interpreting new facts and experiences by way of previous knowledge (memories) and forming a new memory which is linked to previous memories.

Earlier in the book I told you the Zulu word for elephant. I introduced it as a meaningless word; then afterwards I explained what concept it was the key to. Only when you had read the explanation would the word have made much sense to you. You probably remembered the word for long enough to be unfazed when it recurred in the same chapter, but by now you have probably forgotten it. Why should you remember it? It is highly unlikely that you will have a use for it ever again.

Personally I am a lazy reader, and if I were a non-Zulu-speaking reader of this book I would not have remembered the Zulu word for elephant. When reading this page, I would not have referred back to find out what the Zulu word was (notice, I have not repeated it here), which means that I would still not know it. On the other hand, perhaps you as a reader are sufficiently diligent to have flicked back through the book, trying to locate that wretched word. If you are not, doubtless some others are. Each time they read the Zulu word for elephant, these people probably 'sounded' it to themselves. All these processes would have led to their retaining it in their memory, at least for a while longer than I would have done. If it turned up again on the last page of the book, they would probably think (perhaps you will now think), 'Ah – that's the Zulu word for elephant.'

I am trying to demonstrate that memories stay for a while, then fade, but can be refreshed.

MEMORIZING USELESS INFORMATION

Let me show you some memory experiments. You do not need to do them yourself (though you are welcome to), but you will hopefully appreciate them by analogy with things you remember doing in the past.

The first memory experiment was done by Ebbinghaus. He wrote down a list of words made up of nonsense syllables (like the list in Table 9.1) and tried to learn the list to perfection by repeating it to himself.

There are various ways of trying to learn the list: you might read through silently, or read it out loud, or write it down. Whichever way you choose, it is likely to take several rehearsals before you can repeat it to perfection.

Table 9.1 *A list of nonsense words to memorize*

Goeie
More
Dit
Is
'n
Mooi
Dag

Try again tomorrow, with the same list, and you will not be able to remember it as well as you do after several rehearsals today. You can make yourself recall it again, but it will take some more rehearsals. However, each day it will take fewer rehearsals than it did the day before.

I can make things somewhat easier for you by giving you an English word that matches the 'nonsense' word, as in Table 9.2.

This time your learning strategy will become very different. Most likely you will first recall the English sentence, then attempt to recall the 'nonsense' equivalents. You will notice that there is a similarity in sound and appearance between some of the pairs of words, and will use this as part of your recall strategy. You will also tend to remember the words that are most similar to the English equivalents (such as 'is' and 'dag') first.

The words on the left are actually not 'nonsense': they are all Afrikaans words, so one thing that is being demonstrated here is the process through which most grown-ups learn a new language. Children tend not to learn a new language by rote as we do, but by incidental exposure.

What this means in terms of the mechanisms of the mind is that the more links there are between existing neuronal systems and the 'new' memory's neuronal system, the more easily the new system will become embedded in your memory.

Table 9.2 *The memory test, part 2*

Goeie	Good
More	Morning
Dit	It
Is	Is
'n	A
Mooi	Beautiful
Dag	Day

As an example to demonstrate this even better, just imagine how long it would take you to (memorize) any of the lists in the columns of Table 9.3.

These are all common computer fonts. The ones that produce alphabetic characters are pretty easy to learn, but it is not so easy to learn the ones like Webdings and Windings that produce non-alphabetic characters. In fact, the best learning strategy is to first learn the Webdings and Windings characters corresponding to each letter, then to remember that the sentence you are memorizing is 'Good morning it is a beautiful day', then to transpose each character one by one.

Table 9.3 *The memory test, part 3*

Bauhaus 93	BELL MT	Vladimir Script	*Vivaldi*
Good	Good	Good	*Good*
Morning	Morning	Morning	*Morning*
It	It	It	*It*
Is	Is	Is	*Is*
A	A	A	*A*
Beautiful	Beautiful	Beautiful	*Beautiful*
Day	Day	Day	*Day*

The way people memorize has been studied extensively, and all the studies show that the way to memorize better is to start by forming associations, as between the Afrikaans and English words. It becomes even easier when the English words form a sentence rather than being at random. If I had changed the sequence of the list to: 'Morning is a beautiful good it day', you would have found that you had to rehearse it a few times more, because it is not a grammatical sentence, and your knowledge of grammar that made the previous sentence a little easier to learn would not have come into play.

WHAT PROFESSOR BAHRICK TAUGHT ME

I came to meet Professor Harry P Bahrick of Ohio by a very circuitous route. I had realized in the early 1990s that I would need to understand more about human memory if I ever wanted to understand advertising and advertising research, so I read a few books on the subject, and found the most user-friendly of them to be Alan Baddeley's *Your Memory: A user's guide* (1990). When I travelled to the UK (for other reasons) I thought it might be useful to talk to Professor Baddeley, fully expecting that he would be on a retainer to advertising agencies and research companies. To my surprise (and this strikes me as an indictment of the whole advertising and research industry) he told me no advertising agency, research house or student of advertising had approached him before. I explained to him the issues that advertising researchers are grappling with, and he referred me to Professor Bahrick as the person most knowledgeable about the issue of 'learning rehearsals' – what we call 'frequency of exposure'.

In 1991 I travelled to New York, and took the relatively short hop to Ohio to see Professor Bahrick. (He too had not been approached by anyone involved in advertising before.) Over breakfast he explained the 'response curve' to me on a napkin – and all the empirical research done by advertisers made sense to me for the first time.

As I explained to him, in 1979 Mike Naples published a book entitled *Effective Frequency*, which stated that the response to advertising is s-shaped. People do not respond at the first exposure, and there is very little response at the second. Then there is a big response at the third exposure, and thereafter the response decreases for each subsequent exposure. This led to the recommendation (see Chapter 18) that media schedulers should try to arrange their schedules so that the maximum number of people receive more than three exposures to any advertisement. I explained too how Erwin Ephron, influenced by Professor John Philip Jones, had 'disproved' this, claiming that the maximum response came from the first exposure, and that all subsequent exposures (within a short, say seven-day, period) produce less response, and are therefore wasted money.

Professor Bahrick looked at the two curves, s-shaped and convex, that I drew on the napkin and said, 'Both of them are right! What they both lack is a time perspective. What you advertising people call a "response curve" is what we call a "learning curve".' How much simpler life would have been had advertising researchers in the United States afforded themselves a breakfast in Ohio!

To illustrate this, he asked me if I remembered learning to ride my first bicycle. I got on and immediately fell off. I got on again and immediately fell off. I did this 10 times, and then managed to progress 4 yards before falling off. I got on again and gained 6 yards, and then 8 yards, and then 10, and then 11. And then my mother called me in, because it was time to go to bed. My learning curve for that first day was s-shaped, as in Figure 9.1. The vertical axis shows 'performance' and the horizontal axis shows 'repetitions'.

The next day, being excited about my bicycle, I got on again. I fell off once or twice, but quite quickly got to the level I was at the day before, and then continued to improve, again at a 'diminishing return' rate – see Figure 9.2. Then the next day I did not fall off at all, so my learning curve appeared to be convex, as in Figure 9.3.

To generalize out from me and my bike, for a newly acquired skill the learning curve is s-shaped. There are a number of rehearsals required and then an apparent 'Aha!' effect when the message gets through. After this threshold level there is some success, and this increases with each subsequent rehearsal (see Figure 9.3). The performance itself is just the building-up of the memory of what to do.

You will realize, of course, that Ebbinghaus's experiment (discussed above) was an example of the same phenomenon. And you will appreciate too that with each rehearsal the neurons in the brain are laying down sensitivities in the synapses, so next time around you are more likely to remember the right syllable, or the 'right' way to ride the bike.

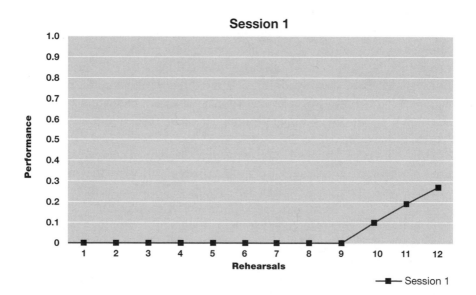

Figure 9.1 *The learning curve*

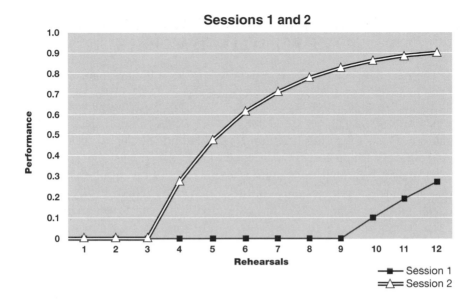

Figure 9.2 *The convex learning curve*

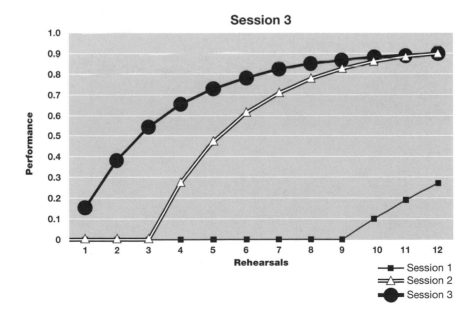

Figure 9.3 *The learning curve changing with practise*

THE LEARNING CURVE WHEN THERE ARE SOME RELATED MEMORIES

Professor Bahrick is well over 60, short and sinewy, while in 1991 I was in my mid-forties and played squash twice a week, although I confess I was a bit overweight. He asked me whether I ever roller-bladed, which I had not. He had then just taken up roller-blading, and he asked me what our relative learning curves would look like.

I took into account my previous experience with roller skates and resultant sprained knees, and told him that mine would be disastrous, requiring many rehearsals (and hospitalization), and that his would be even worse because at his age he would tend to find new learning very difficult.

Figure 9.4 is not my prediction of how easy he would find it to learn compared with me; it was Professor Bahrick's prediction. What I did not know when I made my prediction was that he spent each winter skiing in the Rockies. I have never skied or skated: living in South Africa, I have only seen snow twice in my life.

It only took Professor Bahrick one rehearsal to be reasonably proficient at roller-blading. The point he made was that while roller-blading might be a new experience for both him and me, he had a much better memory structure to call on than I did, so he could expect to have fewer disastrous

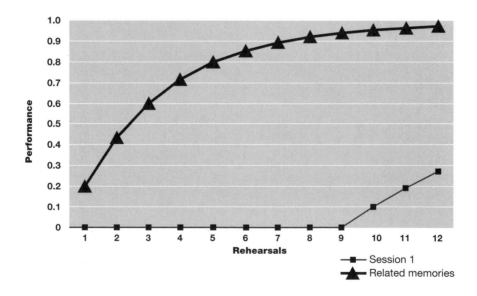

Figure 9.4 *The learning curve with related memories*

experiences than me. In other words, the rate of learning is not fixed for everyone. People learn at different rates, depending at least partly on what they already know.

LEARNING AND THE RATE OF FORGETTING

Professor Bahrick also dealt with another issue: how to relate the rate of learning – which is dependent on rehearsals – to the rate of forgetting, which is time-dependent. He explained that learning and forgetting need to be combined in the same model. (The napkin he used probably would have the same significance to advertising as the napkin Picasso drew on, but unfortunately I lost it.)

One of the features of the learning curve model in Figure 9.5 is that it shows not only learning, but forgetting too. With each rehearsal a memory trace is put down, but with each gap between rehearsals, some forgetting occurs. You might like to think of there being three axes to the graph: competence on the vertical axis, rehearsals on the horizontal axis, and 'time' on the third axis. Figure 9.5 uses an artificial example. Let us

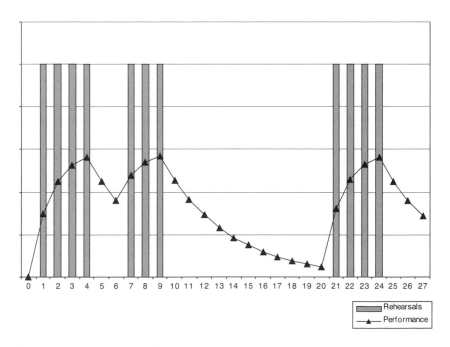

Figure 9.5 *Learning and forgetting*

assume that every hour, on the hour, you read the list of words in Table 9.1 once, then write down those you can remember. You do this on the hour for six consecutive hours, then you go away for six hours, then you do it every hour, on the hour six more times. For each rehearsal session you start from a higher point of competence than at the start of the previous session, but not as high as at the end of the previous session, because you have forgotten some of what you learnt in the meantime.

THE OPTIMAL RATE OF REHEARSAL
FOR LEARNING

Professor Bahrick then told me something that to the best of my knowledge has never been tested in advertising research. I asked him whether he could tell me whether the optimal frequency of exposures to advertisements was three-plus in a week, as Naples claimed, or once every week, as Jones argued. This was his answer.

At the moment the view of cognitive scientists is that the best way for students to revise their work is this. Each day, when they get home from class, they should read everything that was taught in class that day. They should re-read it a day later, then two days later, then again four days later, and then again eight days later. In other words, the frequency of exposure should be relatively high at the start, but then reduce exponentially. I can see no reason why this should not apply to advertising as well.

10

From brains to advertisements

I have tried so far in the book to put together research and understanding from a number of different fields more or less closely connected with the study of the human brain, in order to outline a paradigm that will help us make greater sense of how advertising works, and how to make it work better. At this point, perhaps it would be useful to summarize the argument I am putting forward.

How and why do we think? How do we determine what out of the vast amount of sensory input we receive is worth paying attention to? The psychologists' view that I looked at in Chapter 3 puts forward two entities called a 'central executive' and a 'supervisory attentioning system', as part of a model of thinking processes. This ties in with a number of aspects of what we might call the 'old paradigm', and in particular with some very important ideas that can be dated back to the French philosopher René Descartes.

Proposition one is that there is some higher entity in us, a 'homunculus', as Descartes called it, which directs the activities of our brains, and through our brains, of our bodies. Perhaps another way of saying the same thing is that there are two different things: the brain, which can be taken to be physical, and the mind, which can be taken to be a non-material entity that directs the workings of the physical brain.

Proposition two is that emotion and rational thought are separate, and opposed; that emotion has no role in a rational process of directing thoughts and making decisions.

If we put these propositions together, we come up with a hypothesis that the central executive and the supervisory attentioning system are entirely rationally based, and in no way concerned with emotion. This is, in effect, the paradigm on which work in psychology, and in advertising research, was based for a long time.

We also looked at the work that neurologists have been doing in analysing what goes on in the brain, and at the work of 'mechanism of mind' scientists in trying to develop parallels to brain operation in artificial systems. Neurologists have analysed the structure of the brain, and identified areas and components that seem to have specific functions. Among these functional areas are some whose activity appears to be primarily concerned with 'emotion', working on an instinctive level that is closely tied in with our bodily response to positive and negative stimuli. Other areas appear to be primarily concerned with the 'rational': that is, with detailed conceptualization, language, and the higher thought processes. However, neurologists have not identified anything that looks like a 'central executive' or a 'supervisory attentioning system' in the sense that the psychological model proposes. Instead, what they have shown is that our instinctive and emotional reactions and our higher thought processes are deeply and inextricably linked to each other. What is more, our instinctive emotional reactions come first, and they appear to play a major part in determining what we pay attention to, and in shaping our conscious thought processes.

The model that the neurologists are leading us to is not one in which the 'supervisory attentioning system' is a non-emotional logical entity. On the contrary, it is one in which the system that focuses our attention, in ways that are probably part hard-wired and part conditioned by past experience, is driven primarily by our instinctive and emotional responses.

At the same time, the very endeavour of the 'mechanism of mind' school is based on the assumption that, crude as the current experiments are, it is in theory possible to produce a kind of 'artificial intelligence' in which learning, and something that can genuinely be described as thought, take place; and that this kind of system can be built out of simple physical components. Arguably the only kind of 'programming' that is needed is some kind of equivalent of emotion: a predisposition to be drawn to some things, and to pull away from others.

None of this is intended to suggest that 'the spirit' does not exist, or that all of life is entirely physical. But it *is* intended to suggest that we need to rethink the role of emotion, and to reconsider how 'paying attention' actually takes place.

This is the core of what I am suggesting:

> *Emotion not only shapes our unconscious reactions; it also feeds into, shapes and controls our conscious thought.*

The relevance of this to our industry is blatantly obvious:

> *Emotion not only shapes our unconscious reactions to advertising; it also feeds into, shapes and controls our conscious thought about brands, products and services.*

If the first part of my argument is concerned with paying attention, the second part of it is concerned with learning and remembering. What we pay attention to, we remember; that is, it has a permanent impact on the contents of our brain. And what we have paid attention to and remembered in the past, we are more likely to pay attention to in the future, so attention and memory create a feedback system. So the second part of my thesis goes like this:

> *The first task of advertising is to ensure that it is noticed, and to this purpose it has to be designed to attract an emotional response from us. The second task of advertising is to ensure that it is remembered, and this is intimately tied in with* how often we see it.

Finally there is a third part to my thesis, which goes like this:

> *For an advertisement to be noticed and remembered is in itself not sufficient. It also has to shape consumers' buying behaviour, and in order to ensure that it does so, we need to pay attention both to the connection between the advertisement and the brand, and to the buying process, and the role of memory within it.*

In short, the task of advertisers is:

▌ To devise advertisements that will attract attention.
▌ To ensure that these advertisements are seen and noticed sufficiently often to become memorable.
▌ To ensure that these advertisements influence customer buying behaviour.

Does it sound simple? You know it is not! But my task now is to draw out some pointers to how it can best be done.

11

Why should advertising be researched?

It is a common lament by advertising agencies that research kills creativity. This is simply not true. What the advertising agencies mean is that research sometimes kills ideas the agencies hoped to get past their clients. In any case, the statement implies that 'creativity is king', when we all know that 'the consumer is king'. What does creativity count, if the advertisement does not work with consumers?

In this second part of the book, we need to look at how to create advertisements that attract attention. This implies that we need to research which advertisements work, and which do not. However, not all advertising gets researched at present, and as I suggested in Chapter 1, there is still a fair amount of resistance to 'copy testing': to trying to find out in advance whether advertisements are likely to work. At this point, I would like to put forward some of the arguments in favour of copy testing.

Copy testing, of course, is only one aspect of advertising research. The other aspect is tracking: finding out after the event whether advertisements are recognized or recalled, and whether they have had an impact on brand awareness and on sales. I look at these issues later in the book.

WHAT I LEARNT FROM A ZULU MINER WITH LITTLE FORMAL EDUCATION ABOUT COMMUNICATION THEORIES

Before I give a more empirically reasoned argument in favour of copy testing advertisements, I should like to share an experience of mine.

When I am asked where I learnt most about advertising theories, the answer is not a book about the brain, or a book about advertising, or any journal paper, or a specific professor. I learnt the most about advertising from a miner.

In 1994 South Africa had its first democratic election, which effectively moved power from the mainly Afrikaans white government to a black government. Obviously emotions were running high, especially because (since there were many more black than white voters) the outcome of the election was a foregone conclusion. Afrikaners felt threatened by what the future might hold for them, and blacks felt liberated and able to make aggressive statements in public showing their new-found 'power'. Afrikaners in rural areas felt especially threatened. During this time I was asked to do research among the black miners in a rural coal mine, to establish what they saw as their major problems. I did this under the condition that the results would be shown to representatives of their management (white) and trade union (black) at the same time.

To my dismay the black miners rated as their third biggest problem the fact that 'White managers insist on giving their instructions in Afrikaans'. I was dismayed because I knew, from my experience with focus groups, that the black miners spoke better Afrikaans than English. They preferred to speak Afrikaans rather than English, and to listen to Afrikaans programmes on television. So why would they want the management to give them instructions in English? It seemed obvious to me that the only reason for their giving this problem such a priority was that they were making a political statement. This was not an unlikely explanation at that time.

Because mining is such a physically demanding job, both managers and face workers tend to be big, strong people. As an Afrikaner, I felt rather uneasy at the prospect of presenting this politically sensitive result in a meeting of these big people in a small room. I tried to gloss over the point in my presentation. The leader of the trade union asked me to go over it again more slowly. I tried to gloss over it again, and he again called on me to spend more time discussing it. I told him outright that I believed it was a political point-scoring exercise, and best left out of the meeting.

He then proceeded to give me a lesson in communication, which I still rate as the most valuable I have ever had. His words went something like this:

It is true that most of us Zulus are more proficient in Afrikaans than in English.

However, Afrikaans is our third language and English is our fourth. Most of us speak two native African languages better than we speak either Afrikaans or English.

Afrikaans is the managers' first language. When a manager gives an instruction in Afrikaans he will give a concise instruction, believing he has expressed himself clearly, and then be upset when we do the wrong thing.

When a manager gives an instruction in his second language he feels more insecure. He will probably repeat the instruction a few times, using different words, and will use a lot of body language to demonstrate what he means. Then he will ask us whether we understand – and patiently re-explain if we don't.

The difference is that when he instructs in his first language he believes *he has done a good job of communicating, but when he does it in a language we are both less proficient in, he really* does *a good job of communicating!*

We all tend to forget that the people that create advertising, the agencies and marketers, are doing this in their first language (so to speak). They have been trained in the language of advertising, they have a lot of experience in the language of advertising, and they know the product very well. The people they are creating the communication for are not steeped in either the language of the product or the language of advertising. In fact, they mostly cannot be bothered to learn either.

This does not mean that the message has to be simplistic or aimed at the lowest common denominator among the target audience. It simply means that the advertisers need to make sure that the target audience understands the message as it was intended. In fact, achieving this is something that requires true creativity.

A MORE EMPIRICAL (RATIONAL) ARGUMENT IN FAVOUR OF COPY TESTING

In Chapter 1, I outlined research by Professor John Philip Jones on the effectiveness of advertisements in changing consumer behaviour. (See Table 1.1, page 15.) For the 78 brands that were tracked by the research, he found that when a household had been exposed to a commercial the subsequent market share of the brand was on average 24 per cent higher than in the non-exposed households.

However, averages are dangerous things. What Professor Jones also found was that not all advertising is created equal:

▌ For one out of five advertisements the effects were magnificent: there was a 94 per cent increase in share of market in the short term.
▌ For two out of five advertisements, the effect was positive.

▌ For one out of five advertisements the effect was minimal.

▌ For one out of five advertisements the effect was negative – the house-holds that had been exposed to the advertisement bought less than those that had not. Possibly the advertisement was not that bad, but these households had also seen more effective advertising by rival brands, while the non-exposed households had not seen either advertisement. (This was something Professor Jones did not investigate.) The more worrying possibility is that the advertising had a negative effect, and dissuaded some of those who had seen it from trying the brand.

Quite simply, this means that in 60 per cent of the cases the advertisers benefited from their advertising effort, but 20 per cent of advertisers might as well not have bothered, while 20 per cent spent money and lost even more money as a result.

Now let us look at what might happen as a result of a copy test. In my experience there are three possible outcomes:

▌ The advertisement flops with the test audience, and the only recom-mendation that can be made is to scrap it and start again. In our experi-ence this happens in about 20–30 per cent of cases.

▌ The advertisement scores well in some ways, but less well in others, and recommendations are made to improve it. This happens in about 40 per cent of cases.

▌ For the final 30–40 per cent, the advertisement is passed with no changes.

Impartial feedback tends to be a lot better than the hunches of the clients and creatives. In many cases very good advertisements are not recognized as such by the whole management team on client side. Some people in management will cast doubts on even the best creative advertisement. There is a lot of benefit in *knowing* that one has a winning advertisement, and also a lot of benefit in getting unbiased feedback if there are differ-ences of opinion between the client and the advertising agency.

It is also important to bear in mind the impact of the whole copy-testing process on the design and production process. I suspect that when agencies know that there will be a copy-test, they tend to make a better advertisement than when they know they are not going to get such rigorous feedback.

Figure 11.1 summarizes this argument in graphical form.

One practical argument is that the problem with some copy tests is that they take a lot of time, and for most advertisements there is just not enough time to do a decent copy test. However, the best research compa-nies have developed ways to get around this objection. My company,

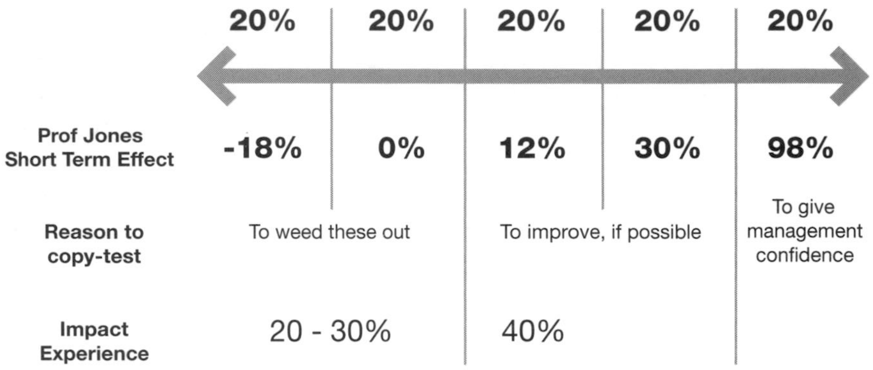

20%	20%	20%	20%	20%

Prof Jones Short Term Effect	-18%	0%	12%	30%	98%
Reason to copy-test	To weed these out		To improve, if possible		To give management confidence
Impact Experience	20 - 30%		40%		

Figure 11.1 *Advertising effectiveness*

Millward Brown South Africa, built its own theatre copy-testing equipment, which reduces the time required to conduct a copy test to just three days. This means that even this objection to conducting copy testing has disappeared. So is there any argument for not researching the effect of advertising? My conclusion is that there is none at all.

12

It is getting more difficult to be memorable

INTRODUCTION

I have tried to show why it is important for advertisements to attract attention, and to be remembered. However, it is not as easy as one would have thought to attract attention; and it is becoming more difficult! At this point it is worth looking at some of the reasons for this.

In his book *Advertising Effectiveness* (1994) Professor Giep Franzen discusses the reasons for this, and provides evidence of the information explosion that the average viewer is exposed to. He also presents evidence that it has become increasingly difficult to create an advertising memory. Most of the results mentioned here come from his book.

EMPIRICAL EVIDENCE

An experiment by a company named Burke showed how the percentage of people who can remember the last commercial that was shown on the television, when phoned while watching the television, has declined in the United States. (See Table 12.1.) GfK found the same in West Germany for 150 campaigns that it followed (see Table 12.2).

Table 12.1 *Percentage of viewers remembering the last commercial they have seen on television in the United States*

1965	18
1974	12
1981	7
1986	7
1990	4

Source: Burke

Table 12.2 *Percentage of viewers remembering the last commercial they have seen on television in West Germany*

1985	18
1986	17
1987	17
1988	15
1989	14

Source: GfK

THE ADTRACK DATABASE

At this stage I would like to introduce you to the Adtrack database, which is unique, and by far the largest advertising database in the world. In 1985 Impact Information (South Africa) started to measure the in-market ad-awareness of all non-retail advertising in the country, and in the same year the South African Broadcasting Corporation (which then controlled the only television channels in the country) provided, as a service to advertisers, a list of all the advertisements that had appeared for the first time in the previous week. Impact used this list to compile a question-naire, every week. It asked a sample of 200 respondents each week the following questions:

1. Have you seen any new television commercials recently?
2. (For every new commercial) Have you seen a commercial for…?
3. (If the answer was yes to question 2) Please describe this for me (veri-fied noting).
4. (If a reasonably correct description was given) Please give it points out of 10 in terms of how much you like it.

South Africa has a good television audience measurement system. It has been using people meters since 1989, so that flighting details can be married to each commercial. Telmar in South Africa also provides a service whereby every spot is linked to the audience data, so it was possible to pick up the actual audiences for every commercial up to the point just before it was measured in the Adtrack research. The core of the database is simply the verified noting of the commercial in the third week of its life, and the TV GRPs up to that stage. At the time of writing, the database contains 30,000 commercials, all dated and measured at the same time – three weeks after their first appearance – along with their media data.

Adtrack's research shows the same trend as is apparent in the Burke and GfK research (see Figure 12.1). On average, advertisements were recalled by 26.5 per cent of people in 1985. By 1994 this had declined to 14 per cent.

During 1995 the format of television in South Africa changed. Until then there had been three terrestrial channels, all government owned, with two transmitting in languages spoken mostly by whites and one in black-oriented languages. As in other countries, people tended to leave the television on while they continued with their other activities. It became a form of background noise, but they might occasionally register when something of interest came on and take notice of it.

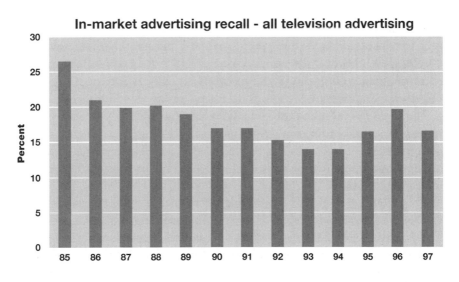

Figure 12.1 *In-market advertising recall in South Africa (for all televison advertising)*

In 1995 all three channels became multi-lingual. This meant that during the evening there would be, for example, a programme in English followed by a programme in Zulu, followed by another English programme, on all three channels. The advertising community predicted that this would lead to a fragmentation of audiences and a decrease in the effectiveness of the medium.

The advertising community was right. During this period actual audiences declined, and the cost per GRP increased. However, as Figure 12.1 shows, despite the decreased audience, the effectiveness of the medium in delivering advertising penetration increased! We believe the reason was that the channels attracted more attention during the first years of this format. For example, people would have the television set tuned to an English programme, perhaps not paying much attention to it, then it would be followed by a programme in a language they did not understand. They would need to switch channels, and this forced them to pay attention to the set for a moment or two. Viewers also had to start planning their viewing. They could no longer simply leave the set on to 'see what was on', unless they could accept the irritation of a programme they could not understand playing in the background. Again this meant that people were giving more attention to their set.

The lesson to be learnt from this is that 'audience' is a much over-rated concept. What matters is not how many people are in the room when the advertising appears on the screen, but how many people are giving attention when the advertising is on the screen.

In many countries the advertisers have become more interested in GRPs than in 'effective GRPs'. They employ organizations to do their media planning on the strength of their buying power, and evaluate media schedules mainly on the cost per GRP. It is possible to have a media schedule with a lot of cheap GRPs, but still waste most (or all) of the advertising budget.

The objective of an advertising schedule should be to create memory traces, not simply to provide an opportunity for many people to see the advertisement. Therefore the evaluation of the media schedule should be on the basis of whether memory traces are formed, not the size of the audience that is reached.

This declining ability of advertising to create a memory trace is not only true of television advertising. Professor Franzen presents evidence in his book of the same effect applying for magazine and newspaper advertisements. Millward Brown has multinational evidence of this phenomenon, and below I reproduce a paper on the subject by Andy Farr, Group Research and Development Director.

HOW ADVERTISING CLUTTER AFFECTS TV'S POWER

In most markets TV is still the lead medium for big advertisers' brand building activity. It is able to communicate in a multi-faceted way through visuals, sound and movement; to convey information and emotion; and to communicate quickly and relatively simply to a mass audience.

However, a number of factors are starting to weigh against TV. The cost of air time and production has been escalating in many markets, whilst at the same time the audience has been fragmenting, making planning more complex. TV may also be falling victim to its own success. Some TV networks have increased the amount of air time devoted to advertising to meet demand.

This may appear to be good for advertisers, but what does this do for the effectiveness of TV as an advertising medium when advertising has reached over 20 minutes per hour, as it has in some day-parts within the US?

Andrew Cracknell, Executive Creative Director Bates, wrote recently: 'There is an unwritten, unspoken contract between advertiser and advertisee, and we could be coming closer to breaking it. That contract states that there needs to be a climate of acceptability, not just in content but in volume, for advertising to work at its most efficient. It has to be not just tolerated but welcome, other wise it gets "cut out" and we get diminishing return on our investment.'

Is that contract being broken? Is the level of ad clutter leading to a decline in the effectiveness of TV advertising?

Millward Brown has looked at the evidence for the effect of advertising clutter on one of the most basic goals of advertising – its ability to create impact and log a recollection in the mind of the viewer that a brand has advertised. The study was done in two ways – by looking across countries and by looking over time in one market where the volume of advertising has increased dramatically over the past 10 years.

The number of ads an 'average shopper' is exposed to in a week varies hugely around the world. For example, in Belgium and Denmark, it is likely to be fewer than 200 ads (Figure 12.2), whereas in the US it is nearly 1,000, and even more in Japan. For people in one of those Northern European markets, such high levels would be startling,

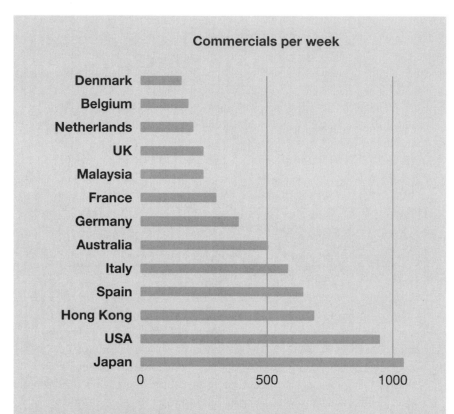

Figure 12.2 *Number of commercials shown per week in different countries*

but according to the American Association of Advertising Agencies, this number is still rising in the US despite the slowing economy. In addition, over 100 stations are now using technology that compresses the length of TV shows, and potentially commercials themselves, by deleting repeated frames. This technology allows stations/networks to squeeze even more commercials into every hour of programming.

So how does this relate to advertising response?

Looking at the average response per GRP in terms of advertising impact, more ads on air means less effect on average. For each of the markets where ad clutter information was available and the audience measurement data was felt to be reliable, Millward Brown conducted an analysis of the average response per Gross Rating Points (GRP/TVR/TARP) in terms of advertising impact. The advertising impact score was calculated using Millward Brown's advertising awareness model. This model calculates the increase in advertising awareness per hundred GRPs, removing the effects due to media weight, diminishing returns and advertising history. In other words, providing a level playing field for measuring advertising impact.

Based on the scores across a range of different advertisers an average for each country was calculated. To aid comparison this was then indexed back to the average of all these countries (Figure 12.3).

All of the countries with above average impact were also countries with below average clutter. In four of the most cluttered markets – Italy, Spain, Japan and Hong Kong – the average response is half that of the less cluttered markets. Or put another way, it would require twice as many GRPs in Japan to generate the same response as the

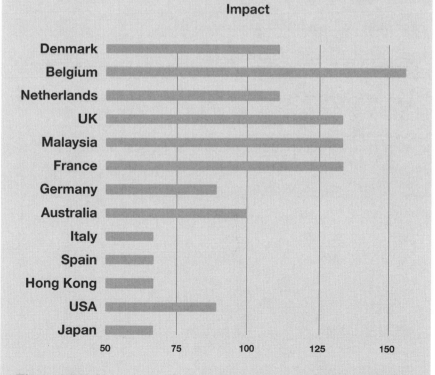

Figure 12.3 *Increase in advertising awareness per hundred GRPs in different countries*

UK. The more ads there are vying for a viewer's attention. the harder it is for each advertisement to get its message across.

To quantify this further, Millward Brown created a simple model of average impact based on the level of ad clutter. Based on this set of countries, ad clutter explains nearly three-quarters of the variation in overall advertising impact. And showed that an increase in clutter from 400 to 500 ads per week would result in an 8 per cent decline in average advertising impact.

One of the markets where the TV environment has changed most dramatically is Spain. Because of the growth in the number of new stations over the past 10 years, the volume of advertising shown per year has increased 10 fold. We don't have sufficient tracking information to go back over the past 10 years, however, we can look at the last five years. Over that period we have seen that the rise in volume of ad clutter has been mirrored by a decline of 30 per cent in terms of the average level of advertising impact (Figure 12.4).

So what are the implications of this?

We believe they fall into two areas.

▮ Firstly, there are some very clear practical implications. On top of existing considerations about the size of the market and relative costs per thousand, advertisers now need to think about the effect of clutter when it comes to planning international campaigns. Rules of thumb about media exposure levels or GRP levels do not

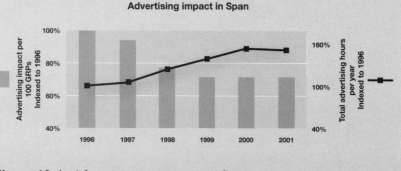

Figure 12.4 *Advertising awareness in Spain*

work across borders. The optimal level of media exposure in a cluttered market will not be the same as that in a low clutter environment. Clearly this is an important factor to consider when deciding how to divide up the media budget across both markets, and across channels within those markets.

▌ The second set of implications are more general. By increasing the amount of time devoted to advertising, the TV broadcasters could quite simply be 'killing their golden goose' – starting a dangerous spiral that will be very difficult to stop.

If the amount of clutter is allowed to increase to create more advertising air time, brands will have to buy more spots to achieve their objectives, which will in turn put more pressure on air time. At the same time, this puts a strain on the contract between viewer and TV station/network. Not only will the advertising have less impact, the irritated viewer will be more inclined to stop watching TV, or avoid advertising using technology such as PVRs, or subscribe to non-advertising channels. Without concerted pressure from advertisers, the power of TV as a brand building medium could be severely diminished.

There is, however, one factor that we need to remember in all this. The effects of clutter we have been looking at are at the aggregate level. In every market the best 10 per cent of ads are more than five times more effective than the weakest 10 per cent (Figure 12.5). For example, the best 10 per cent of ads in Japan and the US still generate many times more impact than the weakest 10 per cent in the UK.

Strength of copy

Advertising clutter is an important factor, but the strength of the copy is still the most important determinant of success. This highlights the importance of research at all stages of the advertising development to ensure that the opportunity available in each market is being maximized.

Author: Andy Farr
Date: September 2002
(This article appeared in Millward Brown's *Perspectives* newsletter, Issue 20, September 2002)

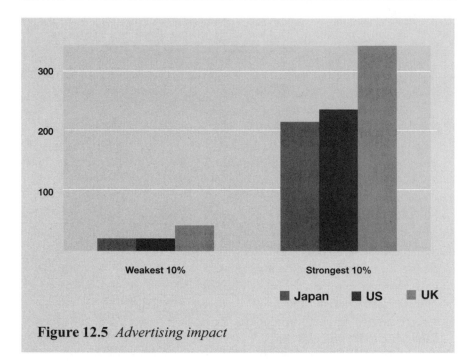

Figure 12.5 *Advertising impact*

DECLINING ADVERTISING MEMORABILITY IS NOT NECESSARILY DECLINING ADVERTISING EFFECTIVENESS

When confronted with statistics like those Farr cites, some advertisers interpret them to mean that advertising itself is becoming ineffective. This would be a vast over-simplification of how one should interpret these findings. We believe it is equally important to take note of these points:

▮ Remember that the studies showing advertising works by Professor Jones and SPOT (see Chapter 1) were done in the early 1990s, after the declines shown above.

▮ If all advertisements were remembered by everyone, then all advertisements would be equally effective: they would simply cancel out each other's effects. All the studies quoted above measure memories, not purchases (as do Jones and SPOT).

▮ The important implication of these statistics is that it is becoming increasingly incumbent on advertisers to ensure that their advertising is effective advertising.

But exactly how do we ensure that our advertising *is* effective?

13

Advertising, learning and memory

Let's take one more stage in the exploration of how to ensure that advertising is effective, by trying to tie together the issues of learning and memory that we looked at in the first half of the book with some more specific insight into how advertising works.

For advertising to have an effect at all, it must have an effect on memory. It is fairly obvious that it should be possible to increase an advertisement's ability to create a memory by making it longer, bigger, louder or whatever. In this chapter we briefly consider the evidence that this is in fact what happens, then go on to look at some other aspects of advertising and memory.

The most measured aspects of advertising are relationships of the physical aspects of commercials to people's memory of them. For example there are studies looking at whether longer advertisements create better memories than shorter advertisements. One reason is that it is probably the easiest thing to measure about advertising: anyone can time the length of a commercial, then devise some measure of its memorability. Another reason is that media owners would prefer advertisers to buy slots for longer rather than shorter commercials, and advertising agency creative departments prefer to make longer television commercials. (A much larger proportion of the budget spent on production is made up of profit than of the budget for media buying. This is especially true where one company produces the advertisement and a different company profits from booking the media.) So it is not surprising that many media owners worldwide have invested money in researching the relationship between advertisement length and memorability, and also in publicizing the results when they are to the advantage of longer advertisements.

THE ADTRACK DATABASE

At this stage I would like to reintroduce you to the Adtrack database, which is unique, and by far the largest advertising database in the world. (I first introduced it on page 114.) At the time of writing, the database contains 30,000 commercials, all dated and measured at the same time – three weeks after their first appearance – along with their media data. Here are some results from our database.

TELEVISION ADVERTISEMENT LENGTH

Figure 13.1 shows the relationship between the length of a commercial and the percentage of the sample who could describe the commercial to the extent that the interviewer was satisfied that they had seen it, within three weeks after the first appearance of the commercial.

As you can see, there is a strong correlation between advertisement length and advertisement memorability. This result is not amazing: it simply replicates what has been found in many similar studies worldwide. In fact, if the study had not found this relationship, it would have been

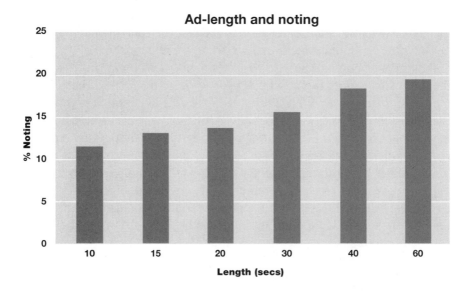

Figure 13.1 *Relationship between advertisement length and percentage of respondents remembering it*

Table 13.1 *Percentage of respondents with spontaneous and aided recall of advertisements, by length of advertisement*

	15 sec	20 sec	30 sec	45 sec	60 sec
Spontaneous recall	20	21	28	40	39
Aided recall	55	56	63	70	70

worthy of comment. Another study that shows much the same effect, by NIPO in Holland, is summarized in Table 13.1.

Some advertisers believe the right lesson to take from these results is that 30-second advertisements are more cost-effective than 60-second commercials, because longer advertisements show diminishing returns (that is, the increase in recall is not proportionate to the increase in length). We do not subscribe to this argument, for two reasons. First, the cost of advertising time is also not proportionate: a 60-second commercial is less than twice as expensive to run as a 30-second one; and second, the effectiveness of a commercial is much more dependent on its content (message) than on its length. If the creative execution requires 60 seconds to work, it makes sense to make a 60-second commercial. However, if the creative content can be put across in 30 seconds, only a fool would spin it out to make a 60-second commercial.

The main reason for citing these empirical results here is because they fit in well with our model of the physical workings of the brain. The longer a commercial is, the longer the time during which the brain receives information from it, thus the longer the relevant neurons will be stimulated and the more sensitive their synapses will become. This in turn will lead to increased memorability, so the advertising results and the model of neuronal activity validate each other.

TELEVISION FREQUENCY EFFECT

Figure 13.2 also shows results from the Adtrack database, this time on ad-awareness (again measured in the third week after the appearance of each commercial) analysed by the length of the commercial and the GRPs applied during the first two weeks of the commercial's life. It again shows an increase in the recall of longer and higher-GRP commercials among the sample, and again there is a diminishing return for both length and media pressure.

To remind you, a GRP is simply a cumulative measure of the percentage of the total potential audience reached by the media plan. When a campaign is built up, each spot adds GRPs to the accumulated total, depending on the size of the audience it reaches. Total GRPs mathematically represent the reach of a campaign multiplied by its frequency. Thus a campaign with 100 GRPs could reach either 50 per cent of the potential audience on average twice, or 25 per cent of the potential audience on average four times. In practice, the first spots (when GRP is below 100) tend to add reach to the schedule (that is, more people see the commercial for the first time), but very soon (by the time the GRP is over 200, say) the schedule only adds frequency (that is, people who have already seen the commercial once see it more and more times).

Again this seems to fit well with what we learnt earlier in the book about neural networks and how memories are laid down: memory laydown increases not only with length of exposure, but also with the number of times the exposure is repeated.

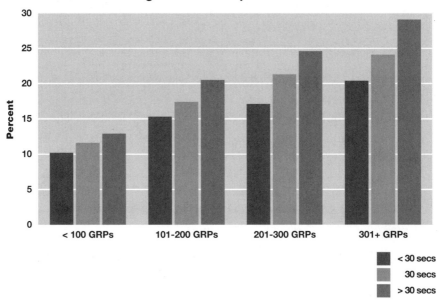

Effect of ad-length and media pressure on in-market recall

Figure 13.2 *Television ad-awareness (three weeks after first transmission) by length of commercial and number of GRPs during the first two weeks of advertising*

PRINT

In print, the measures do of course need to be different, but we can expect the results to be analogous: that bigger advertisements and advertisements with more colour will attract attention better, and therefore lead to better recall. This is in fact what all studies have found. Typical results are those that Giep Franzen showed using the Starch INRA Hooper results for ad noting in business magazines (see Table 13.2).

In Chapter 7 I explained how, according to Professor Susan Greenfield, the ability for a stimulus to become a part of the individual's consciousness depends on:

▌ the arousal level of the person – that is, how awake he or she is;
▌ the existing neural networks that can be stimulated;
▌ the loudness or size of the stimulus.

Again, this is a very good fit with Professor Franzen's findings. However, things are not always that simple. Let us look at some other pieces of information.

Werner Kroeber-Riel of the University of Saarland has published a lot of eye-scanner work (measuring how long people focus on an item) in this regard. He concluded that the average time a reader spends on a print advertisement is 2 seconds, although again this varies by size of advertisement (see Table 13.3).

Research by von Keitz extends these figures to consider also the percentage of the potential audience who actually look at an advertisement. His German study, again using eye-tracking research to find out the average reading time for different sizes of advertisement, also found an average time close to 2 seconds. (See Table 13.4.)

Table 13.2 *How size and use of colour affect percentage of advertisement recall in business magazines*

	Black and white % recall	Full colour % recall
1/3 page	21	25
1/2 page	22	32
Full page	29	42
Double spread	34	52

Source: Franzen (1994)

Table 13.3 *Eye-scanner figures for time spent reviewing advertisements, by advertisement size*

Double spread	2.8 sec
3/4 page and full page	1.9 sec
1/2 page or less	0.6 sec

Source: Kroeber-Riel (1990)

Table 13.4 *Average audience and reading time for print advertisements*

	Average percentage looking at advertisement	Average reading time
3/4 page and larger	89%	5.0 sec
1/2 page to 3/4 page	67%	2.4 sec
1/4 page to 1/2 page	52%	2.1 sec
Smaller than 1/4 page	47%	1.5 sec
Average		2.8 sec

Source: von Keitz (1985)

Two quite different aspects are being measured here: the ability of the advertisement to attract attention, and the ability of it to retain attention. Obviously it needs to attract at least a minimal amount of attention before there is any memory laydown, and then we can hypothesize again that the longer attention is retained for, the stronger the memory trace will be.

You might think that there is a very simple explanation for the difference in attention span: longer advertisements contain more wording, so they take longer to read. Surprisingly, however, advertisements with more words do not attract attention for the additional time it would take to read all the text. On the contrary, a researcher called Laufer found that the more words in a print advertisement, the lower the recognition and the recall (see Table 13.5). So the message is that viewers do not give attention to

Table 13.5 *Recognition of and recall of text-oriented advertisements*

	Recognition	Recall
Advertisements with little or no text	100	100
Text up to 1/3 of space	86	82
Text 1/3 to 1/2 of space	77	73
Text 1/2 to entire space	60	61

advertisements with a lot of words, perhaps because these tend to be advertisements that fail to make an emotional impact.

TIME AND ATTENTION

From the above it is clear that we need to differentiate between an advertisement's ability to get attention and its ability to keep attention.

In Chapter 6 we saw how one part of the physiological process of attentioning has been measured as activity in the posterior regions of the brain. In other words, a cycle of activity is apparent when a stimulus is 'seen' and then 300 milliseconds later when the posterior regions receive instructions to attend to the stimulus again.

Some work has been done to research the time people take to decide whether or not to give attention to an advertisement. Since a print advertisement is exposed to the reader as a complete stimulus, and a television commercial is revealed over time, there has to be a difference between the way people decide whether to read a print advertisement and the way they decide whether to continue watching a television commercial.

I mentioned above some research using eye-scan measurements of how long people spend looking at a print advertisement. An interesting experiment using this technology was done by NIPO. People were given magazines to read, and while they were reading the eye scanner determined where they were looking on the page, and for how long. Subsequently the respondents were shown advertisements from the magazines and asked whether they had seen them while reading. The researchers found that the respondents claimed they had seen only 70 per cent of the advertisements that the scanner readings showed they had glanced at.

The majority (23 per cent) of the difference could be explained by the fact that the observation time for the commercials that were not remembered was less than 0.75 second. For the observed viewing and the recognition of the advertisement to tally, the advertisement had to have been viewed for longer than 2.75 seconds.

A researcher named Kover (whose work has been described by the philosopher A J Ayer) believes that television viewers give a commercial 3 seconds to prove that it is worthy of their attention. Herbert Krugman used pupil dilation measures, in experiments analogous to the magazine eye-scanner experiments, and concluded that the viewer's attention in the first 4 to 10 seconds of a television commercial shows with 83 per cent accuracy whether he or she will give it attention over the entire 60 seconds.

The important advertising principle that is emerging from these studies, and from our knowledge of the physiology of the brain, is that time is all-important. This is because, first, the advertisement has to get attention, and second, the longer a commercial can retain attention, the better the memory laydown. This is true for both print and television advertising.

It is important to note that at this point we are not discussing the issue of content, or the message a commercial is trying to communicate, although clearly content will have some bearing on whether attention is caught and retained. We are simply discussing the issue of creating a memory trace. And the message is that a print advertisement has less than a second in which to make readers pay attention to it, after which it is has to hold their attention for more than a second if it is to leave any trace in their memory. A television commercial has only a little more time to grab the viewer.

Some advertisers mistakenly believe that what they need to do for their commercial to achieve this is to shout or shock in the first seconds. This is not what we are talking about. We are talking about using emotion to draw attention, but it is worth bearing in mind that there is not much to be said for the advertisement to be associated with *negative* emotion; and that *positive* emotion has little to do with shouting. Just as we can notice a friend in a crowded room without their shouting at us, so our attention can be drawn to an advertisement without its needing to 'shout' unduly.

MULTI-MEDIA EFFECTS

About eight years ago one of the newspaper groups in South Africa asked my organization if we could track the effect in our database when television advertisers also ran advertisements in their medium. Our first response was that we were measuring television advertising, and therefore were not geared to measure the impact of print advertisements (a typical researcher response). Our second response was to run an experiment, which had results that amazed us.

In South Africa there are two major Sunday papers, and advertisers that advertise in one generally also advertise in the other. About 50 per cent of our weekly Adtrack sample reads one or both of the Sunday papers, so we simply asked our respondents whether they were Sunday paper readers or not. After six months we looked at all the ad-awareness figures (remember we were tracking television ad-awareness) among people who had read a Sunday paper in the week before being interviewed, and compared it with awareness among those who had not.

Our clients asked us to research 17 campaigns that they believed had appeared both on television and in their paper. We found that for most advertisements there was no significant difference in recall between people who read Sunday papers, and those who did not. However, for the 17 campaigns we were asked to research, there was double the non-reader awareness of the television campaign among the readers.

The research threw up five more campaigns for which a similar difference was apparent. We asked the advertisers to check whether print advertisements had also been run for these products, and found that they had.

Media synergy is a very big issue, and this is not the place for a full discussion of it, but even so these results seem worth taking into account. What we believe we observed was that although the media were completely different, the advertisements in the two media stimulated the same neuronal sets and intensified the same memory. In other words, the advertisements in the paper acted as another exposure to the advertising campaign, and directly impacted recall of the television commercials. Again, it seems that this fits well with the neurologists' model of how the brain lays down memories.

CONSCIOUS AND UNCONSCIOUS LEARNING

There are certainly some instances in which people look to consciously learn from advertising. Before making major 'high involvement' purchases, for example, many people seek out information to help them select the right product, or right brand (if it is a branded product). Someone interested in a high-tech product like a computer, a video camera or a car, might well opt to buy a specialist magazine, or watch a specialist television programme, or check out producers' Web sites, to find out as much information as possible about the rival offerings before making a choice. Someone looking to buy a house will almost certainly go looking for suitable houses, and will be guided by advertising material from agents in that process. One role for advertisers is to place information in the path of those who are actively looking for it. But for low-involvement purchases few of us go looking for much information, and the information that we do acquire is acquired incidentally. We do not consciously try to watch the advertisements for washing powder on the television, for instance, but we are probably exposed to a fair few of them over the course of a week's programme watching, and we will acquire information as a result.

Both conscious and incidental learning work by means of repetition, or rehearsal. (We saw this for example in Ebbinghaus's experiments, briefly described in Chapter 3.) And as well as direct repetition, they work by accretion: we add new learning to the basis of what we already knew, as Professor Bahrick explained (in Chapter 18).

THE WORKINGS OF MEMORY

You will recall from Chapter 5 how memories are formed, and used for interpretation; and that this is largely involuntary. When someone gives attention to a commercial it forms a part of his or her memory. The more intense, the longer or more frequent the attention that is given, the stronger the memory trace will be.

We also briefly hinted at how the process of perception (seeing) is fundamentally a process of interpretation. This process too is driven by experience – that is, by our *memories* of previous experience, which enable us to make sense of what we see. These processes happen during the advertising and purchase cycle, as in all other types of activity.

Thus the process of seeing brands on a shelf is also the process of interpreting what is seen. Our brain automatically draws on relevant previous experience to make the interpretation, on all levels from 'this is toothpaste, it's used for cleaning teeth, it's available in tubes and pump cylinders, and I tend to buy the tubes because they are cheaper' to 'this is the pack for Colgate's new toothpaste which I saw advertised recently'. And this is how advertising memories come to the fore to be 'used'.

The phrase 'consumers use advertising' might make it seem as if there is a complex mechanism that stores advertising memories, and that when the consumer makes a cogitated brand choice these memories are recalled for use, but (according to our current understanding of how the brain works) this is not so. The laying down of advertising memories is mostly involuntary, and occurs by way of their attracting our attention, however fleetingly. The recall of these memories is also involuntary, occurring by way of attention being given to the brands on display.

From an advertiser's point of view what matters is that when the consumer thinks of the brands in the category, there should be links back to the memory of their advertising. In other words, the advertising 'comes to the fore' via the process of neural recruitment.

DIRECT RESPONSE ADVERTISING

The one obvious exception to the process of memorizing of advertisements followed by a purchase process is direct response television advertising, where viewers are invited to contact the seller and buy the product immediately. This type of advertising is aimed at moving the audience to action at the time the advertisement is on the air. 'Action' might be calling the phone number given, or it might just be a step in that direction, such as writing down the number, or actively memorizing it.

These advertisements tend to be much longer than advertisements that are not designed to prompt a direct response. They are much more based on relevant news (setting out a problem and the solution to it), and there is an emphasis on the reasons to respond immediately: perhaps a discount available only for a short time.

YOU INTERPRET ADVERTISING USING YOUR OWN MEMORIES

When you look at a commercial you use your memory to interpret it. British television viewers are familiar with a long series of advertisements for Hamlet cigars that use the same tune. Any advertisement using that tune will bring forth so many memories to the average British viewer that it is barely necessary to name the brand. Viewers from countries where the advertisements have not been shown would, however, find the minimally branded ones thoroughly confusing.

Many companies boycotted South Africa until a few years ago. Now that they are entering its market they cannot run the same campaigns as they are using in the United States or the UK, because South African viewers do not share the brand memories that would enable them to interpret the advertisements.

Woolworths in South Africa is a store similar to Marks & Spencer in Britain. South Africans are confused when they visit a Woolworths in the UK: its brand image is completely different. They would be just as confused if Marks & Spencer were to open a store in South Africa. The memories are wrong.

All your knowledge is made up of your memories. Your memories comprise the sum total of your knowledge. You only behave the way you do because of your memories. People *are* their memories.

Top athletes train in their memories. A high jumper will stand before the jump 'seeing' it in his mind's eye. He will rehearse the whole action in his mind. What he is doing is bringing forth the memories in his mind, so that when he executes the jump the memories that guide his actions are fresh.

INTERNET ADVERTISING

Predictions about the future of online advertising varied from hailing it as the medium that will become the most popular to it being a total waste of time. Print advertising has the advantage for consumers that they can spend as much time as they want reading the advertising, and even store it somewhere to read again at a later stage. Obviously this includes their deciding to spend zero time on the advertisement. Television advertising has the benefit to consumers that advertisements have movement and sound, but viewers cannot determine the rate at which they watch them, or store them or review them. Internet advertising has the advantages of both print and television advertising. The question is whether the benefits really work, and how this fits in with what we know about the way the brain works.

Nigel Hollis presented a paper at the ESOMAR Conference in Mexico City in 2001 entitled 'Is bigger really better?' in which empirical evidence was given about the performance of online advertising. The main thrust of this paper was to evaluate whether streaming advertisements (that is, advertisements with movement) differ from banner advertisements (static). He commented:

1. *One finding is clear, many people do not even remember seeing the ad banner they were exposed to only minutes earlier.*

   On average, the percentage of people who claim to have seen the ad banner before, when it is shown again during the survey, only increases by 8% points between test (who were exposed to the test ad) and control cell (who saw an ad for another brand). While the maximum score was 32%, this data implies that much of the potential brand building power of an ad banner can be lost, simply because it is not noticed.

2. *The question used in BrandImpact to measure brand-linked ad aware-ness is the same as that used by Millward Brown to track the effects of other media. It does have a proven relationship with attitudinal change and sales effects. Online we see a wide range of results, just as with traditional media, but the degree of brand-linked ad awareness created by ad banners is typically only a third that of the recognition. This demonstrates that the ad banners that created strong increases in*

brand-linked ad awareness on average create an increase in brand awareness over ten times as strong as the poor performers.

This is very much in line with the results we have shown from Adtrack data for television advertising, and again stresses the problem advertisers have to get the brand name linked to their advertising memories.

3. *So how do the new ad formats perform compared to ad banners? Well there is little doubt that they are more noticeable! On average, big impression ads create recognition levels twice that of an ad banner. Streaming ads generate an increase almost four times as great.*

Which is what one would hope for: increased size attracts attention, and adding movement should also increase attention.

4. *However, as I noted, recognition is only the first hurdle. The most important question is whether or not the ad delivers a branded impact. The results for brand-linked ad awareness are even more positive. Big impression ads create three times the lift that banners do, and streaming ads six times. This obviously suggests that the new ad formats are more effective brand building vehicles than the traditional ad banner.*

This is a very important finding which implies that because of the size or movement effects, people's attention is not only caught but probably also held for longer, which increases the chance for the brand name to register. Obviously this will also enhance the chance for the intended message to register, and that, after all, is part of our core intention.

14

The attention continuum

In chapter 13 we looked at the results of many independent studies relating physical features of advertisements (their length, size and so on) to their ability to be noticed. Underlying these results is the fact that people have to spend time giving attention to the advertisement in order for them to remember it. Advertisers spend money to increase the odds of people giving attention to the advertisement by adding colour to the advertisement, increasing its size or length, and so on. These aspects of the game are what we look at in this chapter.

The media planning sum is simple:

Cost of Media Schedule = Number of People Reached × Frequency × Attentioning Enhancements

where:

Number of People Reached = People exposed to the advertisement (Reach)

Frequency = How often they are exposed

Attentioning Enhancements = The extra cost of bigger space, longer time, colours added, sound added, and the like. (All media charge more for bigger or longer.)

All the research we have quoted here has been used with the objective of justifying these extra costs, or even of finding ways to calculate these extra charges. We have used this empirical evidence to point out how these results from empirical advertising research do support the neurological insights of scientists. The longer sets of neurons are activated, the lower the limen of the synapses between these neurons becomes, and the more likely the neurons are to fire in harmony again – which means, the better the memory formulation.

All the evidence, including the evidence on clutter in the media, points to people giving very little attention to any advertisements. In fact, it would be a revolutionary advertising theorist who suggested that people give active attention to most advertisements.

However we should not be amazed at the low level of attention that people give advertising. The fact is that we give very little attention to anything at any point in time, yet we remember a lot of what we are exposed to at such a low level of attentioning. We all know that we give real quality attention when we are trying to consciously learn something, or that we give good attention to something if we are reading it – like this book.

But there are other levels of attention-giving that are a lot less conscious, but also work very well. I recently bought an I-Pod and have so far loaded 1,881 songs onto it. These are all old songs from my CD collection and as I now listen to them I can sing along for the great bulk of these songs. At no stage in my life did I sit down and try to memorize these songs, nor did I ever give active attention to most of them. In many cases I only need to read the title of the song, and the lyrics as well as tune will come to mind. (But keep in mind that these songs are generally between three and five minutes long, and I would have listened to the CD a lot at the time it was new.)

The point is really that we are looking at a *continuum of attention*. The top end of the scale consists of situations where we consciously work at trying to form memories by giving quality attention for a long period repeatedly, down to a point where we give little attention but memories are still formed quite effectively, and at the lower end where we give virtually no attention, to the point on the scale where we give no attention. This continuum of attention is largely reflective of the extent to which we kept a set of neurons firing simultaneously, and thereby decrease the limen between these neurons.

Advertising, by its very nature, works at the lower end of this continuum. And, over time, it appears as if the same ad typically slips further down the continuum.

Advertisers, their agencies and the creative directors see their major challenge being to create advertising that operates at as high a level on this continuum as possible. They do this by, for example:

▪ paying a premium to make longer, bigger, more colourful advertisements;
▪ making very 'creative' advertisements;
▪ incorporating emotional appeals.

Not surprisingly a lot of money is invested in doing research before making the advertisement, to assist the creative directors in finding ways towards better creativity, and a lot of money is invested in evaluating creative ideas pre-production, and a lot of money is invested in evaluating whether the final product is getting attention.

From what we know about neurology, it is impossible for someone to give attention to anything without a memory being formed. The act of giving attention – even very little attention – causes limens to be decreased, which is memory formation.

CAN AN ADVERTISEMENT WORK IF IT GETS NO ATTENTION?

Robert Heath published a book in 2001 entitled *The Hidden Power of Advertising: How low involvement processing influences the way we choose brands*. He has subsequently changed the name of his model from 'low involvement processing' to 'low attention processing' (LAP), because people confused his model with the FCB Brain Grid model, which is about low-involvement products, a quite different issue.

The basis argument of Heath's book is that:

1. People give little attention to advertisements.
2. This is especially so after the first few exposures.
3. Therefore measuring memories of advertising is not a good idea.
4. It is especially advertising with emotional appeals that Heath believes works like this.

He quotes the following campaigns as examples of advertisements that, in his judgement, fall into the LAP category:

▊ Nike – the swoosh symbol;
▊ Benson & Hedges – Gold Campaign;
▊ Andrex;
▊ Heineken;
▊ Renault Clio;
▊ Castrol GTX;
▊ Budweiser.

Unfortunately these were all very well-remembered campaigns in the UK back in 2001, and are so even now in 2004, and as examples they seem to defeat the thesis of the low-attention model.

While it is counter-intuitive to think that advertising can work without any attention being given to it, this is a proposition that one should consider in the light of the neurological evidence. I believe that it is theoretically possible, but only under certain circumstances and in a limited way.

In the first section of this book we used examples of how we 'switch attention', in situations like:

▌ Someone mentioning your name at a party while you are not talking to them, yet you switch attention to the conversation where your name was mentioned.

▌ You talk and drive giving no attention to the difficult task of driving, yet switch your attention the moment something on the road demands your attention.

▌ If you see a snake in your path (or even something that might be a snake), your attention will shift, even if you gave no attention to the path before.

The point is that everything your senses experience is transmitted unedited to your brain for interpretation. The process of interpretation occurs by way of neuronal recruitment. We have shown how this process of recruitment occurs for sight from the rear of the brain (occipital region) towards the frontal lobes, and how a half-developed interpretation will contain emotional memories by the time (measured in microseconds) that the process reaches the limbic system. Thus, for everything you see (or hear) the process of interpretation has started. The reason for this is that a 'decision' has to be made whether you should give attention to the observation (such as the snake appearing at the periphery of your sight). If the decision to give attention is *not* made, the developing neuronal cloud just dissipates.

However, even if the decision to give attention is not made, and no further attention is given, the neuronal circuits required to interpret the observation have been activated. When neuronal groups are activated the limen is affected, and memories are refreshed. This is why I believe there can be an effect from advertising that is not given attention, if there exist memories that are available to be refreshed. However, this process has not yet been empirically researched to the extent that it has even begun to be understood.

If I were tasked to develop a research process to investigate the positive effects of advertising that superficially appear to be ignored, where would I start?

1. I would not use a 'recall' measure, but rather a 'recognition' measure (see Chapter 16 for a discussion of the difference between these). Recall measures rely on the advertisement memory being integrated with the brand memory. However, if an advertisement receives

extremely low attention, it will be unlikely that the brand name has been noticed.

2. I would look among non-user segments of the market. Since they are non-users they would probably decide early in the interpretation process that the advertisement had nothing to do with them.
3. I would look among advertisements that are not really emotionally driven. Good emotionally driven advertisements attract attention, and this will create memories of the advertisement, and probably the brand.
4. In spite of the point I made above, I would look for effects on brand awareness measures. This might surprise you: but if the advertisement is brand-linked, then part of the reason for not giving it attention might be that you are not interested in the brand.
5. I would look for the effect in a laboratory setting, or in a personal interview where I can interview the respondent very quickly after exposure. The reason is that memories that have been stimulated only to the extent that a decision to not give attention is taken can only be very transient (because in these cases, the synapses will only have been activated for milliseconds).

These options apply most obviously when the advertisement is relatively new. There is another situation in which advertisements work with very little attention being given to them, which is when the viewer (or listener) experiences wear-out. (In the next chapter I outline a model called COMMAP, and use the term *familiarity* to describe this situation.) While no research has been done on wear-out (in fact the word does not appear in the indexes of any advertising books I have read), it certainly exists, and we all talk about it as a reality.

The mechanism of wear-out is fairly obvious against the background of neurological theories. During the process of interpreting the advertisement, the viewer makes a 'decision' that what is being observed is not important enough for it to be given any attention, because it is already so familiar. Intuitively one would expect that a commercial that is entertaining will take a lot longer to bore its audience than one that concentrates on giving news. And this is exactly what Millward Brown has found in its massive database of tracked advertisements: we can expect a bigger but much more short-term sales reaction from advertisements that are informative than from entertaining commercials. Over time all advertisements become worn out, in the sense that people give them less attention than they did when they were new, but this process will occur at different rates for different advertisements, and for differing advertising styles.

Even an advertisement that has become very worn-out will be interpreted when it is observed. This process of interpretation involves the stimulation of neuronal structures, and in the process the synapses are again strengthened. How effective this stimulation is depends on the way that all the brand associative networks are stimulated. Unless these networks have been well established by the time that the advertisement is in this situation, the low-attention process will be unlikely to work – because there are no neuronal networks to be stimulated.

HEATH'S ERROR

Robert Heath will be surprised to hear that I agree with nearly all the references he uses in his book. He will not be surprised that I disagree with nearly all his conclusions:

▌ Heath explains that all advertisements eventually give rise to low-attention processes. That I agree with. But to then apply his theories to all advertisements at the start of their life is an unwarranted logical jump. Unless a commercial establishes a memory structure in the early part of its life, it cannot 'refresh' this in the later part of its life.

▌ There is no reason to believe that an advertisement can impart anything 'new' when it relies on low-attention processing. Thus a new brand, a new brand position, new news about a brand, even new emotions about a brand are unlikely to occur if the advertisement is processed at a low level of attention.

▌ All advertisements operate at a low level of attention. The desire of all advertisers is to operate at the highest possible level of attention for their commercial – and even then the best achievable will be a relatively low level of attention. What we are all trying to achieve is to increase this level of attention a bit.

▌ All the evidence about 'emotional appeals in advertising' shows that their main role is to attract attention, therefore it is unlikely that the more emotional an advertisement is, the more it will become low-attention processed.

WHAT THE REST OF THE BOOK IS ABOUT

No one, apart from researchers and academics, studies advertising, but we all learn from it just the same. Much of what we know about the world is learnt incidentally, without much attention, and most of us pay little attention to advertising. It is important to realize, however, that paying little attention is not the same as paying no attention. As I hope you will have learnt by reading this far, the anticipation of a positive experience will automatically engage a higher degree of attention. Compared with deliberately studying for an exam or learning to ride a bike, the degree of attention is low, but the resulting memory trace is directly influenced by the strength of that attention. Advertising cannot work without attention, since without it there would be no memory trace, but it is a common misconception that advertising can work this way.

In the remainder of this book we will consider:

1. Evidence from large-scale industry studies that emotion in advertising has a bigger influence on getting attention than any other 'bought' dimension – that is, it is more effective than the premium paid for size, length, colour and the like.
2. What emotions are in advertising, how they can be used in account planning and creative strategies, and how can they be measured.
3. What to do with an advertisement in the media when it has been created.
4. How to adapt advertising media strategies over time.

What we have done up to this stage is set the background against which advertising has to work, initially by focusing on the brain. We have outlined a mountain of research considering intrinsic aspects of an advertisement (its length, size, placement, colour and so on). Many of the results one would intuitively have expected. Now we are going to get more involved in the practical issues of advertising.

Earlier I introduced a simple formula. It can be adapted for the rest of the book to give a simple advertising planning sum:

Cost of Advertising = Number of People Reached × Number of Times Reached × Structural Attentioning Factors × Creative

Where:

Number of People Reached = Reach of the schedule

Number of Times Reached = Frequency of exposure

Structural Attentioning Factors = the extra cost of bigger space, longer time, colours added, sound added and similar factors.

Creativity = the creation of emotions by way of interesting news, aspirations or entertainment, to act as a multiplier.

Obviously I shall be talking a lot about how the last factor in the formula can be measured, to reduce risk for the advertiser and the advertising agency. From an advertising agency perspective, this is where things become critical, because such measurement is where advertisers get the freedom to become creative and achieve greatness – and get their proposals passed by clients.

15

What ad-liking means

We're getting there. Now let us focus seriously on what it really means to like an advertisement.

In the 1980s a major piece of research known as the Copy Research Validation Study (CRVP) was carried out by the American Advertising Research Foundation (ARF). Russ Haley managed the project, and once it was complete he said that the logistics were such that it was unlikely it would ever be repeated.

The research was done during the 1980s. The ARF approached advertisers and asked them to identify pairs of advertisements that had been used for the same brand, where one had been a big success and the other had been a failure. This was not an easy task. The main problem was that few advertisers would admit to having made bad advertisements. It is even probable that few advertisers really knew whether, or which, advertisements were successes or failures.

Eventually eight pairs of advertisements were identified. Haley's team also gathered all the research that had been done on them. It then devised a questionnaire which asked respondents to rate advertisements on every possible measure that can be taken of a commercial in a copy test. As Haley tells it, when the questionnaire was finally ready to be used for fieldwork, someone suggested at the last moment that maybe it should also simply ask people if they 'like the commercial'.

The conclusions that this research drew were that all the major copy-testing measures (which I discuss further in this chapter) are at least to some degree predictive of an advertisement's success, but that *ad-liking is the most predictive*. This was an unexpected result, since whether people liked advertisements did not feature in any of the recognized ways of researching the effectiveness of them. It set the whole advertising industry alight, and was followed by much furious debate.

The most notable reaction was by Alexander Biel. He published a paper in *Admap*, 'Love the ad. Buy the product?' (1990), which took the ARF research and argued that this was a reason for agencies to focus more on making advertisements that would actually be 'liked'. Perhaps understandably, many advertising agencies saw this as a carte blanche to make 'creative' advertising.

American advertising research companies saw this new measure, which none of them had been using, as a new contender on the block and a real threat to their income. So they rapidly re-analysed their databases, and published papers explaining why the ARF results were not valid. Since they had not been using ad-liking measures in the past, they did not have data on these to support their cases, so they had to use surrogate measures, and judicious choice of these helped them prove their point.

Despite the negative reception American research companies gave the news about ad-liking, the evidence in favour of this measure kept coming in. Two particularly interesting papers appeared which commented on ad-liking as a measure of effectiveness. One, by Professor Esther Thorsen, discussed the run-up to the discovery of ad-liking, and the other, by Professor John Philip Jones tied the concept of ad-liking to his large empirical database.

RESEARCH BY ESTHER THORSEN AND JOHN PHILIP JONES

Esther Thorsen's paper showed that academic research during the 10 years before the ARF study had in fact consistently found advertising likeability to be a very strong predictive measure of advertising effectiveness.

John Philip Jones looked at the characteristics of effective advertisements and concluded that they:

▌ are likeable: that is, they offer a reward for watching;
▌ are visual rather than verbal;
▌ say something important and meaningful about the brand.

However, his assessment of likeability was 'impression based' rather than based on research, because nowhere in his research did Jones actually ask other people whether or how much they liked commercials, in preference to judging them by whether he liked them himself.

SPOT AND ADTRACK

An industry study in the Netherlands, SPOT tracked 23 commercials and attempted to assess their impact on both in-market awareness and purchase intent. The conclusion the researchers reached was that more than 40 per cent of the variation in effectiveness was explained simply by ad-liking scores.

We began to see in the early part of the book how emotion plays a role in directing our attention, and in setting the context for the interpretation of sensory input. The question that comes to the fore now is how liking an advertisement works to affect its impact. Does it give the commercial greater power to attract attention, or does it affect how favourably we look on the information given in the commercial, or on the brand that is being advertised? Or does it work in both these ways? (See Figure 15.1.)

An example might make this clearer. Let us take an advertisement which achieves 10 per cent audience awareness for every 100 GRPs. Now let us assume that 30 per cent of those who recall the commercial then go on to buy the brand. In other words, for every 100 GRPs, about 3 per cent of the audience will buy the product.

If the advertisement is liked, then (let us say) its ability to create awareness doubles. So for every 100 GRPs, 20 per cent of people will become aware of the commercial (that is, acquire a memory of it). Again, 30 per cent of those with recall will buy the brand, so this time around 6 per cent of the audience will buy.

Alternatively, let us say that the fact the commercial is liked has no impact on awareness creation, but it does have a major effect on the purchase intent. So this time, only 10 per cent retain a memory of the commercial, but twice as many of them – 6 per cent – buy the product. In both examples the effect of liking doubles purchases, but the reason this happened is different in each case.

We can begin to see which of these effects is real by looking at the Adtrack database, where respondents are asked to give all advertisements a 'points out of 10' liking score. Figure 15.2 shows the effect of ad-liking on the in-market ad-awareness of 11,400 advertisements that were shown

Figure 15.1 *How ad-liking might work*

Effect of ad-linking on noting

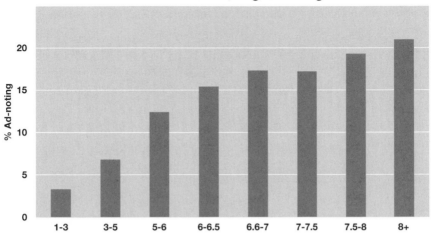

Figure 15.2 *The effect of ad-liking on in-market ad-awareness*

in South Africa. We repeated the same study in England for 180 advertisements, and the same relationship was exhibited there.

Dr Mike Ewing of Curtin University in Australia did an analysis on the food advertising in the Adtrack database, which was published in the *Journal of Advertising Research*. His conclusion was that ad-liking explains 58 per cent of the variance in people's memory of food advertising, the length of the advertisement only 2 per cent, and media variables virtually nothing.

The Dutch SPOT study calculated the increase in awareness per 100 GRPs and also the increase in stated purchase intent per 100 GRPs, relating this to the liking scores of the advertisements:

▌ If the liking score was 5/10, the impact on in-market ad-recall was 3 per cent per 100 GRPs.
▌ If the liking score was 6/10, the impact on in-market ad-recall was 10 per cent per 100 GRPs.
▌ If the liking score was 7/10, the impact on in-market ad-recall was 33 per cent per 100 GRPs.

These studies show that there is little doubt ad-liking has an effect on the ability of a commercial to get attention, and as a result to lodge itself in consumers' memories. Every advertiser should try to make advertising that consumers like, for a very simple reason: it acts as a multiplier of the effectiveness of the media budget!

The ARF study made no comments on whether liking works on people's attention or via persuasion; it noted only that it worked on the final outcome – sales. Our Adtrack database cannot comment on the persuasive ability of commercials that are liked, but can give evidence about the attentioning abilities of the commercials.

The SPOT study, however, did comment on both the attentioning effect and the effect on purchase intent that resulted from ad-liking. It found that ads with high ad-liking have a big effect on purchase intent per 100 GRPs, and ads with lower ad-liking have a lower effect on purchase intent per 100 GRPs. So the available evidence is that ad-liking has a twofold effect on the advertising process (a double whammy, so to speak) (see Figure 15.3).

Despite the fact that the established research houses have a vested interest in 'disproving' ad-liking as an important measure of advertising, the evidence in favour of ad-liking keeps coming in from reputable studies. There is no way that advertisers can ignore or downplay this evidence any more.

However, ad-liking is not just a 'licence to creative irresponsibility', as the creatives in advertising agencies initially liked to think that it was. Ad-liking is a well-defined construct. A lot of the arguments about whether or not it is important, or even relevant, would have been avoided if advertising researchers had only taken some time out to find out what ad-liking *is*. Unfortunately most people simply think of ad-liking as

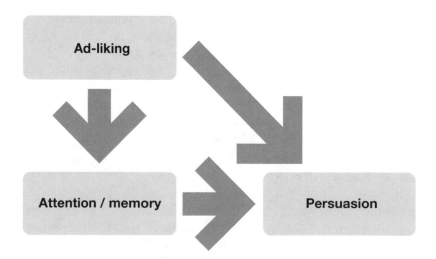

Figure 15.3 *The double effect of ad-liking*

entertainment, or even more simplistically as humour. If ad-liking simply meant that consumers were asking to be entertained by the advertising, it would indeed be realistic to doubt whether ad-liking is a useful measure – after all, the prime purpose of advertising is to sell, not entertain. However, that is not the case.

THE COMMAP MODEL

When we at Impact Information discovered from our Adtrack database that 'ad-liking created ad-noting' (that is, that people remembered best the advertisements they liked the best), we too also thought initially that ad-liking meant respondents found the advertisements entertaining. However, since we did Adtrack studies for all the advertisements that appeared on South African television, and as a result we had a liking score for every advertisement in the country, we pretty soon learnt that many advertisements that were not particularly entertaining obtained high liking scores. We therefore set out to get a better understanding of what advertising likeability is.

We identified seven published studies (using data from the United States) that had as their objective to determine the dimensions of advertising communications. Typically these resulted in a battery of statements that could be applied to measure responses to advertising. Alexander Biel compared these studies in the *Journal of Advertising Research* and concluded that they all arrived at very similar results. For our experiment we used the Viewer Response Profile (VRP) developed by Professor Mary Jane Schlinger in conjunction with Leo Burnett.

In this research, Professor Schlinger first analysed the open-ended responses generated in copy tests that had been conducted, to compile a list of statements that reflect the ways in which 'viewers responded to advertisements': for example, 'The characters (persons) in the commercial capture your attention', 'I know that the advertised company/brand is dependable and reliable' and 'The commercial gave me a new idea.' She then used these statements as a basis for asking consumers to give ratings to a battery of advertisements. The measures were then factor-analysed to establish the underlying dimensions that explain how viewers respond to advertising. The result was a battery of 32 statements on which any advertisement can be measured. These statements are summarized by seven factors – or to put it differently, they embody seven different dimensions – Entertainment, Relevant news, Empathy, Brand reinforcement, Confusion, Familiarity and Alienation.

Adtrack researchers took seven advertisements for which we knew the liking scores from the Adtrack database, and asked 400 respondents to rate them using the 32 statements. (The details are reported in a paper in the *Journal of Advertising Research*; Du Plessis, 1994b.) We then did a correspondence analysis of the result. The output of this was a map which described the interactions between the variables used in the analysis.

At the end of our experiment we had a mathematical model that was predictive of an advertisement's 'likeability'. We subsequently used this model in copy testing, and when we had completed 23,000 interviews in about 200 copy tests, we validated the model at a respondent level. That is, we could predict how an individual respondent would rate an advertisement for 'likeability' from his or her responses to the set of statements. We achieved a high level of accuracy in our predictions: $r^2 =$ 0.86. We called this the COMMAP model (COMmunication-style MAP) (see Figure 15.4).

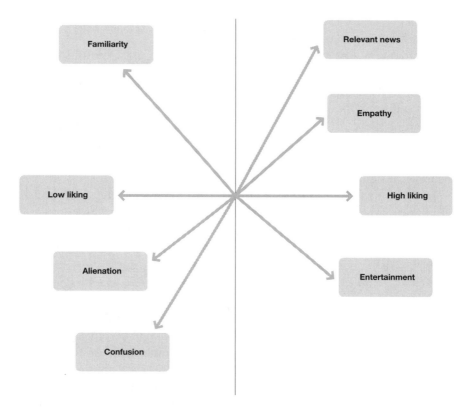

Figure 15.4 *The COMMAP model of communication*

UNDERSTANDING THE DIMENSIONS IN THE COMMAP MODEL

Each of the dimensions in the model comprises several items: those on which Professor Schlinger measured her advertisements, which we then used to measure our advertisements. Factor analysis had showed Professor Schlinger which items correlate (that is, give the same pattern of measurements, or measure closely related aspects of something). These correlated items formed a dimension of the model, and each dimension was given a name by her: Entertainment, Empathy and so on. A dimension is therefore defined by the items that were used to construct it.

These names of these dimensions are likely to be familiar to you, since they basically reveal a typology of advertisement types: Entertaining types of advertising, advertising that creates Empathy, advertising that is Familiar, and so on. However, inside the dimensions (the broad types of advertisements) there exist sub-categories, and to appreciate what is included in the broad typology, it is necessary to look at the items that make up the dimension.

Entertainment items

1. The commercial was lots of fun to watch and listen to.
2. I thought it was clever and quite entertaining.
3. The enthusiasm of the commercial is catching – it picks you up.
4. The commercial wasn't just selling the product – it was also entertaining me. I appreciated that.
5. The characters (persons) in the commercial capture your attention.
6. It's the kind of commercial that keeps running through your mind after you've seen it.
7. I just laughed at it – I thought it was very funny.

Most people, when we talk about entertaining advertising, automatically think we are talking about humour. This is only one of the possibilities. Entertainment can be achieved by humour, but it is also achieved by the use of arresting characters, by sheer enthusiasm in the presentation, and in several other ways.

Relevant news items

12. The commercial gave me a new idea.
13. The commercial reminded me that I'm dissatisfied with the product I'm using now and I'm looking for something better.
14. I learnt something from the commercial that I didn't know before.
15. The commercial told me about the product and I think I'd like to try it.
16. During the commercial I thought how this product might be useful to me.

This dimension does not simply classify the commercial as containing new information (news), but looks especially at whether the news has any relevance to the consumer. Maybe we can rephrase this: it asks whether the news is presented in a way that makes it relevant to the consumer. Problem–solution type advertising especially falls into this typology. It should be self-evident that this is an especially good style of advertising for new products.

Note that the item that indicates the likelihood of the consumer trying the product – number 15 – forms part of this dimension. Because it covers this kind of aspect, this dimension can be thought of as a 'persuasion' measure, and there is a real sense in which the earlier concept of persuasion (see Chapter 16) is incorporated in the COMMAP model. From a different perspective, the fact that the persuasion measurement is only one of 32 in the COMMAP model shows how inadequate it is as a complete descriptor of the effectiveness of an advertisement.

Empathy items

19. The commercial was very realistic – that is, it was true to life.
20. I felt that the commercial was acting out what I feel at times.
21. I felt as though I was right there in the commercial experiencing the same thing.
22. That's my idea – the kind of life that the commercial showed.
23. I liked the commercial because it was personal and intimate.

This broad typology applies especially to lifestyle-type advertising, and also to aspirational advertising: commercials that show people the kind of goods they might possess, the kinds of experience they might have, the kind of lifestyle to which they can reasonably aspire.

Brand reinforcement items

17. The company/brand is a good company/brand and I wouldn't hesitate to recommend it to others.
18. I know that the advertised company/brand is dependable and reliable.

Later in the book I talk a lot about the impact the brand has on the effect of advertising. An advertisement does not only affect consumers' perception of the brand; their existing perception of the brand also affects consumers' perception of its advertising! In Damasio's terms (see Chapter 8), the soma of the brand affects the interpretation of the advertisement. A major implication of this is that if the brand has a positive soma, the objective of 'reminder advertising' is totally valid. Each time the consumer is reminded of the brand, the neuronal systems that store the brand soma are strengthened. Of course the opposite is also true: if the brand has a nega-tive soma, this too affects the way the advertising is received, and the soma might well become even more negative as a result.

Confusion items

8. It was distracting trying to watch and listen at the same time.
9. It required a lot of effort to follow the commercial.
10. It was too complex. I was not sure what was going on.
11. I was so busy watching the screen, I didn't listen to the words.

I refer often to Confusion in the rest of this chapter, as it is the most common mistake creatives make in designing advertisements. The four statements Mary Jane Schlinger identified are a remarkably good summary of the main sources of Confusion in advertising.

Familiarity items

24. This kind of commercial has been done many times before – it's the same old thing.
25. I've seen this commercial so many times, I'm tired of it.
26. I think this is an unusual commercial – I'm not sure I've seen another one like it.

As is clear from these statements, the Familiarity dimension basically measures how boring advertisements are. One aspect of this (but only one) is whether a specific advertisement has been around for a long time and has 'worn out'. As Item 24 emphasizes, even a new commercial can be considered to be worn out if it is an original approach for the specific product category but if something similar has been done in other product categories.

Alienation items

27. What they showed didn't demonstrate the claims they were trying to make about the product.
28. The commercial didn't have anything to do with me or my needs.
29. The commercial did not show me anything that would make me want to use the product.
30. The commercial made exaggerated claims. The product would not live up to what it said or implied.
31. It was an unrealistic commercial – very far-fetched.
32. The commercial irritated me – it was annoying.

It is amazing in how many ways advertisers can irritate – and hence alienate – consumers. Our experience shows that advertising that is confusing is mostly just ignored by the audience: at the worst, the media budget is wasted. However, advertising that alienates is not ignored: it just creates a negative soma for the brand and advertising in general. This means the media budget is spent to achieve a negative effect!

Any conversation about advertising, whether it is a structured conversation in a research context or a casual chat over dinner, tends to bring up mention of advertisements that irritate the hell out of people. Every time someone mentions a pet hate advertisement, my automatic thought is, why don't they just ignore it? The answer is simple: they cannot. Just as paying attention to an advertisement is not entirely a matter of conscious choice, so ignoring it is not something we can do deliberately either.

THE INTERACTION BETWEEN THE COMMAP DIMENSIONS

The horizontal axis in the COMMAP model (again, see Figure 15.4) is a scale with low ad-liking on the left and high ad-liking on the right. The arrows indicate aspects of the advertisement that cause it to be more liked (or less liked).

▌ **Entertainment.** As might be expected, if an advertisement entertains, it will be liked.

▌ **Familiarity.** The opposite is also true: things they have seen a lot of before seldom entertain people. Familiarity causes a decrease in liking. A commercial that is very similar to many earlier commercials is unlikely to be well liked.

▌ **Empathy.** However, it is not only entertainment that creates liking. People like advertisements they can empathize with. They like to see situations they would like to be in, or that they can aspire to.

▌ **Alienation.** People dislike advertisements that alienate them (this is probably saying the obvious).

▌ **Relevant news.** It is important to note that people like advertisements that give them information that is relevant to them.

▌ **Confusion.** However, when an advertisement is confusing it cannot give relevant news. It will also fail to entertain or create empathy.

The COMMAP model is being used here as a vehicle for analysing advertising, but in fact nothing in it is specific to the advertising sector: it is a general model of communication. It could just as well be applied to this book, for example. As a reader, you will probably like the book if you feel it is telling you something new and relevant. You might be alienated by some of the views expressed, particularly if they contradict your long-held beliefs about advertising; alternatively you might find yourself empathizing if you find that I manage to spell out insights you had been groping towards yourself. The book is not meant to be entertaining in the humorous sense, but obviously I hope it is not boring to read. Maybe you will find parts of it confusing; if so, you are liable to like it less as a result. Conference papers, newspapers, even inter-office memos will be 'likeable' or not on the same dimensions.

The power of the COMMAP model is that it describes in measurable terms something (which we call 'likeability') that has a definite correlation with the tendency of a commercial to be remembered, and to have an impact on consumers' intention to purchase.

SPOT and what ad-liking is

The Dutch industry study SPOT, which I have already mentioned, also investigated what ad-liking means. It concluded that high liking derives from Relevant news, Empathy and Entertainment, and low liking results from Alienation, Confusion and Familiarity.

RACHEL KENNEDY REPLICATES COMMAP IN AUSTRALIA

A possible criticism of the COMMAP model is that it is very limited in its cultural base: all the research on which it is based is South African, and even then it draws on only one of the many cultures of that country. True, the Viewer Response Profile on which the model is based is from the United States, but that does not of itself prove that COMMAP is applicable in a variety of cultural settings. SPOT is Dutch, but the Dutch and South African cultures have close links, and I was also involved in the design of that study (though not the analysis), so this cannot be taken as much of a broadening of the applicability of the theory.

I was conscious of these limitations, and during the mid-1990s I visited Professor Andrew Ehrenberg in London to find out what he thought. Unfortunately his research interests did not really dovetail with my own, but he did me a favour by introducing me to the delightful Dr Rachel Kennedy, one of his assistants. She read the *Journal of Advertising Research* paper explaining the COMMAP model, and for her PhD, under Professor Byron Sharpe in Australia, she set out to see whether the model held true in a different country, using different statistical approaches. It did, although we only learnt this several years after she had completed her research.

From the research to date, there is a great consistency in results from the United States, South Africa, Australia and the Netherlands.

EARLIER EVIDENCE ABOUT THE IMPORTANCE OF AD-LIKING

I have already mentioned, Professor Esther Thorsen's research, which identified papers about the importance of ad-liking going back more than a decade before the ARF study was published. This prompted us to see if we could identify any even earlier evidence of advertising researchers identifying the importance of ad-liking.

The oldest evidence we found was a paper by David W Olson delivered at an EMAC/ESOMAR conference in Copenhagen in 1984. At that stage he worked for Leo Burnett, and his paper, 'Validation of copy-testing measures based on in-market performance: an analysis of new product ads', seems to me still to be one of the best studies of copy-testing that has been written.

One of the troubles with measuring advertising is that it operates in the real world where there are many other variables at work. This is particularly so for established products, where sales are obviously heavily affected by the intrinsic performance of the product, and people's experience of it and the organization that produces it. Research into advertising for product launches tends to be more reliable because in these cases the product's prior performance does not have an impact. Advertising is the main source for consumers of knowledge about new products, and the main prompt for them to try it.

Olson collected information from the Leo Burnett offices on new products they had launched over 15 years for which there was some research data available: feedback from copy-testing, and trial rates measured in test markets. A wide variety of copy-testing methodologies was being used by Burnett clients, and this made it difficult to find a big enough sample of new products for analysis, but Olsen's team managed to identify 65 that had been measured using the Schlinger VRP battery. (As you will recall, this was the basis of the seven dimensions used in COMMAP, and this makes it relatively easy to compare Olson's results with our own research into ad-liking.)

As a first step in the analysis Olson considered the media pressure. From the test market data he calculated a trial rate per GRP, then he classified the advertisements into high trial, medium trial and low trial (which might be taken to mean, successful, moderately successful and less successful). He analysed these categories by the dimensions of the VRP , and found that two dimensions explained the difference between a high trial rate and a low trial rate: Relevant news and Entertainment (although Olson called this dimension Stimulation). Relevant news was the most important factor in an advertisement's success, and Stimulation was also important, but secondary. The results were presented graphically, and are reproduced in Figure 15.5.

If you compare this figure with Figure 15.4, you will see how it represents one part of the COMMAP model. You should also note that the high-trial brands appear to be 'rated' on a 45-degree line, which is the same line found in the COMMAP model between Entertainment and Relevant News. (That is, they fit the 'ad-liking' line.) So what Olson really showed is that high ad-liking (in a sense that includes not just Entertainment, but also factors such as Relevant news) leads to a high level of trial for new products.

APPLYING THE COMMAP MODEL

My organization has been using this model of communication for about 20 years now, and over that time we have learnt a lot. These are our main discoveries.

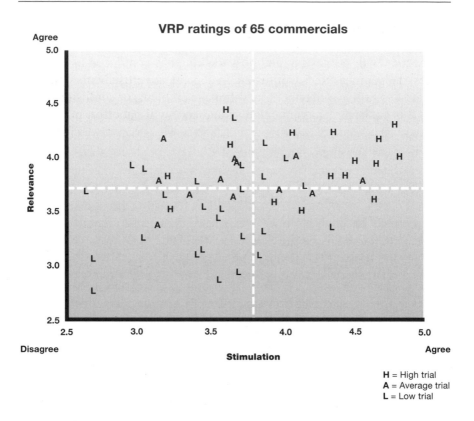

Figure 15.5 *VRP ratings and trial rates for commercials*

The model has to be seeded with normative data

It is not good enough just to indicate to a client that its advertising scores low or high on any of the dimensions. It is necessary to compare an advertisement's scores with those of other advertisements. The average scores on the dimensions are quite different: for instance, scores on Confusion tend to be very low, so even a fairly low (but higher than average) score on this dimension can be a danger signal. I once read a report on a focus group which commented that 'only' two of the seven respondents had expressed confusion about the advertisement being tested. This should not have been taken to mean there were no confusion problems with the advertisement: clearly there were, for a significant number of the respondents.

Confusion is the biggest danger

Experience with pre-testing and post-tracking has convinced us that the biggest danger measure is Confusion. In general, advertisements with low impact rates suffer from either brand-linkage problems or confusion problems. It is a mistake to assume that an audience will put effort into figuring out what a commercial is about. Usually they will not: if they feel even slightly confused, they just ignore the commercial.

A multitude of scenes creates confusion

From our experience we can safely state that too many scenes in an advertisement create confusion, and lead to low impact rates. This often happens when the advertisers try to create empathy by providing a wide variety of associations, or linking the product to a variety of lifestyles. Invariably these crowded commercials simply confuse the audience.

Too many objectives lead to confusion

Because the model indicates that high ad-liking is created by Entertainment, Empathy and Relevant News, many advertisers seem to believe that if they try all three in a commercial they will get the highest possible score. Unfortunately, with rare exceptions the opposite is true. The culprit mostly appears to be Entertainment – especially humour. If an advertiser has Relevant News to share with the audience, it should not confuse them by also using humour, or too much Entertainment. It is better just to tell them the news. Then when the news is not so new, the strategy can change and the focus swing from Relevant News to Entertainment.

Relevant news can decline rapidly

We have on occasion seen the measure for Relevant News decline even while the copy test is being carried out. For example, Benson & Hedges used to sponsor One-Day Cricket in South Africa. Legislation was introduced to ban cigarette sponsorship, and Standard Bank took over. Two advertisements were created to announce this. They were shown and rated sequentially. The first obtained a very high Relevant News rating, but the second got a much lower score. It was not a bad advertisement in itself, but it was doing a job that had already been done by the first advertisement in the test.

An advertisement competes against all other advertising

One of our clients insisted that its new advertisements be compared with its own earlier advertisements, not with the competition. The rationale was that it was continuously striving to improve its advertising, and wanted feedback on whether it was succeeding. It seemed to us much more relevant that the average scores of all their advertisements were well below the average for all advertising, and below competitors, on just about all dimensions. What the client was really doing was perpetuating its below-average status.

Some clients want to compare their campaigns with competitors' campaigns, not with advertising in other categories. However, this does not take account of how and why consumers pay attention. Consumers do not think this is the best bank advertisement, or this is the best toilet paper advertisement. They just look at advertising they like to look at.

We have seen advertisers try a creative approach that they believe to be new for their product category, even though it has already been used widely in other categories. This subtlety seems to be lost on consumers. They rate advertisements like these high on Familiarity, which means, low on ad-liking.

Humour can be a two-edged sword

There is no doubt that humour is a very powerful creative medium, and when it works, humorous advertisements achieve good Entertainment scores. However humour has its dangers, and we have seen this often in our research.

Humour is very often culture-dependent: what seems funny to an South African of English origin might not be funny to an Afrikaner or a Zulu in the same country, let alone to someone from a different continent. The same is true for the diverse cultural groups in the United States and the UK, and everywhere else. Attempted humour that fails to connect with the audience can be a great source of Confusion – and when audiences are confused, they give up on attention.

Unfortunately, sometimes creatives think it is humorous to make a joke at the expense of another culture or group. This is an incredibly dangerous practice. Although some of the audience might rate the advertisement Entertaining, many will rate it as Alienating, so overall it might well do more harm than good to the product's soma.

In today's climate of political correctness, racially or socially denigratory humour might not only offend the group who are the butt of the joke. We tested one commercial in which a banker confesses to a Catholic priest that he charges the lowest interest rates. This was challenged at the Advertising Standards Authority for denigrating Catholics. Our research showed that Catholics did not feel insulted, but Presbyterians felt that Catholics would be insulted, and they reacted negatively to the advertisement.

COMMAP VERSUS LINK

COMMAP is a communication-style model that has been adapted to be used for copy-testing. Millward Brown's Link is a copy-testing methodology. The two are, not surprisingly, very similar. Both Impact and Millward Brown were doing advertising tracking and developed an insight into the dynamics of how advertising works. Both experienced the deficiencies in existing copy-testing methodologies. Both worked toward methodologies that could predict Impact Rate (Awareness Index) and look for the common mistakes in advertising (such as a failure to link the brand adequately with the memory of the advertisement).

COMMAP was developed using a very stringent theoretical-academic approach. If the aim is to develop a descriptive model of a market (like a perceptual map), a good way to start is by doing qualitative work to develop yardsticks, then take quantitative measures of the products using those yardsticks, then do factor analysis and correspondence analysis. This is what we did, using Professor Schlinger's work as the basis for the qualitative part of the project.

In contrast Link, developed by Gordon Brown and Nigel Hollis, started with their sitting down and using their experience from tracking and copy testing to work out what needed to be measured. Only then did they design the measurements.

Because COMMAP is a general communications methodology that is being used as a copy-testing methodology, and Link started its life as a dedicated copy-testing methodology, COMMAP is also much more cumbersome than Link and we have now adopted Link as our standard in South Africa.

AD-LIKING AND PRINT ADVERTISING

Somewhat naively I used to feel that the issue of emotion, especially as measured by liking, mainly applies to television and cinema advertising, and not really to print advertising. In other words I was still thinking along the lines of the old paradigm that sees between emotions and rational processes as opposites.

There is a theory by Herbert Krugman that print works on the logical side of the brain, and television on the emotional side of the brain, and therefore one should use recognition and recall to access the different hemispheres of the brain – recognition to search for memories of television advertising (emotion) and recall to search for memories of print advertising (see Chapter 16). After I talked at the 2004 Advertising Effectiveness Conference in Barcelona about emotions and advertising effectiveness, Patrick Hermie, the marketing manager at Medialogue, the advertising sales house of Sanoma Magazines Belgium, which is the leading magazines publisher in Belgium, approached me with a manuscript (in Dutch) reporting on a large-scale empirical research project on the importance of ad-liking in print advertising. This manuscript will be launched in February 2005 in Belgium (Hermie *et al*, 2005). Patrick has worked as a researcher and marketing manager in the advertising sales business for magazines for almost 15 years, and Medialogue has been measuring about 300 print advertisements each year since 1996, yielding a total database of 3,000 advertisements. This research helped to crystallize my own ideas on recognition and recall.

It should have been obvious to me that ad-liking would play the same role in print advertising as it does for television:

▌ Emotions cause attention.
▌ Print advertising is as much dependent on attention to work as is television advertising.
▌ As research has shown (see Chapter 13), a minimum of 2.75 seconds' attention is required for a print advertisement to lay down a memory trace.
▌ The COMMAP model suggests that ad-liking is caused by things like humour, characters, aspirational situations, and news that is relevant to the reader. All of this applies to print advertising as much as it does to television.

Medialogue's research was done for one specific edition of a publication, on a sample of 100 readers of that edition. The test material is the specific edition being measured, with all the branding removed from the advertisements. Respondents are asked which advertisements they recognize, and then also to name the brand. Next the respondent is shown a version of the publication in which the brands have not been removed, and is asked questions about the advertisements: whether he or she likes them, and what he or she thinks about their originality, informativeness, suitability to the magazine and so on. For each advertisement in the database a host of other information is also kept, such as the format, the colours used, clutter in the edition, and whether the advertisement appears on a left- or right-hand page. The researchers also carried out a regression analysis to determine the relative importance of the influencers on the scores.

Medialogue considers three scores as being important to report on:

▌ *Recognition*: the percentage of readers that claim to have seen the advertisement.
▌ *Attribution*: of those, the percentage that assigned the correct brand to the advertisement.
▌ *Effective score*: a combination of the above two scores.

The most important building block of both recognition and attribution is whether people liked the advertisement. In fact 80 per cent of the variation in recognition is determined by ad-liking, and 51 per cent of the variation in attribution is explained by ad-liking! So everything comes back to ad-liking, which is why, I argue, it is the core element on which advertisers should focus.

In the next chapter I look briefly at some other ways in which researchers have analysed advertising, then we go on to consider another crucial issue, the link between the advertisement and the product it is trying to sell.

16

Recognition, recall and persuasion

The phenomena that advertisers describe as 'recognition' and 'recall' both figure heavily in the history of copy testing techniques, and it is worth looking in a little more depth at these measures, and the newer criterion of *persuasion*. A more comprehensive review by Alexander Biel of the issues I briefly explore here can be found in *Admap*, May 1993.

MEASURING HOW ADVERTISEMENTS ARE REMEMBERED

Both recognition and recall are techniques that dredge memory for traces of awareness of an advertisement or brand, but recognition is a direct technique, while recall approaches the memory indirectly.

In other words, *recognition* is the term for trying to access a memory of something by prompting with that concept: so a prompt using the actual advertisement, trying to access any memory of having seen it before, is searching for recognition. *Recall* is the term used when one prompts with a brand name while looking for feedback on the memory of the advertisement; or conversely, prompts with the unbranded advertisement while looking for feedback on the brand that is being advertised.

In practice there are a number of ways in which it is possible to put these techniques into practice, and dredge a consumer's memory for traces of an advertisement or brand. A researcher might:

- show respondents the advertisement and ask straight out if they remember it;
- remove the branding from the commercial, show it to respondents and then ask them to name the brand;
- describe the commercial to the respondents, omitting to mention the brand, and then ask them if they have seen it, and what brand it is for;
- ask the respondents if they remember seeing a commercial for brand A;
- ask the respondents to describe the most recent commercial for brand A.

Each of these techniques impacts differently on respondents' memories, so a researcher who applied different memory-dredging techniques to different sets of 100 respondents (for the same commercial) would be likely to get different results each time. Ignoring the statistical vagaries that can throw up the occasional wildly atypical sample, these different techniques give increasingly lower results as one use a technique lower on the list above: so a researcher who shows respondents the advertisement and asks if they have seen it before will get the highest proportion of positive responses, while a researcher who asks respondents to describe the commercial, without showing it at all or prompting them about its contents, will get the lowest proportion.

This does not mean that people have different 'memories' of an advertisement. It *does* mean that the same pattern of connectivity in the brain (the same 'memory') is stimulated in different ways by different prompts. If the prompt material is 'rich', and triggers lots of neural activity, the output (the memory triggered) is also likely to be rich. A stingy or indirect prompt (like the brand name) will generate relatively little output.

In 1932 Dr Daniel Starch started to measure the recognition of print advertisements in the United States. Starch was followed by Gallup and his partner Claude Robinson, who adapted Starch's initial *recognition* measure to a *recall* measure for television advertising. Alexander Biel has said that this started the greatest and longest-running debate in advertising measurement. The two organizations argued the relative merits of their approaches, other research companies adapted these approaches and entered the debate, and client companies supporting the different approaches also entered the debate.

The next development in advertising measurement (in the United States) was in the late 1940s, when Horace Schwerin introduced a 'persuasion' measure. This was based on asking consumers about their brand preferences before and after exposure to a commercial. If a shift in preference occurred, this was evidence that the advertisement had 'persuaded' the customer of the merits of the brand.

As Alexander Biel states, while there are now many research firms in the United States that provide measures of advertisement effectiveness, they almost all use variants of the methodologies pioneered by Starch, Gallup and Schwerin. To this day there is a lot of debate about the relative merits of recognition, recall and persuasion at US advertising measurement conferences. The UK seems to ignore this debate, other than criticizing the measures, but certainly runs the risk of throwing the baby out with the bath water by doing so.

LEFT- AND RIGHT-BRAIN MEMORIES

Possibly the most interesting turn that this debate took was in the 1970s, when Herbert Krugman related the measurements of recognition and recall to brain hemispheric theories (based on the differences between the 'right brain' and 'left brain': see Chapter 8). His 1977 paper is particularly interesting in this context, because it is the first attempt I am aware of to relate a view of how the brain works to how advertising works.

Krugman argued that:

▌ Recognition is an emotional task, and recall is a logical task. In other words, recognition makes use of the right hemisphere of the brain, which appears to be primarily concerned with emotional matters, and recall makes use of the left hemisphere, where there is most activity when logical thought is required.

▌ Print advertising tends to be logical, and television advertising tends to be emotional, in its appeal. (Therefore, according to Krugman's reasoning, print stimulates the left hemisphere and television the right hemisphere.)

▌ Therefore recognition is the correct method to use for television, and recall is the correct measure for print.

Soon after Krugman's paper, Zielske published a paper (1982) which provided empirical evidence that recall penalizes 'emotional' advertising: that is, that recall techniques rate emotional advertising as less successful than it actually is. This is, he suggested, what Krugman's theory implied would happen. Then a paper entitled 'Not recall' was published by Larry Gibson (1994). This also purported to provide empirical evidence that recall is a misleading measurement. The closing line, from which the title of the paper is derived, is: 'I don't know what the answer is, but it definitely is not recall.'

Both Zielske's and Gibson's papers have subsequently been 'debunked': that is, the evidence they presented has been shown to be invalid. Nobody has attacked Krugman's paper, largely because it did not offer empirical evidence, but stated a theory. Zielske's paper was criticized by Professor Eve Thorsen, who pointed out that his research was based on measurements of only six commercials, and that if the two extreme results were ignored, it proved exactly the opposite. She conducted a much larger-scale experiment and proved what the mid-scale results from Zielske's research also suggested, that emotional advertisements score better than logical ones on recall measures.

Professor Joel Dubow reanalysed Larry Gibson's data and found that he was guilty of 'sloppy statistics'. There was a brief flutter of excitement when Larry answered Joel, and Joel answered Larry in the *Journal of Advertising Research*. Unfortunately the gist of the 'answering' was that Larry was offended that Joel had not consulted him before making the results public, and Joel had felt he did not need to. At the end of this un-illuminating exchange, many people in the industry still thought that 'Not recall' provided real evidence that recall was not a valid way of measuring the effectiveness of advertising.

To my mind (as you will appreciate, if you have been following my argument this far), these researchers putting forward extremist arguments about memory-dredging techniques are just two gladiators fighting in the mist, and it is all driven by commercial interest. Neither one is right, because:

▎ Although it does seem to be the case that the left and right hemispheres of the brain have recognizably different functions, from what we know about the brain it seems that most memories and concepts include elements that one might describe as both 'emotional' and 'logical'. They are embodied in patterns of neuronal activity that spread widely across the brain, and are not confined to one hemisphere.

▎ There cannot be more than one physical embodiment of the memory of an advertisement, so although different measurement techniques may come up with different answers, they cannot be measuring 'different memories'. It is the techniques that are different, not the memories they access.

▎ Different techniques can only measure different aspects of the same memory.

▎ There is no way that one measurement technique can be 'wrong'. It can only be inapplicable to what is being measured.

RECOGNITION AND RECALL VERSUS PERSUASION

Understandably the whole debate gained a further dimension when Schwerin introduced a measure for persuasion. Suddenly the companies that were selling recognition and recall measures did not only have to fight each other; there was a new contender on the block. The amazing thing about 'commercial interest' is that it seldom stops to consider merits, it simply attacks what it perceives as a threat. Only the academics consider the relative merits of the methods. So, the recall and recognition companies, while fighting each other, also argued against persuasion.

Alexander Biel points out that this is a non-argument:

> *Recognition and recall are memory-dredging techniques largely viewing advertising as a learning process, whereas persuasion is a motivation issue.*

In other words, while recall and recognition are attempts to measure whether or not there is a memory trace (that is, the consumer has a memory of the advertisement and/or the brand), persuasion considers *what effect the ad might have on behaviour*. It looks at the response of the individual to the advertisement, not whether the individual recalls it. There should not be an argument about these issues as being either–or; they must be complementary.

Recall too that advertising does not work immediately, because in most cases the consumer does not make the purchase decision immediately. It is the *memory* of the advertisement that is drawn on when the purchase decision is made.

Many attempts to measure persuasion use a pre-post-exposure evaluation: that is, they ask people whether they intend to purchase something, after they have seen the advertisement but before they have made a purchase. The weakness of this is that it does not take full account of the complex effects of memory and time delays on the impact of the commercial.

We believe that persuasion is a valid measure, and that it does reflect to some degree what impact a commercial might have, if it were recalled at the time of the purchase decision. However, the current research models of many companies that claim to measure persuasion do not reflect this thinking. Our view is that the persuasion model of how advertising works is mainly relevant to direct response-type advertising, and some launch or relaunch advertising. Here the strategy is to communicate relevant news, not to lay down a long-term memory, and an immediate short-term effect is hoped for.

In general, though, it is important for us to be clear how advertisements actually affect people's buying behaviour, and it is by no means clear that recognition and recall provide the whole story there. In the next chapter we start to look at the link between advertisement memories and brand memories, and in the process we put this small debate in a wider context.

17

Advertisement memories and brand linkage

My aim in this chapter is to extend the view of advertising memory that I have already begun to build up, and to look in more depth at the interlinkage between memories of an advertisement and memories of (and predilection to buy) the brand that is being advertised. This ties in with the issues of recognition and recall that we explored in Chapter 16, but goes beyond them in many ways.

INTRODUCTION

You will recall, I hope, that neurologists understand our memories to be stored in patterns of neural activity in the brain, so a memory, or a concept, in a sense is just the sensitivity of some synapses, which makes their neurons more likely to be fired by future stimuli. This is true of the memory of an advertisement, and it is also true of the memory, or concept, of a brand. I also explained that it is not a case of a dedicated set of neurons representing one concept, and another dedicated set representing another concept; rather, there is a dense network of neurons, interlinked by the varying sensitivities of their synapses, and representing an equally dense network of overlapping concepts.

Take the example of someone seeing an advertisement for a brand of computer that features an elephant. One set of neurons that will be stimulated by this exposure is the set that somehow embodies the concept of 'elephant', with pathways that will have been laid down by previous exposure to pictures of elephants, articles about elephants, conversations about elephants, the sight of real elephants in the zoo, and so on. Another set will be the set that somehow embodies the concept of 'computer', with pathways laid down by previous direct and indirect experience of computers. And another set will be related to previous exposure to this particular brand of computer. (The same is true, of course, for all the other concepts into which one could fit this advertisement, including the very concept of 'advertisement', and all the knowledge and understanding that makes us appreciate how flickering lights on a television screen or ink on a page can be designed to encourage us to purchase something.)

In short, we use our existing concept of the brand (our memory of the brand, if you prefer) to help us to decode this advertisement; and in turn, our decoding of the advertisement has an impact on our existing concept of the brand. So (provided the advertisement is not so disastrously obscure that it fails to evoke the brand concept at all, an issue I consider below) there is a direct connection between our memory of the advertisement and our memory of the brand.

The words 'brand linkage' suggest that the memory of the advertisement and that of the brand are linked, which is arguably a misrepresentation. It might make more sense to say that what happens is that the memories of the advertisement *become part* of the brand memories.

MEMORIES AND FORGETFULNESS

Impact Information did an experiment to learn more about the nature of advertising memories, and specifically how the memory-dredging techniques of recognition and recall actually function. In their experiment, respondents were shown commercials and asked whether they remembered having seen them before. Some of the commercials had not been flighted for several years. The average recognition rate was 67 per cent. That high rate is an indication that recognition of visual material is very slow to decay.

This is in sharp contrast to the prevailing wisdom in the advertising industry about the decay of ad-awareness. Adtrack's experience with tracking 30,000 commercials shows that, on average, in-market ad-recall (measured by a technique that uses the brand name as a trigger and requires a description of the advertisement) declines by 20 per cent each week in the absence of advertising support. By contrast, Millward Brown, using only the brand name as a prompt and asking for recent awareness, but not requiring a description, works to an constant rate of decline in awareness of 10 per cent per week. Without further exposure by the end of even one year, let alone several years, ad-awareness on these measures would be minimal. However, the visual memory of the advertisement (as measured by recognition) is clearly still very much there, somewhere in the brain.

Figure 17.1 is one attempt at explaining what is happening here.

∎ If someone is asked for memories of the advertisement but prompted with the brand name, his or her memory of the advertisement is accessed via his or her memory of the brand name – which might provide an access route (that is, might prompt memory of the advertisement) but is not likely to be a very efficient method of prompting the memory of the advertisement.
∎ If the person is shown the advertisement itself, the prompt is directly to the memory of that advertisement, which is likely to be much more efficient.
∎ If the person is shown an unbranded advertisement then asked for the brand name, the route in is via the advertisement memory, but the aim is to access the brand memory: the reverse of the first method above.

As I explained in the previous chapter, advertisers distinguish the direct and indirect-prompt methods using the terms 'recognition' and 'recall'.

It is our experience that advertising agencies and marketers prefer to be given higher numbers when it comes to measuring their advertising, and therefore they prefer methodologies that access the ad-memory directly: that is, methodologies that focus on recognition rather than recall.

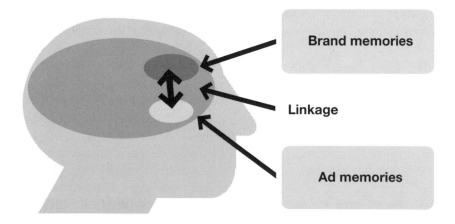

Figure 17.1 *Different access strategies to advertising memories*

However, it can be argued that to test recognition is not really testing how an advertisement works, or indeed how an advertiser wants it to work. The advertisement memory is not an end in itself: its purpose (in a simplified sense: of course, it could have less direct objectives as well) is to prompt the consumer to influence the brand memories – by either strengthening them, or even changing them. As we outlined in Chapter 1, when consumers shop they seldom think directly about the advertisements they have seen. They generally think first about goods (products or services) they want or need, and second about brands of those products. So the purchase is prompted not by the advertisement, but by the brand itself.

What marketers most need to know is not whether the advertisement itself prompts recognition (of itself), but whether it does the job of steering consumers towards the brand. So it makes a lot of sense for an advertiser to want to know whether the prompt of the brand name produces a memory of the advertisement. More generally, what is important is whether there is a good link between the memories of the brand and of the advertisement, and this is something that can be tested by seeing whether the advertisement comes to mind when the consumer is prompted by the brand.

SOME EMPIRICAL EVIDENCE

In the Adtrack system, we investigate recall techniques using both advertisements and brand names as triggers. So sometimes the respondent is asked if he or she can remember the advertising for a brand whose name he or she is given, and sometimes the process is reversed: the respondent is read a description of the advertisement, then asked whether he or she has seen it, and if so, whether he or she can name the brand that was advertised. The two questions are given to different samples of 200 respondents. Figure 17.2 shows the results for 800 commercials tested in the second of these ways.

As you can see, just over half of the sample recognized the advertisement, and of these a little less than half (that is, a quarter of all the respondents) were able to name the correct brand. It is noteworthy that in the normal Adtrack survey we find that where we do a recall test (prompting with the brand name and asking about the advertisement) the result is very close to the 25 per cent in the above chart that recognized and got the brand name right.

The more significant aspect here, however, is just how much advertising *fails* to make the advertisement–brand linkage. More than half the

Brand linkage

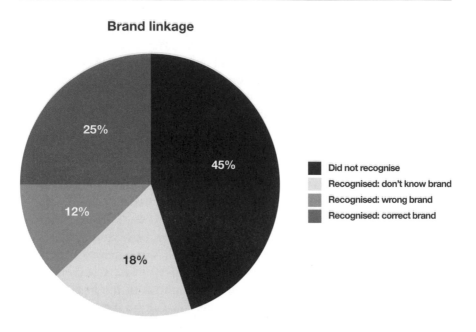

Figure 17.2 *Recognition: respondents who can name a brand once the advertisement has been described*

time, when a respondent recalls the advertisement, he or she cannot recall which brand was being advertised! It is a great waste of the advertising budget if when your advertisement comes to mind, the consumer thinks of your competitor's brand.

Experience has taught us that there can be a number of reasons for poor brand linking. The major culprit, however, remains poor branding in the advertisement.

Stewart and Furse (1986) were the first to develop the concept of 'effective length' of a commercial. The defined this as the length of the commercial from the first moment attention is 'engaged' and the viewer realizes which brand is being advertised. Thus if a 60-second commercial only mentions the brand in the thirtieth second (and the viewer has had no clue which brand is being advertised for those first 30 seconds), its effective length is only 30 seconds.

Impact Information has done the same analysis on its database. Its research too has found that some of the variation in recall from commercial to commercial can be explained by looking at the effective length rather than the real length.

Certainly in South Africa it appears to be fashionable for creative people not to mention the brand early in a commercial. They seem to think that it spoils their creation. However, it is worth bearing these statistics in mind.

We are not suggesting, however, that every commercial should start with pack shots. There are far more subtle (and indeed, creative) ways of establishing the branding early in a commercial. Very often it is only necessary to have some branding in the background, or to use a part of the 'brand image'. Brand images (which include symbols, logos, advertising themes, slogans, jingles, even just a distinctive 'style') are incredibly useful for advertisers. Once the device has been established, this does the work of establishing the branding. (For example, the moment an actor says 'Wasuup', the branding has been done effectively: the audience will realize that Budweiser is being advertised. A slice of purple silk does the same job for Silk Cut cigarettes.) We come back to branding devices later in the book. However, when an advertiser opts to 'set' the branding of a commercial through a device like this, great care has to be taken in the media scheduling to ensure that the device is well established early in the life of the advertising campaign. This might require high-impact scheduling (our term for very high frequency in the media schedule).

NEUROLOGY

Let us tie these insights into the neurological research we discussed earlier in the book. Remember that the memory of the brand will be used to interpret the advertisement. When brand memories (that is, memories of anything that is associated with the brand, and triggers the concept of the brand) are stimulated at the same time as the memories for the advertisement are laid down, the link between these memories is itself formed.

The longer the synapses between the neurons that embody the brand memories and the advertising memories are stimulated, the stronger the laydown of the link between brand memories and ad-memories will be. If a 60-second commercial includes branding devices in the first second, the brand memories will be stimulated for all 60 seconds. If it only mentions the brand in the fortieth second, the brand memories will only be stimulated for 20 seconds. So once again a whole body of empirical advertising research validates aspects of the neurological model of memory; and the neurological model of memory explains a finding of advertising research for us.

ANECDOTAL EVIDENCE

In the 15 years that I and my company have been tracking advertising awareness we have had some unique experiences, and since the people involved in them have moved on, we can now mention the brands involved.

Kelvinator – a manufacturer of white goods such as washing machines and refrigerators – made a commercial that showed a Ford light delivery vehicle with a lot of cardboard boxes on the back driving up the path to a farmhouse. These were then unloaded and the happy family was shown with all their new Kelvinator appliances. We tracked this commercial for several weeks and could hardly find a respondent who could describe the ad when we mentioned Kelvinator appliances. We then realized that the first brand identification in the commercial was in fact the Ford logo on the delivery vehicle. When we asked respondents if they had seen an advertisement for Ford delivery vehicles, they all described the advertisement with the vehicle delivering stuff to the farmhouse.

In terms of the neurological model of memory it is clear that the first neural network embodying the concept of a brand that was activated was for Ford. The advertisement memory became linked to that in the brain, and even though Kelvinator later got plenty of mentions in the advertisement, the linkages to the Kelvinator brand concept were so much weaker that it really did not register. The problem was easily rectified by getting a touch-up artist to remove the branding from the vehicle.

We had an even more amazing experience when Grey Advertising convinced Nedbank to make an advertisement with no brand mention at all. Up to that stage Nedbank had been running a very powerful campaign where the sign-off line for each advertisement was, 'Makes you think, doesn't it?' Not only had the sign-off line become well known in South Africa, the actor used in all the advertising also became a symbol for the bank, a part of its brand image.

The new campaign did not use the actor or the character he had portrayed, however. In fact, the whole advertising style was changed from a 'hard sell' to a 'softer image-building style'. Right at the end of the advertisement the words 'Makes you think, doesn't it?' appeared on the screen, but nowhere in the advertisement was there an explicit brand mention.

We tracked this commercial for several weeks, reporting that virtually no one remembered seeing a campaign for Nedbank. The agency then decided to increase the frequency of exposure substantially. Unfortunately this did not help – we still found very few respondents were aware of the campaign.

At this stage the client insisted that the brand name be added at the end of the commercial. Our tracking showed no difference in the result.

We asked ourselves why this was, naturally, and our thesis was this. Everybody who was ever likely to see the advertisement had seen it several times by this point, so when it appeared on screen no one thought, 'Aha, this is that ad where I couldn't figure out what on earth was being advertised. I'd better watch it again to see if I can find out who it's for.' Instead, people thought, 'Boring ad, didn't seem to be selling anything I'm interested in, no need to watch it again.' The viewers' attention was lost long before the branding at the end of the advertisements, so naturally it had no effect.

We suggested that Nedbank move the branding to the beginning of the commercial. This worked very well.

Here's another example involving Kelvinator. The company made an advertisement for its twin-tub washing machine showing two baby elephants with nappies playing in the mud, then the mother elephant washing the nappies in the Kelvinator twin-tub machine. This was one of the most liked South African commercials at that stage, and was also well remembered.

However, no Kelvinator twin-tubs were sold, and the firm blamed the advertising. The agency asked us to show the Adtrack results to Kelvinator to demonstrate that the advertisement was well remembered and liked. We thought this would be a difficult meeting, one where we had to save the agency's bacon. It turned out to be very much the opposite – the client was now praising the advertising. What had happened was that Kelvinator had thought the twin-tub was such a neat machine that it had had a logo designed specially for it, showing two hearts. This did in fact appear briefly at the end of the advertisement, but it had nothing to do with the story of the two baby elephants.

The commercial had been launched, and the twin-tubs had gone on promotion nationally with promotional material consisting of the two-heart logo. This was the period during which there were very few sales. Then in between our being called in by the agency and our presenting our research to Kelvinator, the company launched a second promotional cycle for the twin-tubs. This time the promotional material consisted of cardboard elephants. The washing machines had record sales.

This example serves as a nice demonstration of how advertising works at the time of purchase. When the promotional material reminded people of the advertisement at the time they were making purchase decisions, the advertisement had a chance to influence the decision. When it did not, the advertisements, though liked in themselves, had no effect.

White goods are not FMCG products, but it looks like the buyer decision-making process here is very much the same one as Gordon Brown proposed (see Chapter 1). Buyers do not go looking for a specific product that has been advertised. Instead they go looking for a type of product they want or need to buy; and when they are faced with a choice between brands, the advertising recall can pitch in to affect their decision.

The Adtrack system sometimes measures advertisements that fail to gain much recall despite a good media schedule backing them. The problem is often that the commercial suffers from branding problems. We have, with a lot of success, advised advertisers in this position to try 'high-impact scheduling' – a term we use for a media schedule that flights the advertisement several times during the same time slot, and sometimes even twice during the same commercial break. High-impact scheduling would be wasteful for most advertisements, and is contrary to all media planning theories. However, when a commercial fails to penetrate consumers' memories, it might be all that can be done. It appears that what happens is that the first exposure does the branding for the second exposure.

THE MILLWARD BROWN 'CREATIVE MAGNIFIER'

Not surprisingly, since their basic business is advertisement tracking (just as Adtrack was the basis of Impact's business), Millward Brown has also become very aware of the brand-linking problem that many advertisements experience. It has come up with a rather elegant approach to the problem, called the Creative Magnifier.

The basis behind this development is the realization that people's memories of a television advertisement are seldom equally strong for every second of the commercial. Almost invariably, only a few seconds of the commercial accounts for most of the memories. An often-used example is an advertisement for Harp beer. A guy arrives at a girl's apartment, she goes to make tea, he plays with her dog and its ball, the ball bounces accidentally through the window, and the dog jumps after the ball through the window. The final scene is of the guy and the dog having a Harp beer in the pub. In copy testing most people could remember the dog going through the window, but few could remember that the advertisement was for Harp.

Anybody involved in advertising will have examples of such commercials, where the core creative device is not really linked with the branding, and so heavily overwhelms the branding that everyone remembers the advertisement, but not the brand.

Millward Brown terms the remembered scene the 'creative magnifier', and sees it as having two functions: first, to make the advertising impression memorable, and second, to make a link between that impression and the brand. This concept is generally shown as a V-diagram, as in Figure 17.3.

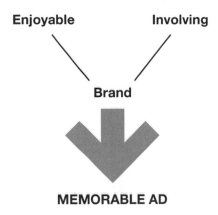

Figure 17.3 *What makes memorable advertising*

Obviously if the creative multiplier does only one of these functions, the advertisement will fail. The extent to which it does both well will be the extent to which the advertisement is 'memorable in the name of the brand'. Obviously, the ideal is that all 30 seconds of a television commercial form the magnifier, not just a few. The extent to which the creative multiplier does its job can be measured quite easily in research.

Again, this fits into the neurological model of memory formation. The creative multiplier is the section of the commercial that attracts attention to it: the section that, as a result, is remembered. But if the *brand* too is to be remembered, it is important that there be laid down a linkage in the brain between the creative multiplier and the concept of the brand. If this does develop, any memory of the creative multiplier will trigger a memory of the brand; but if it does not develop, although the creative multiplier itself will be remembered readily when a trigger is provided, there is no way for this to lead into a strengthening of the brand memory.

That makes a part of my case, I hope: it outlines how we should be looking to design ads that are likeable, to ensure that they attract attention, and that they attract attention to the right thing – that is, the brand that is being advertised. Now I want to look at another core issue for advertisers: just how often we need to repeat this process to ensure that it works.

18

Exposing the consumer to the advertising: media strategy

INTRODUCTION

The studies I have drawn on earlier in the book (particularly Professor Jones's work, the SPOT study, and Adtrack and Millward Brown tracking studies) have shown that, while it is true that advertising works, the extent to which different advertisements are effective varies dramatically. But whether an advertisement works well (or badly, or not at all) is not only affected by its content: it is also affected by its scheduling. This chapter looks at scheduling, and reprises the 'frequency' debate I have referred to a number of times already.

WHAT PROFESSOR BAHRICK TAUGHT ME

In Chapter 9 I described the learning curve, drawing on the work of Professor Bahrick from Ohio, and I have described the advertising response curve, drawing on the work of Mike Naples (see Chapter 1). If you think about it, you should be able to see that the advertising response curve is in fact a specific application of the more general learning curve. (It is also generally one that is aggregated, from the whole population of individuals, while the learning curve tends to be an individuals one.) It details how individuals lay down the memory of an advertisement and are subsequently able to draw on this memory.

The important features of the learning curve are that:

▌ Different people learn different things at different rates.
▌ The first rehearsal sessions are often s-shaped.
▌ The learning curve itself shifts between rehearsal sessions.
▌ The s-shaped curve quite rapidly becomes a convex curve.
▌ More rehearsal sessions increase the slope of the convex curve.

I would argue that if the advertising response curve is an application of the learning curve, more knowledge of it would be likely to show us that it takes the same overall shape. In other words, the response to many advertisements starts out as s-shaped (so the first exposures are in effect 'rehearsal sessions'), but by the second or third burst of advertising, the curve is probably convex in shape.

Empirical evidence to support this argument

Perhaps the best place to start is with the words of Professor Jones himself: 'There is no evidence in our data of an s-shaped response, but, if there is one, then it would be for new advertisements or new products' (Jones, 1998). This suggests that Jones basically took the same view as a result of his own research.

More support comes from research by Andrew Roberts of Taylor Nelson, who tracked brand purchases and advertising exposure using Taylor Nelson's HomeScan panel. Figure 18.1, which summarizes the results, is taken from his paper in *Admap*. His main focus was on the time period over which advertising has an effect, and his conclusion was that the effect is basically limited to the four weeks after exposure. The vertical axis of Figure 18.1 shows the percentage sales increase among people who saw advertising for different brands (which are listed along the horizontal axis) in the four weeks beforehand.

That advertising has a short-term effect should not surprise anyone who has read thus far. Nor should it be at all surprising that different advertisements had different results. What are relevant in this context are the conclusions Roberts drew about brands A to G in the figure. To quote from his paper:

> *The results show some marked differences. All of the seven brands (A–G), which were either new launches, relaunches or had been previously unadvertised, show either a linear or s-shaped curve. Arguably, a linear response is in fact a very attenuated form of an s-shaped curve, and saturation occurs (or would have occurred) beyond the observable range of exposures.*

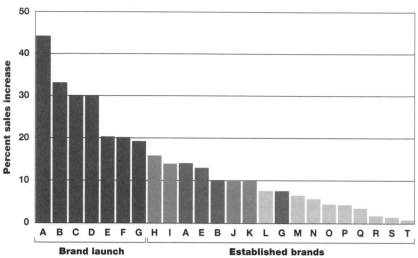

Figure 18.1 *Results from Taylor Nelson's research into short-term sales effects from advertising*

By contrast, virtually all the results for established brands show a convex curve, with saturation effects typically after about 4 or 5 exposures over 4 weeks.

Again, these results suggest that the circumstances of the brand affect how the consumer responds to repeated advertising exposure. If the brand is new, or the advertising has something new to say, then repeating the message over a short space of time has a beneficial effect.

In summary, those who have conducted research on new advertisements or new brands (like Andrew Roberts) have come up with an s-shaped response curve, which provides support for a relatively high-frequency media schedule, while those whose research has focused more on advertising for established brands over a long period of time (like John Philip Jones) conclude that the response function is convex.

This of itself does not add up to evidence that there is a 'magic number three', even for new launches. The threshold (or inflection point: that is, the point at which the curve turns) need not be three exposures. It seems probable that some advertisements (particularly those with a less powerful impact) might require several more exposures before they reach the threshold of significant impact on sales.

Adtrack has measured some (fortunately very few) advertisements that appear to have *no* threshold. It does not matter how high the intensity of exposure is in a burst of advertising, no one seems to register the advertisement.

This leads to two hypotheses. First, the response curve fits different measures for different advertisements; and second, there is a range of response curves that apply to different bursts of advertising. The latter that is shown in Figure 18.2, but it shifts to the left – or towards being a convex curve – in subsequent bursts of advertising.

The fact that the response curve for different bursts varies does not alter the fact that different advertisements are likely to have a different s-shaped response during the first burst. The only rule of thumb for media planning seems to be that all advertisements' response curves will move to the left between bursts.

The obvious conclusion might be that since an advertisement's response curve shifts to the left, in every case it will eventually be a convex curve and therefore it is safe to follow the doctrine of continuity planning. Unfortunately this is not necessarily true. To explain why, we can use Professor Bahrick's example of learning how to ride a bicycle.

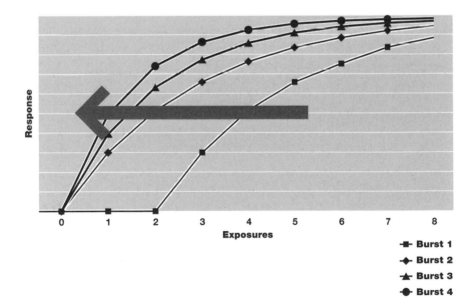

Figure 18.2 *A range of different response curves that might apply to subsequent bursts of advertising*

This supposes you have an over-protective mother, and on the first day you start learning to ride your new bicycle she stops you after two rehearsals in which you have fallen off. The next day you start again, but on that and every subsequent day your mother stops you after two rehearsals.

There is an 'aha!' effect that comes when you realize exactly how to balance and propel yourself on a bike, but it often takes a bit of intensive practice before it kicks in. If you always stop after two falls, maybe you will never experience the 'aha!' effect, because you will never lay down enough memories to progress in each individual session. Because you never exceed the threshold level, your learning curve will not become convex.

This is the danger of all media planning: unless the advertisement gets beyond the threshold level at some point, the response cannot subsequently be convex. If continuity planning is applied from the start of an advertisement's life, and there is no intensive period of exposure, the advertisement might never pass the threshold level, and as a result it might never have any effect.

This is not only true for continuity planning, it could also be true for those still clinging to the old 'rule of three'. Even if the launch burst is planned to give the average consumer three exposures to the advertisement, this might be too few for that particular advertisement to reach its threshold level.

The good news is that if an advertisement has a threshold that requires fairly high levels of exposure, as long as it passes this threshold level in some burst (meaning that thereafter, the response curve will be convex) the problem is resolved. It should be any advertiser's main objective to ensure that an advertisement reaches its threshold hopefully in the launch phase, but if it does not, then to adjust the media schedule so that it does in the next burst of advertising. The only way to ensure that this happens is to have a research system in place that measures whether or not it *has* happened. (This is the objective of Adtrack in South Africa and Millward Brown's *Automatic Tracking Process*.)

IMPACT AND DECAY RATES

Figure 18.3 is a reprise of Figure 9.5, which I used on page 103 to explain how Professor Bahrick explains learning. It shows how there is an increase in performance (indicated by the continuous line) when there is rehearsal (indicated by the bars) of a learning task, and how forgetting takes place when the task is not rehearsed. In other words, this represents the learning

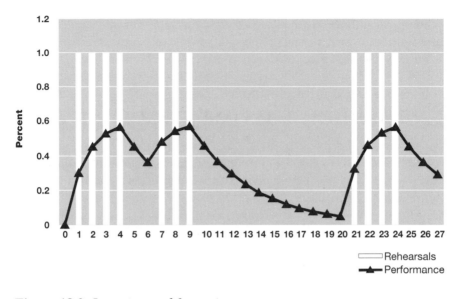

Figure 18.3 *Learning and forgetting*

curve for an individual over time, which is not one convex upwards curve but a series of convex upwards curves, linked by downward slopes where forgetting takes place. This example uses a decay rate of 20 per cent per period: that is, 20 per cent of what has already been learnt is forgotten in each subsequent period, while 80 per cent is remembered.

Most bigger companies have continuous tracking studies in place to measure and model the effects of advertising. All of these show the same general pattern as is shown in Figure 18.3. In other words, there is plenty of empirical evidence that the advertising response curve behaves like an aggregated learning curve.

The effects of advertising over time depend on two variables. The first is the *impact rate*, or the rate at which (individual or aggregate) memories increase when there is advertising, and the second is the *decay rate*, or the speed at which these memories are forgotten when there is no advertising.

There are two alternative ways in which the decay rate can be treated in these models. The first is to treat decay as a variable, or in other words, to assume that different advertisements are forgotten at different rates. (Adtrack uses this assumption.) The alternative is to treat decay as a constant, but use a variable base level. The assumption here is that all advertising memories decay at a fixed rate (generally about 10 per cent per week), but that there is a base below which the recall level does not fall. (Millward Brown uses this assumption.)

In practice, these two approaches yield the same answer, so these are in effect different ways of modelling mathematically a phenomenon which is known from empirical evidence.

RETENTION RATES IMPROVE OVER TIME

The evidence shows that over time there is an improvement in the rate of decay. In other words, fewer people (remember, the response curve is an aggregated model) forget the advertisement after each burst of scheduling. This ties in with what we know from neurology, about the sensitivity of the synapses increasing each time they are stimulated, so that the memory is in effect lodged more firmly in the brain. This also ties in with the 'shifting' learning/response curve. The reason the response shifts to the left with subsequent bursts of exposure is not that the advertisement itself becomes more memorable, it is that the base level on which the memories are laid down is higher with each burst.

Figure 18.4 is based on Figure 18.3, so it is basically the same example of learning and forgetting, but this time the retention rate increases by 10 per cent after each rehearsal session. (In the alternative modelling method, the base level increases each time.) This makes it a more accurate reflection of how learning and forgetting actually take place.

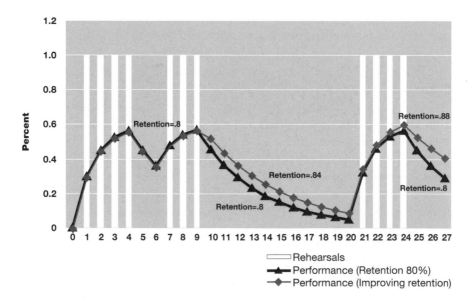

Figure 18.4 *An improved model of forgetting and learning*

THE IMPACT–RETENTION CHART

Adtrack measures the ad-awareness of specific advertisements weekly for the first six weeks of an advertisement's life. This information is then used to model the impact rate and retention rate of the advertisements. The results are shown in Figure 18.5. You might intuitively think that because both of these are basically measures of the memorability of an advertisement, they would be closely correlated, but in fact they are not. (The broken lines in Figure 18.5 show the average impact rate and average retention rate.)

It is important to bear in mind that the data in this chart is only concerned with the launch burst of advertising. It does not look at effects over the longer term of advertising campaigns.

Obviously everybody wants to have an advertisement which has a high impact rate and also a high retention rate, because this is the most media-efficient type of advertisement. Figure 18.5 makes it clear that many advertisers are disappointed. The good news is that advertisements can improve their position on the chart over time, if their media schedule is managed correctly. There is also a consistency in the pattern of change.

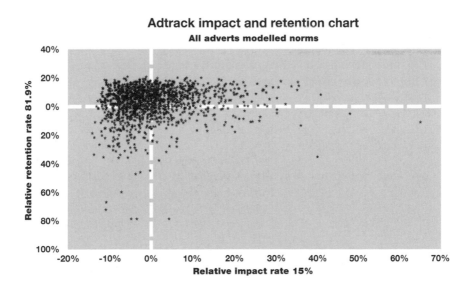

Figure 18.5 *Adtrack's results on impact and retention of advertisements*

Low-impact–low-retention media strategy implications

These are advertisements that fall in the bottom left quadrant of Figure 18.5. They have an s-shaped response curve, which implies that the media pressure during the launch was insufficient to take the advertisement to its threshold for wide recognition. The common reasons for this, in my experience, include:

▌ Poor brand linkage. People do recall the advertisement when prompted by the advertisement, but they fail to remember it when prompted by the name of the brand.
▌ The campaign included several different advertisements which were launched at the same time. Often, when agencies launch multiple advertisement campaigns they do not plan the launch schedule to give enough media pressure to each individual advertisement.
▌ The advertisement had an element of Confusion.
▌ The advertisement was just plain boring, and scored high on the Familiarity measure.
▌ The campaign was a multi-media one and there was not enough linkage between the executions in the different media.

General observations

▌ The good news is that the problem is mostly solvable, if it is recognized and dealt with.
▌ Once this problem is solved it does not come back: in other words, once the threshold on the response curve is passed, people do not need to be pushed past it again.
▌ The tragic news is that if this problem is not recognized and addressed, it does not go away of its own accord.
▌ The even more tragic news is that few companies realize that they have this problem and revise their media plan as a result.

Indicated media strategy

▌ **Increase the frequency of exposure over time.** Since lack of frequency is the problem, more frequency is the solution. The reference to 'time' is of vital importance. It should not be necessary to increase the entire media budget in order to make sure the advertisement gets past its inflection point; however, it absolutely must be got past it, or all the money in the follow-up to the launch burst in the media plan will be wasted. So the answer is usually to take some money from the end of the schedule and move it into the second burst.

It is also a good idea to condense the period over which the burst happens. We have had very good success with high-impact scheduling, even to the extent of having the advertisement appear twice during the commercial breaks for one television programme.

▌ **If necessary consider reducing the reach of the second burst.** As we have seen, scheduling is a question of balancing frequency (how often the audience sees the advertisement) and reach (how large the audience is). This is a difficult issue to make a decision on, but if the budget is tight and the threshold has not yet been achieved, it is probably best to reduce the reach of the whole schedule so that a higher frequency can be obtained, albeit against a smaller audience.

▌ **Cure any brand linkage problems.** Sometimes the problems are obvious with hindsight. If none are obvious, and the advertisement falls in this sector without obvious frequency problems, it is often worth doing some quick research to see if brand linkage is the problem. Adtrack clients know the situation automatically, since Adtrack takes a measure of this during the six weeks of fieldwork.

Reshoots are not always necessary: sometimes the advertisement can be edited using discarded material to improve its brand linkage.

In many cases a brand linkage problem is solved or eased by increased frequency in the second burst.

▌ **If it is a multiple advertisement campaign, relaunch it.** The correct way of launching a multiple advertisement campaign is to launch one of the advertisements first, with sufficient media pressure. Track the results, then when the first advertisement is established, launch the others. If this was not done in the launch burst, the best thing to do is to view the cost as money paid out for gaining experience, and start again, doing it properly.

▌ **Consider what you are doing, or could do, in other media.** If the campaign used a variety of media, and the problem appears to have been the lack of sufficient linkage between the advertisements, it is probably best to shift the money to the primary medium in the second burst. If it did not use a variety of media, it is worth considering whether there is still an opportunity to use other media to create a synergistic effect, and in effect do the job of branding.

▌ **If there is Confusion, edit the advertisement.** Often it is only necessary to edit the voiceover so that the advertisement is better 'explained'.

High-impact–low-retention media strategy implications

Advertisements that fall into this sector are those that have moved past the threshold of the response curve, but where the response curve has not yet started to move to the left. In other words, the process of embedding the memory of the advertisement has not really started. This is not a big problem because it is likely that over time, with more media pressure, the retention rate (or the base level) will improve.

Indicated media strategy

I   One option is to decrease the frequency in the media strategy: that is, to start doing what is indicated for advertisements with high impact and high retention (see below).
I   However, the retention rate is more important to media efficiency than the impact rate, so I would recommend first running another burst with the same frequency as the launch burst, with the specific aim of increasing the retention rate.
I   If the advertiser set the advertising objectives in terms of the base level (or retention rate) that an advertisement should establish itself at, and this level has not been met, it will be necessary at this stage to increase the frequency to establish this base level.

High-impact–high-retention media strategy implications

This is the situation in which everyone would like their advertisement to be, since this is the most media-efficient situation. It means the response curve has become convex, and has a steep gradient. As Figure 18.5 makes clear, many advertisements reach this situation during the launch burst. That those that did not do so initially can be managed towards this situation.

Indicated media strategy

I   Once this point has been reached, the efficient thing to do is to reduce the frequency in the media schedule. In fact the strategies suggested by recency theory now become applicable.
I   The objective of the advertising bursts (which should tend to be mini-bursts, more often, at this stage) should now be to maximize reach.
I   This too is a good point at which to consider other media options. They could have the benefit of extending reach, and by delivering the message in a different way they could increase the depth of consumers' memories.
I   The use of other media (particularly if television was the first-choice medium) can also help to reduce the overall media cost.
I   It is also a good idea to start thinking of making another advertisement with the same theme as the existing one, in order to support it (either to

put across a new message about a different brand benefit, or simply to avoid boredom setting in).

Low-impact–high-retention media strategy implications

This is the situation that most people mean when they talk about wear-out. The advertisement has been around for a long time, and everybody remembers it and therefore gives it very little attention. As a result it migrates from the top-left quadrant to the top-right quadrant.

Neither Impact nor Millward Brown has seen many advertisements shifting into this quadrant over time. The reason is probably that most advertisers decide to make a new advertisement before the existing advertisement has worn out to such a measurable extent – and of course this would be a good decision.

Since Adtrack only measures the first six weeks of an advertisement's life, logic would say that its measurements should place few, if any advertisements in this quadrant, but as you can see from Figure 18.5, that is not the case: quite a large proportion of advertisements fall in this quadrant, though most of them are relatively near the central axes.

The main reasons that an advertisement might fall in this quadrant after launch are:

▎ The launch media schedule had a limited reach, but a good frequency against this small audience. The high frequency would ensure that the audience reached had an high retention of the advertising, but arguably this would not entirely compensate for the small reach. This is a danger for media strategies where the advertisements are placed entirely with a specific type of television programme (only sports, only cookery, only motor review programmes, only soaps...) or in narrow-interest publications.

This is also a particular danger for advertisements launched with a low-cost-per-thousand media strategy. Some marketers have become enamoured with the idea of saving money by looking for a media purchasing strategy that gives the highest GRP for their budget. If this is the objective set for their media departments/agencies, they will generally look to achieve it by placing ads within niche programmes or at non-peak times. By definition this means a limited audience, and in many cases it means reaching the same people time and again. It is difficult to achieve good reach (and a varied audience) without using prime time, or at least good-quality time.

▌ The advertising is only understood by a limited audience. This is a real danger for some advertisements. A humorous advertisement might be rather too sophisticated or 'clever', and a section of the audience will fail to 'get' it, leading to Confusion. Similarly, a 'Relevant news' advertisement might be relaying news that is in fact only relevant to a limited part of the audience.

▌ The advertisement leads to increasing recall of another brand. It is clear from the Adtrack database that sometimes people do not know which brand is being advertised; and sometimes they even assume the wrong brand is being advertised.

▌ The advertisement might be too similar to the previous advertisement. When the advertiser wants to 'just refresh the execution' but keep the feel of an earlier successful campaign, sometimes the changes are not enough to really refresh the advertisement. For the average non-attentive viewer there will not be sufficient difference between the old and new advertisements to avoid Familiarity, and rapid wear-out.

Media strategy implications

For advertisements that start their lives in this quadrant there is no single generalized media strategy recommendation I can give. It is necessary to establish the reason that the advertising is behaving in the media as it does, and work towards a solution from there.

CONCLUSION

By now we have looked at both the content of advertisements and the frequency with which they need to be shown. In the next chapter I continue our slow change of focus, and look at how the brand that is being advertised comes into the equation.

19

Professor Ehrenberg and double jeopardy; or the effect of the brand on the advertising

So far our exploration has really considered advertising, rather than brands. We have specifically looked at the function of emotion in advertising: to generate attention and to generate a soma. We have considered empirical evidence that has been published about the performance dynamics of advertisements, and shown how these empirical results relate to the theories of the first section of the book.

At this stage I want you to start thinking about brands. The aim here is to see whether, and how, the empirical and theoretical work about brands shows the brain mechanisms that we have explored at work. Then we can go on to see how the brain mechanisms in turn can be used to enhance the advertising process.

I starts with the double jeopardy theory of Professor Andrew Ehrenberg, and consider especially whether his theory makes sense against the background of Adtrack's empirical data. Professor Ehrenberg first published his double jeopardy theory in 1979, so it has been around for a good 25 years now. While some marketers do not like it, and many just simply ignore it, the fact is that it remains true for every database that is analysed worldwide. So it is not merely a 'theory', it is a statement of fact that has been validated many times over, in many countries and for many product types.

THE DOUBLE JEOPARDY THEORY

Basically the theory says:

> *The brands with biggest market shares are the biggest because more people buy them, more often!*

It might sound tautological, but in fact it is not. Ehrenberg is making two important points. First, the people who buy the big brands are the people who buy that category of goods and services most often, and second, those people are more brand-loyal than the rest of the population. *That* is why the big brands are big.

▌ People who drink a lot of soft drinks are the ones who drink Coca-Cola most often. (People who buy soft drinks infrequently are more likely to experiment when they do buy them.)
▌ People who buy a lot of take-away burgers buy McDonald's most of the time. (Again, people who infrequently buy take-away burgers are more likely to experiment.)

A core implication of Ehrenberg's findings is that if a marketer wants to find a soft spot in the market, it is *least* likely to be among current heavy users of the category. Heavy users might seem like the best people for a rival brand to target, but they are not the ones who will be most predisposed to try it.

Does this fit the neurological model that was outlined earlier in the book? Of course it does. To understand why, we need to look back at Gordon Brown's model of how people shop, walking down the aisle, considering product categories and picking up their 'usual' brand. (See Chapter 1.)

Let us say you want a beer. If you are like most people, when you decide you feel like drinking a beer, what you really mean is that you feel like drinking a particular brand of beer – your usual brand. People do not go through a great process of rational thinking, considering the alternatives; they know what they like and they ask for that. If you go into an unfamiliar bar and find it does not stock your usual brand, you will have to think what else you are willing to drink, but most of the time it is an automatic process: 'My usual, please.'

I drink whisky. I was brand manager on Bell's whisky and when I sit down in a bar I generally order a glass of Bell's. I am not claiming incipient alcoholism, but I am certainly a higher than average consumer of Bell's. Occasionally, however, I feel like drinking a single malt. That is whisky too, but it is such a different drinking experience that it might as well be considered a different sub-category. I don't drink malts very often, and there is no single brand that I automatically choose. I'd like a malt today, I think, then I ask myself what brand I'd like to try, or look at the shelves behind the bar and see what's in stock.

To paraphrase and generalize this: the occasional category user needs to think about which brand to choose, but the heavy user made a decision long ago. (This is what Professor Ehrenberg proved, way back 25 years ago.)

HABITUAL PURCHASING

We all know that the biggest driving force in terms of brand purchases is the habitual purchase – that is, when people buy the same brand out of habit. The Gordon Brown view of how people shop makes this clear. When consumers stand in front of the washing power shelf in the supermarket, they generally pick up the same brand they used last time. If it did the job, why change it? After all, another brand might not do it as well.

Information overload probably plays a part in this too. There are so many brands in the average Western supermarket, and nobody has time to consider the merits of all of them. Who wants to spend their life thinking what brand of washing powder to buy? We would all seize up if we took decisions like this too seriously. Picking the familiar brand is the easy way out, the way that saves us from making a conscious decision.

I have always envisaged this process as the consumer thinking along these lines:

- I need some toilet paper.
- There are at least a dozen brands on the shelf.
- Which one did I buy last time?
- Was I happy with it?
- Yes? So let's buy it again!

That makes sense to me, but there is an alternative theory about what goes on in these situations. Antonio Damasio and Joseph LeDoux suggest another mental process that might occur, which could be described as the somatic purchase decision:

- I need some toilet paper.
- There are at least a dozen brands on the shelf.
- Which one do I like?

The difference between the two processes is that the second process goes directly to an *emotive* consideration, whereas the first one has two *rational* memory recall steps, 'Which one did I buy last time?' and 'Was I happy with it?'

It looks as if the somatic purchase decision process (the second alternative) is more in line with how the brain really works. The emotion of liking the brand is more readily available to the brain than are the rational considerations which arguably generated that emotion in the first place. The somatic purchase process is also a lot more efficient (that is, shorter) than the rational alternative. There is no need for the consumer to ask *why* he or she likes Brand X; the fact that he or she does so is sufficient.

However, sometimes consumers will ask themselves, 'Which one do I like?' and – as with me and the malt whisky – a single answer does not readily come to mind. Maybe the category is wide enough that special features of the different brands come into play (last time I bought dandruff shampoo, but this time I'd prefer a brand that promises shiny hair; last time I chose Glenfiddich, but I also like the taste of Islay); maybe the consumer does not have much experience in the category, and does not clearly recognize any brand as preferable; maybe the regular brand was a disappointment last time around, and it feels like time to make a change. In cases like these the consumer goes into a 'considered purchase' mode.

This speculation about the role of liking in brand decisions, and what we have known as habitual purchases, opens a lot of doors for new insights and understanding. These are explored in more depth in Chapter 20, which focuses on brand equity. At this stage, just bear in mind that the somatic decision-making model fits very well with the Ehrenberg empirical data:

- The more often consumers use a category, the more they have to make brand choices.
- The more often they choose one particular brand, the better its soma will develop.
- The stronger the soma becomes, the greater the tendency will be to choose that brand again next time, and the less often the decision will be to try something else.

BRAND EQUITY

There is no one agreed definition of the concept of 'brand equity'. To some (especially accountants and management consultants) it is a financial term, to be quantified in monetary terms. (There are various techniques that have been developed to do this.) To some it is a business reality: how much an organization is willing to pay to acquire a brand. In a marketing sense, however, 'brand equity' has a more qualitative definition. I believe the best 'marketing' measure of brand equity is the number of people who will buy the brand 'with the least thinking'.

This implies that the individual has a predefined attitude to the brand: a 'brand memory' which is embodied in a certain set of neurological states. These types of preference can easily be measured.

BRAND LIKING

So far I have talked a lot about ad-liking. I have tried to tie this in with the model of brain functioning that was discussed earlier in the book, and to show how 'liking' (as it was defined in Chapter 15) influences both the attention that is paid to an advertisement and the way it is interpreted. Obviously the implied assumption is that 'liking' the advertisement will set up positive emotions about the product that is being advertised, so 'ad-liking' naturally ties in with 'brand liking'.

Now let us turn to a more complex issue: brand liking, and how brand liking and ad-liking influence each other.

How does brand liking develop? Clearly, it starts when a person is 'exposed' to a brand: we cannot realistically 'like' what we do not know. The person sees the branded product on the supermarket shelf (or website, or high street store window, or wherever); or reads about it, or is told about it by a friend or colleague, or (an important one, this) sees an advertisement for it. The person tries the brand (that is, a branded product or service, although for simplicity I tend to talk about products in this section) and learns at first hand whether it is or is not a good example of the category, whether it suits his or her preferences, whether the experiences he or she has with it and the organization that produces or sells it are positive or negative.

All these activities lay down memory traces to some degree; everything we experience does that, to at least some degree. Over time the natural processes of neuronal recruitment (in other words, the formation of memories and concepts) takes place. This passes through the limbic system, and results in the development in the brain of what we called a soma (positive or negative). In other words, the exposure to the product causes the person to have an emotional attitude to the brand: he or she feels well disposed towards it (brand liking) or if the experiences have been bad, the product poor, feels negatively disposed towards it (brand dislike, we might call it).

It is pretty clear how this translates into a shopping situation. The shopper realizes there are no dog biscuits (for example) in the house, and the dog is making it clear it is getting real hungry, so she (or he) goes to the supermarket to buy some dog biscuits. She finds the dog biscuit section, and looks along the shelves at the different packs of dog biscuits. Probably quite a few of them will be familiar, from advertisements in magazines and on the television, and in some cases at least because she has bought them before. Looking at them will (and this is not a matter of conscious thought, although some of that might be going on too) raise a degree of soma. That is, all her past experiences of the brand (the cute dog advertising one brand, the irritating actor pushing another; her opinion of the price, maybe; memory of whether the dog ate the biscuits eagerly or left them in the dish in disgust last time she bought them) have prompted brain activity which has led in turn to actual physical changes in her synaptic sensitivity. And the sight of the packs triggers a new pattern of brain activity which zips through her synapses in the predisposed pattern, and comes up with an emotional response. Necessarily (unless dog biscuits are a total novelty to this shopper) one brand will generate the biggest positive soma, and other things being equal (enough money in her purse to buy any of the brands, no special offers that sway the decision) that is the one most likely to be picked up.

Picking up the brand, paying for it, using it, all add to the bank of experiences, and further develop the brand's soma – in a positive direction, or so the producer hopes. So habitual brand repeat purchases are easily explained by brand somas, and the more of them there are, the stronger the soma is likely to be.

BRAND USAGE AFFECTS ADVERTISING NOTING

Professor Ehrenberg's double jeopardy effect stretches beyond what happens at the point of purchase, and even into the area of noticing advertising. As well as asking respondents whether they recognize or recall advertisements (in the ways I discussed in Chapter 15) the Adtrack model has been used to ask people which brands they actually use. Figures 19.1 and 19.2 show what impact the use of a brand has, first (Figure 19.1) on respondents' tendency to recognize or recall its advertising, and second (Figure 19.2) on their tendency to say they like that advertising.

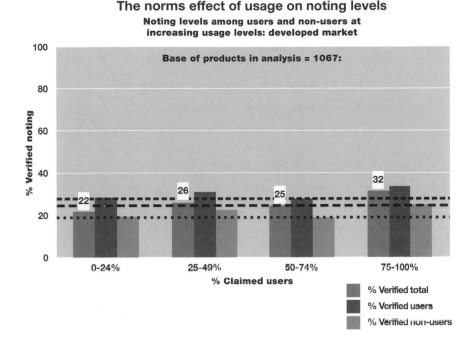

Figure 19.1 *The effect of brand usage on recognition and recall of advertisements*

As you can see, brand users notice the advertising for the brand more than those who do not use it, and also like its advertising more. Of course, it could be argued that there are various factors at play here. (Maybe some of the other respondents do not have a dog, for example: why would they pay attention to advertisements for dog biscuits?) However, this differential applies not only for specific advertisements, some of which are admittedly for products with narrow markets, but over the whole database. This looks to me like another application of Professor Ehrenberg's theory of double jeopardy.

One of the core assumptions we had been working on so far is that:

If people like the advertisement, the advertising soma will rub off on the brand.

As we have seen, there is plenty of empirical evidence that this is in fact the case. Now we have some empirical evidence for the corollary:

If people like the brand, the brand soma rubs off on the advertisement.

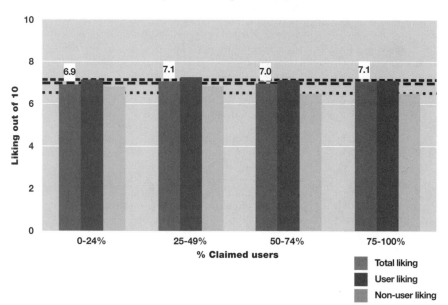

Figure 19.2 *The effect of brand usage on advertising liking*

This is so because the brand memories and the advertising memories are not really separate memories: they are linked, often to such an extent that the advertising memories can realistically be described as a part of the brand memories. When the advertising memories are not part of the brand memories, this phenomenon cannot occur.

We are nearly there now; but there are a few other aspects of brands that we can usefully explore in this context, and I go on to look at those in Chapter 20.

20

The mental world of brands and the objective of advertising

In the first part of this book I led you inexorably towards a 'great thought', a changing paradigm about the brain. It is a paradigm that does not see rational as something diametrically opposed to irrational, or rational as the opposite of emotional; instead, this paradigm posits that the emotional is an essential part of the rational. Emotion is likely to be an older ability of man than rationality, and emotion is probably more important than rationality in the process of living and surviving even today.

Subsequently we have turned to advertising, and I have tried to show how the insights about the brain feed into and illuminate research into advertising. Now I want to introduce you to a concept that is as much a potential paradigmatic shift about advertising, as were the paradigmatic shifts about the function of emotion. Much of this is taken from a book entitled *The Mental World of Brands* by Professor Giep Franzen and Margot Bouwman (1999). (Earlier in the book I introduced Giep's book *Advertising Effectiveness* (1994).) In this book Giep and Margot have this to say about the mental world of the brand:

> *The brand exists as a neural network of memories.*

Perhaps their most important view is buried in the middle of a paragraph on page 312:

> *The authors see the mental response as a synonym of brand representation. The brand name functions as the label of representation.*

They also describe the brand name as 'the key that unlocks memories'. I agree with these statements, but I believe the paradigmatic shift is much more fundamental. The new advertising paradigm I am proposing here is that:

There is only one memory that matters, and that is the memory of the brand.

It seems to me that one thing that is missing from much modern writing on advertising, like Robert Heath's *LIP* (2001) and going all the way back to Larry Gibson's 'Not recall' paper (1983) and Krugman's papers on advertising (1972, 1975, 1977), is that it is advertising-centric, not brand-centric. We all know the reason advertising exists is that producers pay for it to be created and shown, in order to sell their brands, but this is not the issue I am raising here. Rather, my concern is that all the important models, books and papers (with the exception of Professor Jones's *How Advertising Works*) discuss advertising as an objective in itself.

What Franzen and Bouwman started to develop in their book is the view that the 'brand' exists as a neural network of memories, and that these memories are activated by the brand name. This might sounds rather esoteric, but a quick practical example should make it clearer. Look at the following three brand names for one minute:

- Coca-Cola;
- Budweiser;
- Jaguar.

I have no doubt that a lot of information came to your mind in the brief period you spent looking at the three names. The stuff that came to mind immediately probably included knowledge of the product type, a product description, a general feeling of positiveness or negativeness, maybe even something like a pack shot – and since this is a book about advertising you might have recalled one or two advertisements. Just the glancing at these three brand names unlocked a lot of memories, and you will understand that this happened involuntarily as a result of the black text hitting your eyes.

As a second exercise, glance down the list below, as fast as you want, and just notice how much 'comes to mind' at a glance.

- Princess Di;
- Nelson Mandela;
- kangaroo;
- India;
- Wisconsin;

- Orlando;
- Coke;
- Volkswagen;
- Wyatt Earp;
- Dolphin;
- Bath;
- 24/7;
- Cannes;
- Rugby;
- elephant;
- O&M.

When you think about it, it is quite amazing how each one of these words, phrases or acronyms brings a wealth of memories to mind. These memories do not come to the fore in a sequence, you access a whole range of memories – instantaneously! And the longer you look at the word, or just think about it, the more memories you are likely to have come to mind. To use a metaphor I used earlier in the book, the longer you give it attention, the more memories spill out of the cupboard. In fact for any one of these words it would be impossible for you to give me a complete list of what came to mind in the nanosecond after you saw it.

You will understand, I am sure, that this is because your mind is interpreting what it sees, and linking the word on the page to the supporting knowledge in your memory. This is an involuntary process – and very fast. Then the longer you 'think about' something, the more neural networks are stimulated and the more comes to mind. The networked nature of your brain means the knowledge you have forms one entity in your memory, what we called a Gestalt in Chapter 5.

THE 'BRAND MEMORY–ADVERTISING MEMORY' PARADIGM

Although I have tended to write about the advertising memory and the brand memory in this book as if they are two different things, there are not two separate memories in our mind, one for the brand and one for its advertising. We do not have a memory of Coca-Cola the brand and a separate memory of advertisements we have seen for Coca-Cola, we have a continuum, a mixture, of memories that involve both the product and its advertising. We might say that our brain holds the concept 'Coca-Cola', and the brand name 'Coke' is the key or trigger to that memory.

The cupboard metaphor makes sense again at this point:

▌ Our brain involuntarily 'stores' everything our senses absorb regarding Coke.
▌ It is not stored neatly, but as a jumble of interrelated information. In the cupboard of our mind, everything seems to be a mess.
▌ The name 'Coke' opens a door and everything in the cupboard tumbles out. Lots of things fall out virtually immediately, all at the same time, and in no specific order. Lots of things – especially our individual soma for Coke.
▌ Once the memories of Coke spill out, they trigger other memories and thoughts in our brains.
▌ Ultimately there is a key that unlocked this door. It is the brand name that opens the door to the cupboard:
  – The key might have been the word 'Coke' written in the sentence above
  – or seeing a six-pack of Coke on the shelf
  – or seeing an advertisement with the word 'Coke' in it
  – or seeing the distinctive Coke bottle
  – or hearing the words 'vodka and Coke' mentioned in a pub
  – or even something quite different, which just happened to lead to the thought of Coke and (in a sense) the word 'Coke'.
▌ Advertisements form only some of the memories that might come tumbling out when the cupboard is opened.

This is how we need to understand brand memories and advertising memories, because this is the way that the brain works.

ADVERTISING MEMORIES

Most of us like to think of things being logically organized, in our brain just as they are on our computers, or by filing clerks or librarians. However, any logic in our brain is so complex that it is often lost on us. Our brain is certainly not organized in a simple sequential way, where we have one thought and then another thought. Perhaps a closer analogy is the parallel processing in a modern computer, but even that tends to be a lot simpler than our brain activity. It is better still, perhaps, not to think of time as the main organizing factor, but to think of a Gestalt of interrelated information. This is a core part of the new paradigm, the integrated memory.

The issue of 'brand linking' is one that Impact Information picked up early in its career of measuring advertising. It has also become a important concept for Millward Brown, one that has arisen from its extensive world-wide experience in trying to measure the impact of advertising. Advertisers and researchers worldwide understand what is meant by 'brand linking', even if that understanding does not mean that they respect the validity of the concept.

Personally, I do not much like the concept, even though I have used it earlier in this book. It implies that there are two things in the brain, memories of the advertisement and memories of the brand, and some sort of 'bridge' that links them, and as I mentioned above, I think that is a misleading suggestion. It goes back to a sequential model of the brain, with one thought leading logically to the next, and so on. I prefer the notion I used above of a cupboard of memories that open up when the brand is used as a key, some of which are memories of advertising.

Creative directors tend to hate the phrase too, not least because it implies the best way to produce an advertisement is to show pack shots for 30 seconds. That is not the best way to ensure that the advertisement provides a good key to the brand cupboard. (In fact, it is more likely to breed familiarity and boredom – and that is not a positive way to get results, as we saw in Chapter 15.)

WHAT TUMBLES OUT FIRST?

Let us continue the analogy of the brand being a key to an overstuffed cupboard. We said there is no clear sequence in which the memories spill out, not least because everything happens so fast, but even so we can say something about our reactions to the memory-spill. I would suggest that one thing that dominates the memory-spill is its *soma*: the feelings that form part of the Gestalt memory experience.

In other words, our elementary survival instincts mean that we have an instinctive emotional reaction when the key is turned. We might be able to rationalize that emotion and put a variety of different words to our feelings – pain, jealousy, ecstasy, hate or whatever – but our first and deepest instinctive reaction is a much simpler one, a pure negative or positive, as we saw earlier in this book. Then if it needs to, our brain takes automatic action. That speed of instinctive emotional reaction and physical response can at times be life-saving, which is doubtless why we have this ability to react so quickly and automatically.

A choice of washing powder brands hardly comes into the life-saving decisions category, but the same brain mechanisms come into play here; and the first memory that falls out of the 'brand' cupboard is the brand soma, or how we feel about the brand.

ADVERTISING AND BRAND EQUITY

At heart, the task of the marketer is to help ensure that the brand soma is strong and positive, and to orient advertisements in such a way that the 'soma memory' is triggered as effectively as possible. Whether people remember the 'story' of the advertisement is not the point. What matters is that the contents that fall out of the cupboard have a positive soma.

Let us take Coca-Cola as an example again. Ask people what they think about Coca-Cola, and they might put their rational brains to work and come up with descriptions like:

- refreshing;
- carbonated;
- well packaged;
- young;
- modern;
- trendy.

Mention the *word* 'Coca-Cola', though, and the first thing that comes out of the brand cupboard is not a phrase like any of these. It is a positive or negative emotion. We either *like* Coca-Cola or we do not. Only once marketers know that people like Coca-Cola does it become interesting to find out why.

Of course, to 'like' here is nothing as simple as merely liking the taste. Sure, if we do not much like the taste of Coke that will affect our memories and put its mark on the brand soma, but the brand soma has a much wider basis than the objective physical properties of the brand. (That is why, although in blind taste tests people might say they like the taste of Pepsi more than the taste of Coca-Cola, they still 'like' Coca-Cola the most when the brand soma is triggered by a branded taste test.)

It is this instinctive 'liking', this positive emotion (or negative emotion, in some cases) that is the first and often the main determinant of how we act (in this context, which brand we choose to buy). This is not a wild assertion, it is an empirically proven statement, as I showed earlier in the book.

Professor Franzen spends about three pages in his book describing Millward Brown's BrandDynamics model. This model fits very well into the argument of this chapter, because it really considers the soma, rather than specific positioning statements for a brand. The model is built around questions that only relate to the soma that the brand name generates. They might appear very 'rational' at first glance, but the point of the model is not its rationality; rather, its value lies in its ability to provide a measurement of the brand's soma.

As we saw in Chapter 19, brand soma and advertising soma are closely linked. People tend to like the advertising for brands they use more than the advertising for competitor brands, and this is a circular process, with liked advertising feeding into brand liking, and the brand liking feeding back into advertising liking.

In summary, there are two core concerns for advertisers. The first is that the advertising should be properly positioned so that it forms an integral part of the brand concept; and the second is that the advertising should be designed to help reinforce the brand's positive soma.

21

'I told you so'

This chapter is something of an aside. While I was waiting for the proofs of the Dutch edition of this book, Professor Giep Franzen sent me an article by Clive Thompson, published in *The New York Times*, 'There's a sucker born in every medial prefrontal cortex'. The theme of this article is that there is a neurologically-based emotional reaction in the brain when people are exposed to a brand. In other words, what I was predicting in the book has now been measured!

As an introduction to the work being done in this area, let me quote two passages from the article.

> *When he isn't pondering the inner workings of the mind, Read Montague, a 43-year-old neuroscientist at Baylor College of Medicine, has been known to contemplate the other mysteries of life: for instance, the Pepsi Challenge. In the series of TV commercials from the 70's and 80's that pitted Coke against Pepsi in a blind taste test, Pepsi was usually the winner. So why, Montague asked himself not long ago, did Coke appeal so strongly to so many people if it didn't taste any better?*

> *Over several months this past summer, Montague set to work looking for a scientifically convincing answer. He assembled a group of test subjects and, while monitoring their brain activity with an MRI [magnetic resonance imaging] machine, recreated the Pepsi Challenge. His results confirmed those of the TV campaign: Pepsi tended to produce a stronger response than Coke in the brain's ventral putamen, a region thought to process feelings of reward. (Monkeys, for instance, exhibit activity in the ventral putamen when they receive food for completing a task.) Indeed, in people who preferred Pepsi, the ventral putamen was five times as active when drinking Pepsi than that of Coke fans when drinking Coke.*

In the real world, of course, taste is not everything. So Montague tried to gauge the appeal of Coke's image, its 'brand influence,' by repeating the experiment with a small variation: this time, he announced which of the sample tastes were Coke. The outcome was remarkable: almost all the subjects said they preferred Coke. What's more, the brain activity of the subjects was now different. There was also activity in the medial prefrontal cortex, an area of the brain that scientists say governs high-level cognitive powers. Apparently, the subjects were meditating in a more sophisticated way on the taste of Coke, allowing memories and other impressions of the drink – in a word, its brand – to shape their preference.

Pepsi, crucially, couldn't achieve the same effect. When Montague reversed the situation, announcing which tastes were of Pepsi, far fewer of the subjects said they preferred Pepsi. Montague was impressed: he had demonstrated, with a fair degree of neuroscientific precision, the special power of Coke's brand to override our taste buds.

Measuring brand influence might seem like an unusual activity for a neuroscientist, but Montague is just one of a growing breed of researchers who are applying the methods of the neurology lab to the questions of the advertising world. Some of these researchers, like Montague, are purely academic in focus, studying the consumer mind out of intellectual curiosity, with no corporate support. Increasingly, though, there are others – like several of the researchers at the Mind of the Market Laboratory at Harvard Business School – who work as full-fledged 'neuromarketers,' conducting brain research with the help of corporate financing and sharing their results with their sponsors. This summer, when it opened its doors for business, the BrightHouse Institute for Thought Sciences in Atlanta became the first neuromarketing firm to boast a Fortune 500 consumer-products company as a client. (The client's identity is currently a secret.) The institute will scan the brains of a representative sample of its client's prospective customers, assess their reactions to the company's products and advertising and tweak the corporate image accordingly.

I had not heard of the BrightHouse Institute before, so perhaps you have not either. Thompson's article subsequently provides some further insight into what it does:

The BrightHouse Institute's techniques are based, in part, on an experiment that Kilts conducted earlier this year. He gathered a group of test subjects and asked them to look at a series of commercial products, rating how strongly they liked or disliked them. Then, while scanning their brains in an MRI machine, he showed them pictures of the products again. When Kilts looked at the images of their brains, he was struck by one particular result: whenever a subject saw a product he had identified as one he truly loved – something that might prompt him to say,

'That's just so me!' – his brain would show increased activity in the medial prefrontal cortex.

Kilts was excited, for he knew that this region of the brain is commonly associated with our sense of self. Patients with damage in this area of the brain, for instance, often undergo drastic changes in personality; in one famous case, a mild-mannered 19th-century rail worker named Phineas Gage abruptly became belligerent after an accident that destroyed his medial prefrontal cortex. More recently, MRI studies have found increased activity in this region when people are asked if adjectives like 'trustworthy' or 'courageous' apply to them. When the medial prefrontal cortex fires, your brain seems to be engaging, in some manner, with what sort of person you are. If it fires when you see a particular product, Kilts argues, it's most likely to be because the product clicks with your self-image.

Clive Thompson entitled his article 'There's a sucker born in every medial prefrontal cortex', partly because he refers to the big corporations that might be suckered into paying big money to have consumers hooked up to MRI machines while they are consuming specific products and viewing packaging and advertising. He is probably right.

Montague could have obtained the same results without hooking people up to MRI machines because they would have told him their taste preference for the disguised product and the branded product. This is, in fact, what Coke and Pepsi did.

The importance of this research is not that it revealed a new way of interrogating respondents, but that it demonstrates how the brain functions correlate with what we would have found by normal research.

Another important thing to note is how clearly the sites in the brain associated with our emotional responses, as well as those involved in more purely rational activity, show a response to brand stimuli. Of course, that is what we would expect, given all the information that we have put together in this book.

22

The emotional and the rational

I have tried in this book to put forward the shape of a new paradigm for the design of effective advertising. Now I need briefly to suggest how it should be put into effect.

In the past few years much of the debate between advertisers and researchers on how best to make advertising work has focused on whether it should appeal to the emotional or the rational side of consumers. Advertisements have been analysed, and judgements made about whether they are more emotional or rational in their appeal; media characteristics have been brought in to play too. All of this debate is based on the assumption that the brain processes rational information in a quite different way from the way in which it deals with emotions.

The standard communication–feedback model that researchers have propounded is something like the one in Figure 22.1. Let us use this simple model and see what changes we need to make to encompass the new paradigm I have been putting forward in this book, that this dichotomy between the emotional and the rational is not at all a fair representation of the way the two actually interact.

Change 1: Everything is filtered through our emotional responses for interpretation by our rational capabilities

First, let us recap something of what we know about brains, and the consumers who possess them:

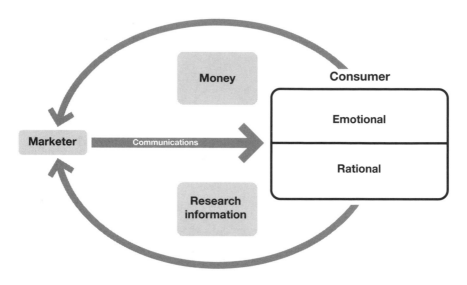

Figure 22.1 *A simple communication–feedback model*

1. The brain has two portals: an input portal through which perceptions (that is, the five senses) enter and an output portal for the neurological signals that govern our behaviour (which includes our speech).
2. Nothing enters the brain except via the senses.
3. What comes out of the brain is behaviour: what people do, say, buy and so on.
4. We know that every perception that enters the brain is in some way interpreted, and that this process involves the recruitment of emotionally coloured memories.
5. These emotional memories determine the amount of attention that the input receives, and also set up the background against which the rational interpretation occurs.
6. All of this happens involuntarily.

All of this leads to a model like the one shown in Figure 22.2.

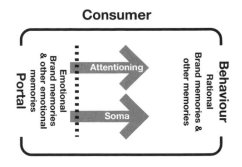

Figure 22.2 *The emotional filter model*

Change 2: This is a general model of communication, but what we need is a specific model of how media work on communication

We still need to show the flow of communication, but we need to recognize that the communications we are particularly interested in (advertisements) are conveyed in specific media. In other words, the medium has the task of ensuring that the communications are presented to the brain's input portal. Figure 22.3 introduces this refinement.

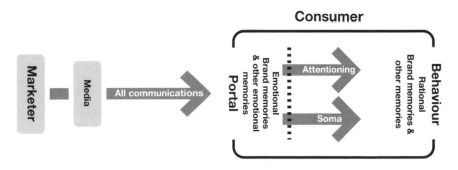

Figure 22.3 *The emotional filter model taking account of media*

Change 3: Now let us apply the model to a specific brand

The emotional filter for perceptions a consumer receives from an advertisement (or from any other key to the brand memory, such as the brand on the shelf, or in the showroom, or the brand being mentioned by someone) draws on the brand's soma: that is, the emotional aspect of the memories the consumer has about the brand. In other words, the communication loop itself is filtered by past memories of the brand. Figure 22.4 accordingly introduces the 'brand as a memory'.

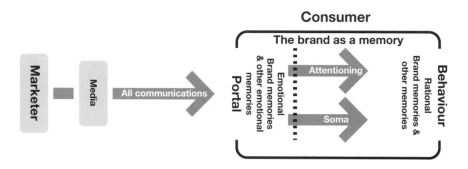

Figure 22.4 *The emotional filter model including both communications media and the brand as a memory*

Change 4: Now let us see how this model feeds into a purchase decision

As we saw in Chapter 1, sometimes the decision which brand to buy is not a fully conscious one. There is little or any rational thought before we make low-involvement repeat purchases, which are driven primarily by practical need for a product mediated by our emotional reaction to the brand (that is, the brand's soma). On other occasions, there is rational consideration before we select a brand. In this case the brain's emotional response to the stimuli serves to prompt our rational mind to give attention to the information that is available, and make the decision.

To reflect this we need to show the brand itself as being outside the initial flow of communication from the advertising, but working as part of a feedback loop that affects the consumer's decision, as in Figure 22.5.

Figure 22.5 includes two further aspects of the model. The first is that the brand purchase provides the consumer with further input (experience of the brand) which will have an impact on future purchase decisions; and

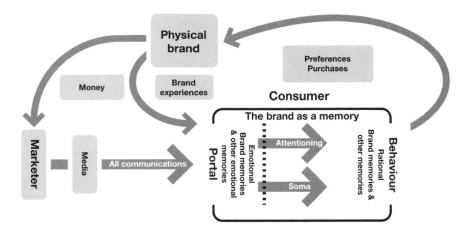

Figure 22.5 *Purchase cycles and the emotional filter model*

the second is that the brand purchase means money flowing to the producer, and in turn to the marketer, prompting a further round of advertising as well as a further round of purchase decisions.

Change 5: Questions from a researcher also act as input to the consumer's brain

All an individual's perceptions – that is, everything that occurs in the individual's environment that has an impact on one or more of the individual's senses – act as input to the brain. They all pass through the emotional filter, which determines which perceptions should be the focus of conscious thought.

This is as true of consumer research as of any other activity. Thus the moment we as researchers mention the brand, or the product category or even a competitive brand, the consumer's mind starts the process of neuronal recruitment: bringing first emotional responses, then rational information, to the process of interpreting what is being shown, said or asked.

We might appear to get a rational answer to a research question (about whether a respondent recalls an advertisement, for instance), but that rational response will still have been mediated by the individual's initial emotional response. In turn, the question and its response act as another feedback loop in the system. Including these refinements makes the model look like Figure 22.6.

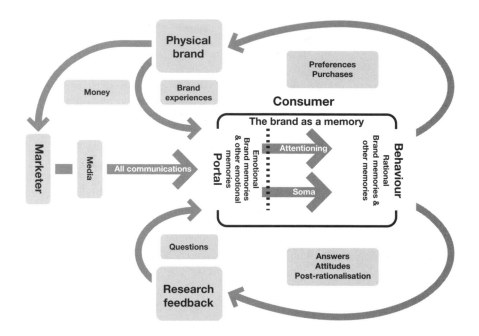

Figure 22.6 *The impact of advertising research on the model*

Change 6: Last of all, we need to show how the research output affects the model

Research has a purpose, of course: in this context, to provide information that shapes the actions of marketers. So the final version of the model shows output from the research exercise feeding back into the process, and shaping the advertising that is the marketer's form of output.

LEARNINGS FROM THE EMOTIONAL FILTER MODEL

What marketing should learn

Since the brain's first response to perceptions is an emotional one, it is of the utmost importance that advertisers understand the emotional response that their output elicits. In other words they need to understand these aspects:

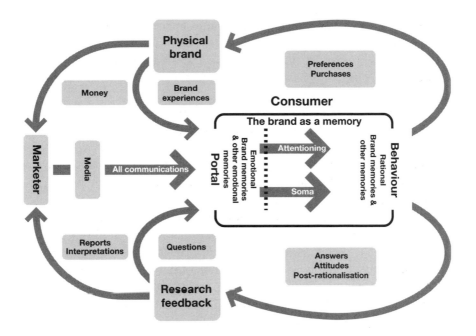

Figure 22.7 *The research feedback in the model*

I What is the emotional response to a mention of the brand name?
I What is the brand memory? That is, against what soma will the advertising message be interpreted?
I What is the emotional response of consumers to the intended advertisement?
I What is the emotional response of consumers on encountering the product itself?
I Against what somatic memories is the brand purchase considered?

Clearly, all these are aspects of the same basic question: what is the brand soma?

It is equally important that advertisers and marketers understand what characteristics the soma has:

- At heart, the soma is a simple limbic reaction (that is, a response from the instinctive centres of the brain: see Chapter 6). On this level, it is not a complex emotional reaction. It might be as simple as a positive or negative, although its strength can vary. Obviously the main issue to a marketer is whether the consumer reacts positively or negatively to the message, and how strongly.
- The rational processes that come into play next generate a more 'complex emotion'. There is upper-brain as well as midbrain activity in a response such as jealousy, desire or fear. Clearly it is important too to understand how consumers rationalize the initial instinctive reaction, and what their full and complex emotional response consists of.
- The 'emotional filter' as we described it above means that not all perceptions lead to rational thought processes; some of them fail to 'attract attention', and little if any memory trace is laid down as a result. The advertiser's first job is to get through the emotional filter and ensure that the advertisement and the product are noticed and remembered.
- 'Liking' seems to play a key role in determining whether an advertisement is remembered, and liking in this sense involves both an emotional and a rational element. Whether the consumer 'likes' the product offering well enough to choose to buy it does not just depend on clever advertising, it also depends on factors such as the quality of the product, its features, and last but not least, its price. There is no point in offering the market a product that everybody loves, if nobody can afford it!

CONCLUSION

We have reached the end of a tour around what has been learned about the brain and its functioning, and around what has been learned about advertising and its functioning. At the end of a tour it is fair to expect the tour guide to provide some sort of summary, to help the tourists to draw their conclusions; and that is what I must now try to do.

Different people will have read this book for different reasons, and each of them will come to conclusions that depend on their existing memory:

both their objective knowledge, and their emotional response to the issues explored. There is no right reaction to my book, and it is not for me to insist on one. But I hope you have found it worthwhile to be given an overview of the exciting new insights into how the human brain works, and of the advertising research that validates and is validated by these findings.

I hope that as well as providing information, the book will help to stimulate broader thinking about advertising: creating advertising, making advertising effective, and measuring how well advertising works. Ours is a fascinating endeavour, and one thing the book should have made clear is that there is still much to learn about how best to ensure people notice, and choose to buy, the products our clients make available.

The book summarizes to the best of my ability the current state of knowledge on the topics I address; but that will never be the final word. Our paradigms today will one day be replaced. We can hope they are better paradigms than those of the past that I have shown to be, in many cases, hopelessly inadequate. They are not perfect, and nor are we. But we are trying to learn, to move forward, and I will have achieved my objective if this book has contributed to that process.

Appendix: Choosing a copy testing methodology

Many readers will be looking to learn from this book which copy-testing methodology works best, and which company they should turn to for testing their campaigns. Here are some issues to take into account. Some of them relate to the technique used, while others are more general.

- The research supplier should have a well spelt-out model (theory) of how advertising works, what the interpretation of the measures should be, and what should be done in the event of different results.
- The client should be confident that the executive presenting the results is knowledgeable about advertising, and not only about research.
- Whatever copy test is used, it must yield an estimate of the impact rate that the advertisement will have in the media when flighted. This is the best way to ensure that the creative strategy and the media strategy are integrated.
- The research executive should be able to talk media terminology, again to help in the integration of creative and media viewpoints.
- The copy test should give an indication of the emotive-attentioning ability of the advertisement.
- The copy test should give a variety of diagnostics about the commercial, and should certainly not be limited to a one-number summary.
- The copy test should not involve a clutter reel, or any 'let's fool the respondent' measures.
- The research supplier should have a normative database against which the individual results can be compared.

Bibliography

Aaker, David A and Myers, John G (1975) *Advertising Management*, Prentice-Hall, Englewood Cliffs, NJ

Aaker, David, A and Stayman, Douglas (1990) Measuring audience perceptions of commercials and relating them to ad impact, *Journal of Advertising Research* **30** (4), pp 7–17

Aleksander, Igor and Morton, Helen (1990) *An Introduction to Neural Computing*, Chapman & Hall, London

Baddeley, Alan (1990) *Human Memory: Theory and practice*, Lawrence Erlbaum Associates, Hove, East Sussex

Baddeley, Alan (1990) *Your Memory: A user's guide*, Penguin, London

Baestaens, Dirk E, Wood, Douglas and Van den Bergh, Willem M (1994) *Neural Network Solutions for Trading in Financial Markets*, Pitman, London

Barnard, N and Ehrenberg, A (1997) Advertising: strongly persuasive or nudging? *Journal of Advertising Research* **37** (1), pp 21–32

Biel, Alexander L (1990) Love the ad. Buy the product? *Admap*, September

Biel, Alexander L (1993) Ad research in the US, *Admap*, May

Biel, Alexander L and Bridgewater, Carol A (1990) Attributes of likable television commercials, *Journal of Advertising Research* **30** (3), pp 38–44

Boden, Margaret A (1987) *Artificial Intelligence and Natural Man*, 2nd edn, MIT Press, London

Broadbent, Simon (1989) *The Advertising Budget*, McGraw-Hill, Maidenhead, Berks

Broadbent, Simon (1997) *Accountable Advertising*, Admap, Henley-on-Thames, Oxfordshire

Brown, Gordon (1992) Some new thinking in the light of modern evidence, in *Proceedings of the British MRS Conference,* MRS, London

Clark, Andy (1997) *Being There: Putting brain, body and world together again*, MIT Press, Cambridge, Mass

Cohen, Gillian, Kiss, George and Le Voi, Martin (1993) *Memory: Current issues*, 2nd edn, Open University Press, Buckingham

Corballis, Michael C (1991) *The Lopsided Ape*, Oxford University Press, New York

Crick, Francis (1995) *The Astonishing Hypothesis: The scientific search for the soul*, Touchstone, New York

Damasio, Antonio R (1994) *Descartes' Error*, Avon, New York

Damasio, Antonio R (1999) *The Feeling of What Happens: Body and emotion in the making of consciousness*, Harcourt Brace, Orlando, Fla

De Bono, Edward (1969) *The Mechanism of Mind*, Simon & Schuster, New York

De Bono, Edward (1986) *Tactics: The art and science of success*, Fontana Paperbacks, UK

De Mooij, Marieke (1994) *Advertising Worldwide*, 2nd edn, Prentice-Hall, Hemel Hempstead, Herts

Du Plessis, E C (1994a) Recognition versus recall, *Journal of Advertising Research* **34** (3), pp 75–91

Du Plessis, E C (1994b) Understanding and using likeability, *Journal of Advertising Research* **34** (5), pp RC3–RC10

Dubow, Joel S (1992) Recall first – but not recall alone, in *Proceedings of the Ninth Annual ARF Copy Research Workshop*, Advertising Research Foundation, New York

Edelman, Gerald M (1992) *Bright Air, Brilliant Fire: On the matter of the mind,* Basic Books, New York

Ehrenberg, A S C, Goodhart, G J and Barwise, T P (1990) Double jeopardy revisited, *Journal of Marketing*, July, pp 82–91

Elman, Jeffrey L, Bates, Elizabeth A, Johnson, Mark H, Karmiloff-Smith, Annette, Parisi, Domenico and Plunkett, Kim (1998) *Rethinking Innateness*, MIT Press, Cambridge, Mass

Ewing, Michael, Napoli, Julie and du Plessis, Erik (1999) Factors affecting in-market recall of food product advertising, *Journal of Advertising Research* **39** (4), pp 29–38

Fehr, B and Russell, J A (1984) Concept of emotion viewed from a prototype perspective, *Journal of Experimental Psychology: General*, **113**, pp 464–86

Franklin, Stan (1997) *Artificial Minds*, MIT Press, Cambridge, Mass

Franzen, Giep (1994) *Advertising Effectiveness*, NTC, Henley-on-Thames, Oxfordshire

Franzen, Giep (1998) *Merken & Reclame: Hoe reclame-effectiviteit brand equity beïnvloedt*, Kluwer BedrijfsInformatie, the Netherlands

Franzen, Giep (1999) *Brands and Advertising*, Admap, Henley-on-Thames, Oxfordshire

Franzen, Giep and Bouwman, Margot (1999) *De Mentale Wereld van Merken* (The Mental World of Brands: Mind, Memory and Brand Success), Samsom, the Netherlands

Gardner, Howard (1987) *The Mind's New Science*, BasicBooks, New York

Gibson, Lawrence D (1983) Not recall, *Journal of Advertising Research* **23** (1), pp 39–46

Goleman, Daniel (1999) *Working with Emotional Intelligence*, Bloomsbury, London

Gordon, William C (1989) *Learning and Memory*, Brooks/Cole, Pacific Grove, Calif

Greene, Robert L (1992) *Human Memory: Paradigms and paradoxes*, Lawrence Erlbaum Associates, Hillsdale, NJ

Greenfield, Susan A (1995) *Journey to the Centers of the Mind*, W H Freeman, New York

Greenfield, Susan A (1996) *The Human Mind Explained*, Henry Holt, New York

Greenfield, Susan, A (1997) *The Human Brain*, Basic Books, New York

Haley, Russell I and Baldinger, Allan L (1991) The ARF Copy Research Validation Project, *Journal of Advertising Research* **31** (2), pp 11–32

Heath, Robert (2001) *The Hidden Power of Advertising: How low involvement processing influences the way we choose brands*, Admap, Henley-on-Thames, Oxfordshire

Hermie, Patrick, Lanckriet, Trui, Lansloot, Koen and Peeters, Stef (2005) *Stop/watch: Everything you wanted to know about the impact of magazine ads*, Medialogue, Brussels, Belgium

Hofstadter, Douglas R and Dennett, Daniel C (1981) *The Mind's I*, BasicBooks, New York

Hollis, N S (1995) Like it or not, liking is not enough, *Journal of Advertising Research* **35** (5), pp 7–16

Hollis, N S (2001) Is bigger, really better?, paper presented at ESOMAR Conference, Mexico City. Paper available from Millward Brown.

Johnston, Victor S (1999) *Why We Feel: The science of human emotions*, Perseus, Reading, Mass

Jones, John Philip (1995) *When Ads Work: New proof that advertising triggers sales*, Lexington, New York

Jones, John Philip (1998) *How Advertising Works*, Sage, Thousand Oaks, Calif

Jones, John Philip (2000) *International Advertising: Realities and myths*, Sage, Thousand Oaks, Calif

Jordaan, W J and Jordaan, J J (1989) *Man in Context*, 2nd edn, Lexicon, Johannesburg

Jugenheimer, Donald W and Turk, Peter, B (1980) *Advertising Media*, Grid, Columbus, Ohio

Kok, A and Boelhouwer, A J W (1997) *Aandacht: Een psychofysiologische benadering*, Van Gorcum, Assen, the Netherlands

Komatsu, Lloyd K (1994) *Experimenting with the Mind*, Brooks/Cole, Pacific Grove, Calif

Kosslyn, Stephen M and Koenig, Olivier (1995) *Wet Mind: The new cognitive neuroscience*, Free Press, New York

Kotulak, Ronald (1996) *Inside the Brain*, Andrews and McMeel, Kansas City, Miss

Kroebel-Riel, W (1990) *Strategie und Technik der Werbung*, Verhaltenswissenschaftliche Ansatze, Kohlhammer, Germany

Krugman, H E (1972) Why three exposures may be enough, *Journal of Advertising Research*, Dec, 11–14

Krugman, H E (1975) What makes advertising effective? *Harvard Business Review*, March–April, 96–104

Krugman, H E (1977) Memory without recall, exposure without perception, *Journal of Advertising Research* **17** (4), pp 7–12

Laufer, J (1986) Erkentnisse aus 10 Jahren Argus, in *Anzeigen-copy tests: Erkentnisse aus 10 Jahren Argus*, Gruner & Jahr, Die Stern Bibliothek

Leakey, Richard and Lewin, Roger (1992) *Origins Reconsidered*, Little, Brown, London

Leckenby, John D and Kim, H (1994) How media directors view reach/frequency estimation: now and a decade ago, *Journal of Advertising Research* **34** (5), pp 9–21

LeDoux, Joseph (1996) *The Emotional Brain: The mysterious underpinnings of emotional life*, Simon & Schuster, New York

Lyon, G Reid and Krasnegor, Norman A (1996) *Attention, Memory, and Executive Function*, Paul H Brookes, Baltimore, Maryland

Mackay, Donald M (1991) *Behind the Eye*, Blackwell, Oxford

McDonald, Colin (1992) *How Advertising Works*, NTC Publications, Henley-on-Thames, Oxfordshire

McDonald, Malcolm and Dunbar, Ian (1995) *Market Segmentation*, Macmillan, Basingstoke

McDonald, Colin (1996) *Advertising Reach and Frequency*, 2nd edn, NTC Business Books, Lincolnwood, Ill

McDonald, Colin (1997) *Pre-Testing Advertisements*, Admap, Henley-on-Thames, Oxfordshire

Millward Brown (1991) *How Advertising Affects the Sales of Packaged Goods Brands: A working hypothesis for the 1990's*, Millward Brown, London (booklet)

Minsky, Marvin (1987) *The Society of Mind*, Heinemann, London

Mitchell, Andrew A (1993) *Advertising Exposure, Memory and Choice*, Lawrence Erlbaum Associates, Hillsdale, NJ

Naples, Michael J (1979) *Effective Frequency: The relationship between frequency and advertising effectiveness*, Association of National Advertisers, New York

Niedenthal, Paula M and Kitayama, Shinobu (1994) *The Heart's Eye*, Academic Press, San Diego, Calif

Oatley, Keith and Jenkins, Jennifer M (1995) *Understanding Emotions*, Blackwell, Oxford

Olson, David W (1984) Validation of copy-testing measures based on in-market performance: an analysis of new product ads, paper presented at the EMAC/ESOMAR Symposium, Copenhagen

Ornstein, Robert (1997) *The Right Mind: Making sense of the hemispheres,* Harcourt Brace, New York

Packard, Vance (1960) *The Hidden Persuaders*, Penguin Books, Victoria, Australia

Posner, Michael I and Raichle, Marcus E (1994) *Images of the Mind*, Scientific American Library, New York

Rice, J (1992) In the mind, out of sight, in *Proceedings of the 1992 SAMRA Convention*, Transkei, South Africa

Rice, J and Bennett, R (1998) The relationship between brand usage and advertising tracking measurements: international findings, *Journal of Advertising Research* **38** (3), pp 58–66

Roberts, Andrew (1999) What do we know about advertising's short-term effects? *Admap*, Feb

Rossiter, J R and Eagleson, G (1994) Conclusions from the ARF's Copy Research Validity Project, *Journal of Advertising Research* **34** (3), pp 19–32

Schacter, Daniel L (1997) *Memory Distortion*, Harvard University Press, Cambridge, Mass

Schlinger, Mary Jane (1979) A profile of responses to commercials, *Journal of Advertising Research* **19** (2), pp 37–46

Shallice, Tim (1988) *From Neuropsychology to Mental Structure*, Cambridge University Press, Cambridge, UK

Smit, Edith (1999) *Mass Media Advertising: Information or wallpaper?* Het Spinhuis, Amsterdam

Stapel, J (1991) Ad effectiveness: like the ad... but does it really interest me? *Admap*, April

Stapel, Jan (1994) A brief observation about likability and interestingness of advertising, *Journal of Advertising Research* **34** (2), pp 79–80

Stapel, J (1998) Recall and recognition: a very close relationship, *Journal of Advertising Research* **38** (4), pp 41–45

Steklis, H D and Harnad, S (1976) From hand to mouth: some critical stages in the evolution of language, in Harnad, S, Steklis, H D and Lancaster, J B (eds), *Origins and Evolution of Language and Speech*, Annals of the New York Academy of Sciences **280**, pp 445–55

Stewart, D W and Furse, D H (1986) *Effective Television Advertising*, Lexington, Toronto

Surmanek, Jim (1996) *Media Planning*, 3rd edn, NTC Business Books, Lincolnwood, Ill

Thompson, Clive (2003) There's a sucker born in every medial prefrontal cortex, *The New York Times*, 26 October

Thorsen, Esther (1991) Likeability: ten years of academic research, Eighth Annual ARF Copy Research Workshop

Thorsen, Esther and Friestad, Marian (1989) The effects of emotion on episodic memory for television commercials, in *Cognitive and Affective Responses to Advertising*, ed P Cafferata and A Tybouts, Lexington, MA

Various (1980) *Mind and Behaviour*, W H Freeman, San Francisco

Von Keitz, B (1985) *Symposium zur Kommunikations-Forschung*, Saarbrucken, 28 June

Williamson, Judith (1978) *Decoding Advertisements: Ideology and meaning in advertising*, Marion Boyars, London

Wundt, W (1897) *Outlines of Psychology*, trans. C H Judd, Stechert, New York

Zielske, H (1982) Does day-after-recall penalize 'feeling' ads? *Journal of Advertising Research* **22** (1), pp 19–22

Zitani, Ron (1992) Commercial likeability: what's it mean? Presentation at the Ninth Annual ARF Copy Research Workshop, New York, Advertising Research Foundation

Index

NB: page numbers in *italic* indicate figures or tables